The First Capital of the Ottoman Empire

The First Capital of the Ottoman Empire

The Religious, Architectural, and Social History of Bursa

Suna Çağaptay

I.B. TAURIS
LONDON · NEW YORK · OXFORD · NEW DELHI · SYDNEY

I.B. TAURIS
Bloomsbury Publishing Plc
50 Bedford Square, London, WC1B 3DP, UK
1385 Broadway, New York, NY 10018, USA
29 Earlsfort Terrace, Dublin 2, Ireland

BLOOMSBURY, I.B. TAURIS and the I.B. Tauris logo are trademarks of Bloomsbury Publishing Plc

First published in Great Britain 2021
This paperback edition published in 2022

Copyright © Suna Cagaptay, 2021

Suna Cagaptay has asserted her right under the Copyright, Designs and Patents Act, 1988, to be identified as Author of this work.

For legal purposes the Acknowledgments on p. x constitute an extension of this copyright page.

All rights reserved. No part of this publication may be reproduced or transmitted in any form or by any means, electronic or mechanical, including photocopying, recording, or any information storage or retrieval system, without prior permission in writing from the publishers.

Bloomsbury Publishing Plc does not have any control over, or responsibility for, any third-party websites referred to or in this book. All internet addresses given in this book were correct at the time of going to press. The author and publisher regret any inconvenience caused if addresses have changed or sites have ceased to exist, but can accept no responsibility for any such changes.

A catalogue record for this book is available from the British Library.

A catalog record for this book is available from the Library of Congress.

ISBN: HB: 978-1-8386-0549-0
PB: 978-0-7556-3543-6
ePDF: 978-1-8386-0552-0
eBook: 978-1-8386-0551-3

Typeset by Deanta Global Publishing Services, Chennai, India

To find out more about our authors and books visit www.bloomsbury.com and sign up for our newsletters.

In loving memory of my mother, Sultan, for teaching me that Malatya is not all about apricots and Bursa is not all about peaches...

Contents

Preface	viii
Acknowledgments	x
List of Illustrations	xiii
Note on Copyright for Previous Publications	xvi
A Note on Spelling, Names, Maps, and Quotations	xvii
Chronological Chart	xviii
Introduction: The First Capital of the Ottoman Empire	1
1 Becoming Bursa	11
2 The City in Transition: Continuity, Conversion, and Reuse	23
3 Contextualizing the Convent-*Masjids* and Friday Mosques: Local Knowledge and Hybridity	47
4 The Roots and Context of the Inverted-T Plan	69
5 Memory and Monuments: The *Külliyes* of the Sultans	79
6 Concluding Remarks on "Invisible Prousa/Bursa"	101
Notes	111
Bibliography	173
Index	203

Preface

This book is about how the Ottomans made the city of Prousa their Bursa. It deals with the first hundred years of the Ottomans, a nomadic tribe of humble origins in Central Asia, as they came into Prousa and began mixing in with the local populace and their new urban setting. During this time, the Ottomans were in the process of creating a cultural identity for themselves, both internally and externally.

Prousa was founded by Prousias I (also known as the Lame or Χωλός) in the third century BC. It was sacked by another Lame ruler, Timur (لنگ ر Temūr(-i) Lang), in 1402. It was the native city of the golden-mouthed Dio, orator and philosopher of the Roman Empire, who constructed a colonnaded street to rival Antioch's in the Roman East. Its holy mountain functioned as a refuge for both Byzantines and Ottomans, and the clergy fleeing from Constantinople in the Iconoclastic period settled there. Its luscious green and verdant landscape gave inspiration to Michael Psellos, an important political and literary figure of the middle Byzantine period. During a year spent at Horaia Pege, the Monastery of Beautiful Spring on Mount Olympus, he wrote letters to John VIII Xiphilinos (1064–75), Patriarch of Constantinople, which included phrases praising his surroundings including "a Platonic lotus, a plane tree, and myrtles."[1] A shrine was built on the foothills of the same mountain to bless the memory of Abdal Murad, an early Ottoman nomad raider–turned-saint. Its *madrasa*s laid the groundwork for Sheikh Bedreddin, an early fifteenth-century influential mystic and theologian, to spread his revolutionary thoughts on promoting a new commune based on the principles of justice, equality, and fraternity. Bedreddin's religious mission and teachings resonated anew in the prose of Nazım Hikmet Ran, a renowned poet who was imprisoned at Bursa in the mid-1940s. The following lines by Ran echo the starting point of this book:

> Galloping full-tilt from furthest Asia,
> craning its mare's head to reach the Mediterranean;
> this land is ours.[2]

So far, several studies have covered the religious, cultural, and political setting of the period. This book tries to do something else. It situates Bursa at an intersection of cultures and peoples and analyzes the character and context of the architectural production. It examines the buildings as cultural artifacts and considers the impact of multiple actors, such as donors, builders, tradesmen, and saintly figures. In the following pages, the reader will learn about the creation of an urban culture in Bursa as a city witnessing the rise of the Ottomans and their assumption of power from the retreating Byzantines. These two cultures were not monolithic, and the transition of power was by no means binary and sudden. Many players, including Greeks, Jews, Turks, Armenians, Rum Seljuks, Latin Crusaders, Genoese, Venetians, Mamluks, Mongol–Ilkhanids, and non-Ottoman Muslim principalities, also played a political role in the peninsula at the time, and the Byzantine to Ottoman "shift" often took the form of a cultural and political marketplace.

This book focuses mostly on the Ottoman urban enterprise, and much of the narrative revolves around the city itself, its walls, and its suburbs. It follows the Ottoman rulers and their expansionist agendas as they made alliances and arranged intermarriages to gain an upper hand in the early fourteenth century. Vignettes will paint pictures of an Ottoman sultan conversing with Byzantine captives or another modeling himself as Alexander the Great; of a French traveler being so captivated by the hot springs of the city that he linked their therapeutic qualities to the foundation myths of the city; and of Genoese tradesmen stopping over to sell and buy products. Rather than looking at Bursa as iconic, this book explores how the city and its fourteenth-century actors of different backgrounds were perceived and imagined. By looking at the multifaceted milieu of its fourteenth-century dynamics, one can see the exchange of skills, ideas, and forms. I hope this book acts as my ultimate tribute to the city's continuity, diversity, and multiplicity in architectural production in the medieval period, allowing the early Ottomans to claim Bursa as their own.

Acknowledgments

Walled cities and towns have always attracted my interest. I grew up living very close to one in eastern Anatolia, and I finished the final corrections of this book while admiring the views of another in Istanbul. I visited Bursa's walled city for the first time in 1993 while working as a nurse for the Turkish Red Crescent Society summer camp. It loomed large when I decided to change careers to archaeology, later earning a PhD in architectural history and theory. I will always remember how the Bursa walls clung tenaciously to the foothills of Mount Olympus and how the city within had beautiful vistas onto the plain. My memory also recalls a mash-up of details belonging to different periods, such as the tombs of the Ottoman founders, which were rebuilt in the nineteenth century on the remains of fourteenth-century conversions of Byzantine religious edifices, the nineteenth-century clock tower, and the cannonballs and tombstones of the Turkish Independence War.

The present book branches out from my dissertation, in which I examined the fourteenth-century cultural transition from Byzantine to Ottoman rule and its reflection on the built environment in Bithynia, with Bursa at its center. Over the years, I have published various sections from my dissertation as articles. Because no comprehensive study exists examining the birth of the first Ottoman capital, I decided herein to narrow my lens to Bursa, narrating the first century of Ottoman-era transformations in the walled city and the suburbs.

I would like to thank Robert Ousterhout for supervising my doctoral studies and dissertation, as well as my committee members, Dede F. Ruggles, Anne D. Hedeman, and Rick Layton. I owe them all my knowledge about art and architectural production in the Byzantine and Medieval worlds (East and West), and I am so deeply grateful. Each also shaped and redirected my approach to teaching and my goal to inspire my students to care about what they are looking at so that they understand why it matters and can grasp the ways cultural and artistic legacy shapes our understanding of the world.

I extend my thanks to Tomasz Hoskins, Rory Gormley, James Tupper, and Yasmin Garcha of I. B. Tauris for carefully editing my work, and Adriana Brioso for designing the elegant cover. I am grateful to Mohammed Raffi, Aarthi Natarajan, and Nandini Sathish for their kind assistance and prompt response in the typesetting process. Many thanks are due to the constructive comments of the anonymous reader. I am also grateful to Jason Warshof for teaching me how to write and also reading almost everything I have written in my postdoctoral years. I thank Alyssa De Villiers for reading and meticulously editing this whole text.

I am also grateful to several institutions for supporting my pre- and postdoctoral fieldwork and archaeological survey in Bursa. These include the Alan K. and Leonarda F. Laing Fellowship at the University of Illinois, the Barakat Trust at the University of Oxford, the Dan David Foundation at Tel Aviv University, the Turkish Cultural Foundation, the American Research Institute in Istanbul, Dumbarton Oaks, the Consulate General of Sweden in Istanbul, and the Anatolian Civilizations Center at Koç University. For granting me a permit to conduct an archaeological study, as well as opening their storage and discussing the results of the salvage excavation notes and visuals with me, I am most grateful to the Ministry of Culture and Tourism and the Bursa Archaeological Museum. The Ministry of Defense in Turkey granted me a permit to carry out my fieldwork on their premises, and the Metropolitan Municipality of Bursa assisted me in the best possible way they could. Asuman Arslan was the representative from the Ministry overseeing my work, and I appreciate her kind assistance in overcoming bureaucratic and fieldwork problems. I did most of the revisions on the book while working as a postdoctoral associate in "The Impact of the Ancient City," a project funded by the European Research Council (Grant/ERC Advanced Grant Agreement n693418) at the Faculty of Classics at the University of Cambridge. I am grateful to the members of the project, especially Andrew Wallace-Hadrill, Elizabeth Key Fowden, and Beth Clark. The project meetings encouraged me to rethink the concepts of the classical versus Islamic city and the formation of the Ottoman city.

Several colleagues, mentors, and friends have shown a genuine interest in, and followed, my work on Bursa. Among them, I would like to extend my heartfelt thanks to Enver Yücel, founder and chairman of Bahçeşehir University, who back in 2010 when I started teaching at Bahçeşehir encouraged me to write a book on the birth of Bursa as an Ottoman city. I am grateful to the former deans, the late Ahmet Eyüce, Sema Esen Soygeniş, and current dean Murat Dündar of the Faculty of Architecture and Design at Bahçeşehir University for their support. Along the way, I have also received exemplary counsel, encouragement, and support from Scott Redford, Amy Singer, Heath Lowry, April Kamp-Whittaker, Larry Conyers, Oya Pancaroğlu, Alessandra Ricci, Maria Cristina Carile, Julia Sienkewicz, Aslı Akışık, Tamara Dubowitz, Lars Karlsson, Karin Ådahl, Ingmar Karlsson, Jesper Blid, Feryal Tansuğ, Angelos Dourlaris, Bülent Erdoğan, Grigor Boykov, Mariya Kiprovska, Elpidophoros Lambrianidis, Sergio Zevi, Pagona Papadopoulou, Şahin Kılıç, Ayşegül Çalı-Kılıç, Nilay Özlü, İpek Aksoy Polat, Ivana Jevtić, Suzan Yalman, Gülru Tanman, İklil Selçuk, Kutlu Akalın, Tuğba Tanyeri-Erdemir, Sotiris Voyadjis, Alia Al-Kadi, Siren Çelik, Robert M. Hayden, Eser Çalıkuşu, Jack Woodford, and Osman Gökhan Baş. These individuals helped me in many different ways. I thank Hidayet Softaoğlu and Oğuz Orkun Doma for their help on the drawings and maps. As always, all remaining mistakes, flaws, and misinterpretations are mine. My heartfelt gratitude goes to Yeliz Yakupoğlu and the late Kamuran Yakupoğlu who hosted me and my GPR team at their beautiful home in the old city of Bursa.

Last but not least, I would like to thank my sisters, Ayten, Gülten, and Hatice, and brothers, Ali, Hüseyin, and Soner, who always stood by me and supported me with their unconditional love and affection, along with financial support, room and board, loans of their cars, rides to the sites, help with bureaucracy when I was out of the country, and especially filling me up with *içli köfte*, *pirpirim cacığı*, *sumaklı çoban salata*, *sütlaç*, and endless cups of coffee. Two of my nephews, Uğur and Deniz, accompanied me on my first trips to Bursa back in 2003 and 2004 purely out of interest in *iskender kebap* and *marron glacé*. Soon after they became fans of the *hans* and the *Ulu Cami*.

Of course, my long-gone parents deserve an acknowledgment. Sultan and Mehmet always advised that a good education would result in life's greatest wisdom. Their perhaps naïve devotion to the pursuit of knowledge coupled with an awareness of the world around them was taken up as a mantra, especially by two of my brothers, Ali and Soner, to whom I cannot express enough gratitude. My mother, in particular, kindled my interest in cities by playing a memory game with me that included naming a fruit or vegetable and a monument or a historic figure for which each Turkish city was famous. Our picnics in Malatya involved visiting the derelict Armenian churches, the tombs of Alevi saints, and the *Ulu Cami* in Malatya.

Rumeli Hisarı (Istanbul)
September 2019

Illustrations

Map

1. Map of Anatolia in the mid-fourteenth century. (Drawn by the author and Oğuz Orkun Doma) — 3

Figures

1. A view into Bursa in 1827 from the west, by Löwenhielm. (Uppsala University, Rare Books Collection) — 2
2. Siting of the socioreligious complexes (*külliyes*), neighborhoods, and landmarks in Bursa. (Google Earth-generated image by Suna Çağaptay) — 16
3. Post-earthquake Cadastral Map of 1862 showing the Old City. (Drawn by Hidayet Softaoğlu based on Ayverdi, *Osmanlı Mimarîsinin*) — 26
4. A view looking into Çekirge, the western suburbs, the Old Bath on the right, and the siting of the Convent-*Masjid* and *Külliye* of Murad I, nineteenth century. (Photo: Sebah & Joaillier, Personal Collection) — 31
5. The 1337 inscription, now immured within the façade of the Şehadet (Martyrdom) Mosque, mentioning the Friday Mosque of Orhan built in the Old City on the left. (Photo: Suna Çağaptay) — 35
6. The sketch showing the tombs of Osman and Orhan. (After J.-P. Grélois *Dr John Covel Voyages en Turquie/Texte établi, annoté et traduit*. Paris, 1998, 146, fig. b4) — 36
7. The Friday Mosque of Orhan in the old city by J. Bernard Fischer von Erlach, 1720s. (University of Heidelberg Rare Books Collection) — 37

8	The Mausolea of Osman (dome in the forefront) and Orhan (higher-domed structure in the middle) by Catenacci, 1835. (Bibliothèque nationale de France Rare Books Collection)	40
9	General view of the Opus Sectile Panel from the Mausoleum of Orhan. (Photo: Suna Çağaptay)	42
10	Plan of the lower city, showing the Convent-*Masjid* of Orhan, 1339, Bayezid I's *Ulu Cami*, and the commercial buildings. (Drawn by Hidayet Softaoğlu based on Ayverdi, *Osmanlı Mimarîsinin*)	51
11	Façade of the Convent-*Masjid* of Orhan. (Photo: Suna Çağaptay)	52
12	Isometric view of the double-storied Convent-*Masjid* of Murad I, 1363–85. (Drawn by Hidayet Softaoğlu based on Orbay, *Bursa*, after Kuzucular, for the *Aga Khan Award*)	54
13	Façade of the Convent-*Masjid* of Murad I, 1363–85. (Photo: Suna Çağaptay)	55
14	The Church of Saint Sophia, Ohrid, Macedonia, 1313–14. (Photo: Suna Çağaptay)	56
15	Façade of the Convent-*Masjid* of Bayezid I (Photo: Suna Çağaptay)	59
16	Plan of Bayezid I's *külliye*. (Drawn by Hidayet Softaoğlu based on Arapi, *Archnet*)	84
17	Irgandı Bridge, the current state of the bridge after the restorations. (Photo: Suna Çağaptay)	97
18	General view into the Cocoon Han. (Photo: Suna Çağaptay)	99
19	Stanislaw Chelebowski's 1878 depiction of the 1402 event when Bayezid I was taken captive by Timur. (Lviv National Art Gallery in Ukraine) (Photo: Suna Çağaptay)	102
20	A view looking into the old city, *Şehadet* (Martyrdom) Mosque on the upper left and the tombs of Osman and Orhan, as well as the *Bey Saray* situated to its right, drawn from the east, possibly from the area of the *Külliyes* of Bayezid I and Mehmed I, by Löwenhielm, 1827. (Uppsala Library Rare Books Collection)	109

Legend Captions for Map 1 and Figures 2, 3, 10, and 16

Map 1   Anatolia in the mid-fourteenth century

Figure 2   Siting of the socioreligious complexes (*külliyes*), neighborhoods, and landmarks from L to R: **(1)** Murad I (aka *Hüdavendigar*); **(2)** Murad II (aka *Muradiye*); **(3)** Old City with the Mausolea of Osman and Orhan, *Şehadet* (Martyrdom) Mosque, as well as *Bey Saray*; **(4)** Grand Mosque (aka *Ulu Cami*) of Bayezid I; **(5)** Orhan; **(6)** Mehmed I (aka Green or *Yeşil*); **(7)** Bayezid I; **(8)** Shrine of Abdal Murad **(9)** Irgandı Bridge

Pictograms for the neighborhoods of the fourteenth-century Bursa: Crescent: Muslim; Star: Jewish; Square cross: Greek Orthodox; and Cross with longer descending arm: Armenian

NB: Numbers 2 and 6 fall beyond the purview of this book and are only mentioned briefly in the text. The extent of the neighborhoods is only tentative.

Figure 3   Post-earthquake Cadastral Map of 1862, showing the Old City
Legends include **(1)** Tomb of Osman; **(2)** Tomb of Orhan; **(3)** *Bey Saray*; **(4)** Friday Mosque of Orhan; **(5)** *Madrasa* of Orhan; **(6)** Orhan's Bathhouse; **(7)** Mosque of Alaeddin; **(8)** Şehadet (Martyrdom) Mosque; **(9)** *Saltanat Kapı*; **(10)** *Kaplıca Kapı* **(11)** *Zindan Kapı*; **(12)** *Su kapı* **(13)** *Yer kapı*; **(14)** *Ortapazar* Street, possibly following the axis of the ancient *decumanus maximus*

N.B. The buildings identified as 4, 5, and 6 do not survive today

Figure 10   Siting of structures in the lower city **(1)** Convent-*Masjid* of Orhan, 1339; **(2)** Bayezid I's *Ulu Cami*; **(3)** *Koza Han* (Cocoon); **(4)** *Emir Han*; **(5)** Bathhouse; **(6)** *Fidan Han*; **(7)** *Geyve Han*; **(8)** *Bedesten*, (Bezasistan); **(9)** *Sipahi Han* (Cavaliers); **(10)** New Market

Figure 16   Siting of Bayezid I's külliye **(1)** Convent-*Masjid* and *Külliye* of Bayezid I, **(2)** Madrasa; **(3)** Tomb; **(4)** Royal Garden Palace; **(5)** Hospice; **(6)** Bathhouse; **(7)** Gate; **(8)** Aqueduct, located in the east suburb of the Old City, 1390s

Note on Copyright for Previous Publications

Some parts of Chapters 2 and 3 have been previously published as the articles noted below. I would like to thank the editors of *BMGS* and *Muqarnas* for permitting me to reprint them.

"Prousa/Bursa, A City within the City: Chorography, Conversion, and Choreography," *Byzantine and Modern Greek Studies* 35.1 (2011): 45–69.

"Frontierscape: Reconsidering Bithynian Structures and Their Builders on the Byzantine-Ottoman Cusp," *Muqarnas* 28 (2011): 155–91.

A Note on Spelling, Names, Maps, and Quotations

This book uses modern Turkish "scholarly" spellings for names and place names. The modern Turkish alphabet has 29 letters, of which three consonants and three vowels are unfamiliar to those who do not know Turkish. These are:

> C as J in Jane
> Ç as Ch in Chalk
> Ğ silent; lengthens the previous vowel
> I as dotted I in Cousin
> Ö as Ö in German Schön
> Ş as Sh in Ship
> Ü as Ü in Tür

Turkish also has a dotted i/İ, which this book uses for Ottoman personal and place names, for example, İznik not Iznik (but not used for Istanbul).

Although the book uses the modern academic spelling for personal names and toponyms, I have used older treatments for names such as Murad, Bayezid, and Mehmed for the Ottoman sultans Murat, Beyazıt, and Mehmet. For architectural terms, for cultural groups, I have followed the spellings in the *Cambridge History of Islam*, such as Rum Seljuks, Aydinids, and Mamluks; for general Islamic architectural terms in Arabic and/or Turkish, without diacritical marks and italicized (*madrasa*, *masjid*, *iwan*, *zaviye* and *imaret*). For toponyms, I have used both Anglicized Greek names and their Ottoman equivalents for the first mention or when a transitional cultural context is implied: see, for example, Prousa/Bursa and Nicaea/İznik. I have used the term Mongol-Ilkhanids when referring to the group in its own realm in Anatolia and Persia, while I have used Mongols in the larger context. For Greek and Latin terms, I follow the spelling in the *Oxford Dictionary of Byzantium*, except for Prousa instead of Prusa, for which I prefer its ancient Greek spelling.

The quotations used in the book have been shortened, and the text has been revised when translated from other languages.

Chronological Chart

Osman (r. 1290s–1324)
Orhan (r. 1324–62)
Murad I (r. 1362–89)
Bayezid I (r. 1389–1402)
Interregnum Period (1402–13)
Mehmed I (r. 1413–21)
Murad II (r. 1421–44 and 1446–51)

Introduction

The First Capital of the Ottoman Empire

A moon arose from the holy man's breast and came to sink in Osman Ghazi's breast. A tree then sprouted from his navel, and its shade compassed the world... [When Osman awoke] he went and told the story to the sheikh, who said, "Osman, my son, congratulations for the imperial office [bestowed by God] on you and your descendants."

Aşıkpaşazade, *Osmanoğulları'nın Tarihi*, 9–10.

Osman, the eponymous founder of the Ottoman Empire, is famed for having had the dream recounted above, in which a tree "sprouting from his navel" becomes fully grown, symbolizing the stamina of his successors and the domains they would conquer.[1] With this dream, Osman took on the mantle of responsibility for leading his people. This dream became a myth, it probably was always one. But the rise to power of the Ottomans several decades later required more than myth or the intervention of a divine hand—it necessitated the conquest of people, villages, and cities.[2]

Situated on a hilltop nestled against Mount Olympus, a walled city known to the Byzantines as Prousa[3] (Figure 1) was conquered by the Ottomans in 1326, whose impressive topography was beautifully drawn by the Swedish diplomat and artist Carl Gustaf Löwenhielm in 1825. It quickly became an important urban center while serving as the first capital (*ilk payitaht* in Turkish) of the Ottoman Empire.[4] The city was also known as *yeşil Bursa* (lit. green Bursa), given its importance in the hierarchy of Ottoman capitals and its verdant landscape.[5] Ibn Battuta, traveling in 1331, just five years after the conquest, praised the city for its vibrant commercial life and "fine bazaars, and wide streets, surrounded on all sides by gardens and running springs."[6] The mountain backdrop and the built environment led the French botanist Joseph de Tournefort to compare it, in 1701, to Granada, Spain.[7]

Figure 1 A view into Bursa in 1827 from the west, by Löwenhielm. (Uppsala University, Rare Books Collection).

The city was a commercial center where textiles and spices were exchanged between east and west. For example, Bertrandon de la Broquière reported leaving Bursa for Istanbul "with three Genoese merchants who were taking spices to Pera," the district today known as Beyoğlu, in Istanbul.[8] Travelers from the fourteenth century onward emphasized the city's impressive practices of moriculture and sericulture (raising mulberries for silkworms).[9] Johannes Schiltberger, a Bavarian captive in the city in 1397, compared Bursa's silk industry with that of Crimean Caffa and Damascus.[10] The city's therapeutic waters were also praised by many. In 1665, Jean Thevénot wrote, "The castle has been founded by the daughter of the Byzantine emperor, who suffers from leper, for being miraculously cured by the natural hot springs." He continued: "Waters that run through the town are so hot that they easily boil eggs."[11] Evliya Çelebi noted that houses had running water and is often quoted as having said, "In sum, Bursa consists of water."[12]

Despite these fascinating details and its status as the first capital of the Ottomans, no comprehensive study of the city during this period exists. Furthermore, descriptions of the rise of Ottoman Bursa have largely ignored how the city's sui generis early Ottoman identity was shaped by the synthesis of Byzantine and Ottoman cultures, two major ethno-religious cultures at that time. This book thus takes on the task of reconstructing Bursa's Ottoman identity in the fourteenth century.

The Ottoman buildings of this period reveal different functions and design concepts compared to their Byzantine counterparts; at the same time, much can be learned from the similarities. Considering the involvement of Greek masons and builders from Bithynia (northwestern Turkey, the region where Bursa is located; see Map 1) who worked for the Ottomans, as well as evidence on construction practices and materials used, the relationship between the two cultures can be regarded as fruitful. I therefore discuss how cross-cultural and cross-religious borrowing and integration played into the creation of the built environment of Ottoman Bursa. I also focus on the impact of individual builders and workshop practices, in contrast to an emphasis on patronage. My discussion does cover patronage-related material, but mainly as a means of allowing for complete discussion of the overall subject matter. The emphasis on hybrid culture, meanwhile, allows me to escape the bind of previous scholars who were overreliant on patronage. My portrait strives to avoid the rigid typologies of the past, instead depicting dynamic contributors to the transitional capital of a rising empire.

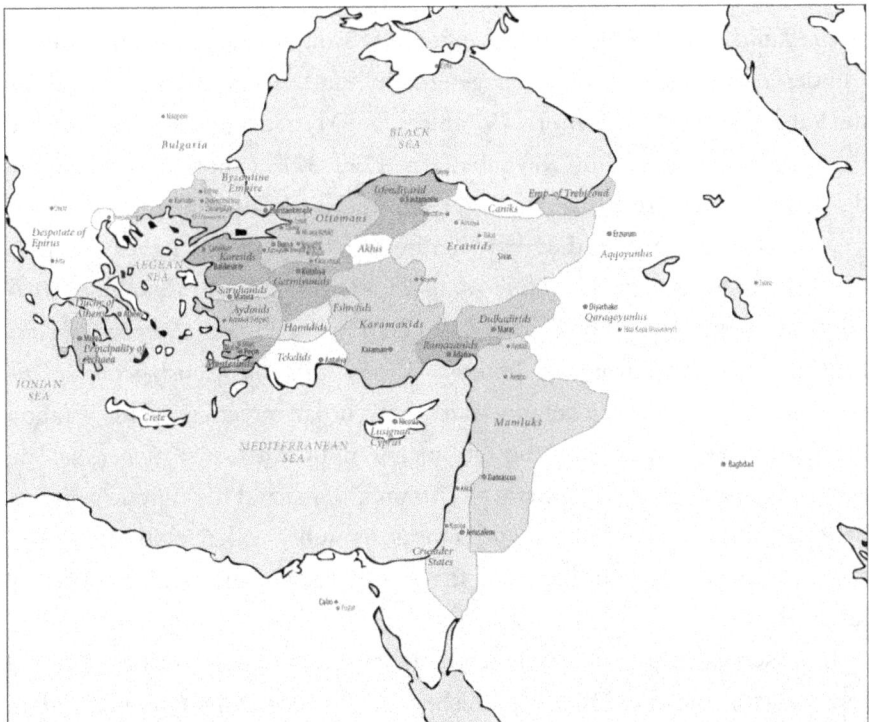

Map 1 Map of Anatolia in the mid-fourteenth century. (Drawn by the author and Oğuz Orkun Doma).

Previous and Current Scholarship

Historian Colin Imber has called the fourteenth century a "black hole"[13] in the formation of the Ottoman state in Bursa, owing to a paucity of textual evidence. Perhaps for this reason, no book has ever been devoted to Bursa during the transition from Byzantine to Ottoman rule. This book draws from the limited textual record noted by Imber, but more notably it examines structures and the stories they tell. It also complements several recent monographs (published books and dissertations) that show nuance, critical thinking, and scholarly rigor. These include Rachel Goshgarian's "Beyond the Social and the Spiritual: Redefining the Urban Confraternities of Late Medieval Anatolia" (unpublished doctoral dissertation, Harvard University, 2008) on methods of conquest and *ahis* (guilds, linked to inverted-T structures, that briefly ruled in fourteenth-century Anatolia); İklil Selçuk's "State and Society in the Marketplace: A Study of Late Fifteenth-Century Bursa" (unpublished doctoral dissertation, Harvard University, 2009) on state-sponsored economic life and the *ahis*; Buket Kitapçı Bayrı's *Warriors, Martyrs, and Dervishes: Moving Frontiers, Shifting Identities in the Land of Rome (13th–15th centuries)*, Brill, 2019) on Turkish-Muslim frontier narratives, identity, and geography; and Suzan Yalman's "Building the Sultanate of Rum: Memory, Urbanism and Mysticism in the Architectural Patronage of 'Ala al-Din Kayqubad (r. 1220–37)" (unpublished doctoral dissertation, Harvard University, 2011) on Rum-Seljuk urbanism.

Several important studies have addressed the topic of larger Anatolia, but Patricia Blessing's *Rebuilding Anatolia after the Mongol Conquest* (2016) omits the period my book covers. Çiğdem Kafescioğlu's *Constantinopolis/Istanbul: Cultural Encounter, Imperial Vision, and the Construction of the Ottoman Capital* (2009) demonstrates how urban practices made Istanbul the representational face of the Ottoman Empire. In a sort of parallel, my book attempts to recount the rise of Ottoman Bursa and the unique synthesis between Byzantine and Ottoman cultures, as well as other cultural shapers, such as Latinized Byzantium and the Mamluks, that have affected Bursa's urban identity.

Most scholarship has encouraged nationalism on one side or the other.[14] A century ago, Herbert Gibbons published *The History of the Ottoman Empire* (1916), which posits that the mix of "wild Asiatic" and "European" ethnicity foreordained the greatness of the empire. In texts published in 1922 (*Anadolu'da*

İslamiyet; Islam in Anatolia) and 1935 (*Les origines de l'empire ottoman*), M. Fuat Köprülü rejected Gibbons's claim to a Byzantine contribution to Ottoman greatness, focusing instead on Mongol-Ilkhanid and Rum Seljuk origins. Just a few years later, Paul Wittek (*The Rise of the Ottoman Empire*) explained the Ottoman rise in terms of the *Gazi* thesis, a desire to expand Islam.[15]

Wittek's paradigm endured for several decades, as historians identified Ottoman military, political, and societal aspirations. Most recently, Heath Lowry has argued that Wittek saw Ahmedi, a fourteenth-century literary figure who cited *gaza* or *gazis* in his verses, as an indication of actual events.[16] Lowry contends that Wittek's flawed conception of Ahmedi as the "versified chronicler" of the period, along with his errant transliteration of the "1337 inscription,"[17] does not justify the claim that what united Anatolian Muslims was a common desire to vanquish the infidels.[18] Indeed, Wittek's *Gazi* thesis drew counterarguments from many, among them Speros Vryonis, who contended that Islam's rise in the region long predated the emergence of the Ottomans.[19] Rudi Paul Lindner, in rigorous if imperfect fashion,[20] demonstrated the tribal nature of the Ottomans, noting the Christian contribution to their rise.[21] Other critics include Colin Heywood, in his reading of Wittek's autobiography; Colin Imber, in line with his aforementioned famous quotation citing a lack of textual evidence;[22] Cemal Kafadar,[23] who tapped new fifteenth- and sixteenth-century sources, as well as Turkish and non-Turkish scholarship, to reconstruct the Anatolian frontier; and Heath Lowry, again, who argued for the emergence of a "confederate brotherhood" based on (1) the Byzantine and Balkan nobility and (2) Christian peasant life in the fourteenth century.[24]

While historians were busy discussing the *Gazi* thesis, art and architectural historians turned to the buildings and sites to understand the broader context, producing a new wave of scholarship on the cultural transition from Byzantine to Ottoman. In this sense, the first seeds of this book were planted in 1968, six years before I was born. That year, leading Byzantinists Cyril Mango and Ihor Ševčenko initiated a three-year project to study Byzantine churches and monasteries surviving on the southern shore of the Sea of Marmara. Following in the footsteps of F. W. Hasluck, who suggested continuity in construction techniques from the Byzantine to Ottoman periods,[25] Mango and Ševčenko drew attention to the similarities between late Byzantine architecture and Ottoman architecture in Bithynia, and particularly the role of Bursa in this transition.[26] This work was taken up by Slobodan Ćurčić and Robert

Ousterhout, the latter studying late Byzantine and early Ottoman monuments side by side in order to understand cultural continuity and the role of masons in that transition.[27]

On the Ottoman studies front, Albert Gabriel's two-volume monograph from 1958 is among the most comprehensive publications in the field.[28] Around the same time, Turkish scholar Ekrem Hakkı Ayverdi undertook a major study of early Ottoman architecture.[29] He categorized it as purely Turkish and Ottoman and strictly opposed suggestions of any sort of Byzantine impact. Ayverdi and his school ignored the Byzantine contribution to the emerging Ottoman architecture in Bursa, part of a broader perpetual neglect of the impact of Byzantine culture in wider cultural studies.[30] This approach, rooted mainly in ideology, also reached literary circles.[31] Poet and novelist Ahmet H. Tanpınar, writing *Five Cities* in the mid-1940s, claimed that Bursa is an Ottoman city whose very identity lies in its fourteenth-century "spirit."[32] He said, "Whatever the changes, disasters or neglect, whatever progressive or felicitous stages it (Bursa) might have gone through, it has always preserved the spirit of its formative age, it conserves with us through it and breathes its poetry."[33]

Outline and Structure of the Book

To chronicle the architectural transition in Bursa, the book is divided into six chapters focusing on (1) the *historical framework* during the rise of the Ottomans and Bursa as an *Ottoman city*; (2) the roles of continuity, conversion, and reuse in this urban scene; (3) the *Sultanic mosques* in local context; (4) the roots and context for the *inverted-T* form in architecture; (5) an exploration of theory on *memory and monuments*; and (6) concluding remarks on "invisible Prousa."

This book's thematic organization owes much to scholarship by Dede Fairchild Ruggles on Hispano-Umayyad Spain,[34] in which she examines the social meaning of the constructed landscape as it transitions from one culture to another: claiming, legitimizing, and inhabiting. Chapters 2, 3, and 4 revolve around these systems (in that order). To Ruggles' triad, I add a fourth dimension: the expansion of the city into suburban areas and control of the land, the focus of Chapters 5 and 6.

As Chapter 1 explains, by the mid-thirteenth century Byzantine power in Anatolia was in decline. The Byzantines held just the northwestern area known as Bithynia, which had only ever been controlled by the Rum Seljuks for a sixteen-year period in the late eleventh century. Elsewhere in the region, the Mongol-Ilkhanids began to replace the Rum Seljuk state, most dramatically at the Battle of Kösedağ in 1243. Although most of Anatolia was subsequently officially ruled by the Mongol-Ilkhanid court, the situation on the ground was fluid, with clusters of Byzantines, Armenians, Mongol-Ilkhanids, Rum Seljuks, and Muslim principalities holding on to power in different areas and sometimes cooperating. It was against such a backdrop that the Ottoman Turks seized Prousa in the early fourteenth century from the Greeks, then led by the local Byzantine potentate Saroz.[35] A decade-long siege preceded the final capture of the city, at which time the Ottomans began developing a new urban vocabulary to match their imperial ambitions.

In Chapter 2, I look at textual and archaeological sources to reconstruct the city of Prousa. I examine it in its first stages of transformation into Bursa upon its conquest by the Ottomans, covering the reuse and conversion of existing buildings, new construction, and attitudes toward ancient and Byzantine buildings. The overall intent is to gain a clearer sense of the chorographic treatments of the Ottoman landscape. The Byzantine city of Prousa had mainly been confined to a citadel on a promontory with a palace and four Byzantine monastic establishments.[36] When the Ottomans took control, they converted two monastery buildings into mausolea for the founders of the Ottoman state, restored the palace and the fortification walls, created residential areas, and constructed buildings. The Ottomanization of the city was a twofold project. In the first stage, architectural conversions took place at sites of former Byzantine splendor, with the attendant reuse and adaptation of Byzantine spaces. The Ottomans then transformed the existing urban order by adding new structures and reviving elements of the ancient Greek, Roman, and Byzantine layers. In other words, Bursa's reinventers "Ottomanized the past" as they built their capital city into a metropolis.

Some scholars have labeled the recycling and spoliation of Byzantine buildings by the Muslim conquerors "utilitarian opportunism" or "triumphalist appropriation" based on a perceived common Islamic practice. The ideas of urban transformation, conversion, and rebuilding loom large in the conquest of cities and the conversion of their inhabitants to Islam in the medieval

Anatolian context.³⁷ One such example is the *Danişmendname,* an epic narrative of conquest and conversion, originally written in 1265 and rewritten in 1360. This work describes how Hilfat Gazi, a son of Christian converts, demolished the church built by his grandfather and transformed it into a *madrasa* in Amasya.³⁸ The architectural and political conversion went hand in hand. The Ottoman chronicle known as *Düsturname,* written by Enveri in the mid-fifteenth century, refers to the Aydinid ruler of Birgi, Mehmed Bey and how "He converted many churches into mosques."³⁹ This account also compiles the deeds of the heroic Aydinid ruler and raider Umur Bey (d. 1348), as well as other authors and popular epic legends, and shows how the *gazis* of Anatolia, such as the Aydinids and Ottomans, succeeded due to their commitment to the holy war against the infidels as well as their cooperation with them, achieving a political superiority over their rivals.⁴⁰

These accounts reveal important details about dismantling and reusing buildings and incorporating them into the evolving design in medieval Anatolia. But rather than seeing these examples as "utilitarian opportunism" or "triumphalist appropriation," I highlight, instead, the creative and integrative nature of the Ottoman civilization. In doing so, I examine patterns of conversion and the transposition of buildings from one cultural setting to another. The Ottomans accommodated the city's visual legacy by preserving local forms with historical referents. A distinct, local urban-visual language thus emerged, a new architectural idiom. My argument is supported by new evidence. An 1855 earthquake obliterated much of early Ottoman Bursa, which has made reconstructing the city a challenge for historians today,⁴¹ but this book includes the results of the first ground-penetrating radar survey (end of Chapter 2) to address this challenge in the citadel, helping to bring to light Bursa's early Ottoman urban fabric and identity.

The next three chapters examine the second stage of Ottomanization, building anew in the old city and suburbs. Accordingly, the third chapter examines the wall construction techniques and decorative details of the early Ottoman buildings. It discusses how Bursa gradually acquired an Ottoman character while still retaining many traits of the local architectural characteristics of Bithynia, including brick-and-stone masonry and banded voussoirs, suggesting continuity and resilience amid the turmoil brought by changes in leadership. Although the architectural style of the convent-*masjids* of Orhan (r. 1324–1362) and Murad I (r. 1362–89) has been identified as both "hybrid" and "semi-Byzantine," previous comparisons between Byzantine and Ottoman buildings fail to go beyond superficial similarities such as the development of the portico façade. A closer look at the city's grand structures reveals links to the broader Mediterranean, including Dalmatia, Apulia, and Emilia-Romagna, regions also affected by the Mamluk hand in the Levant—and, in turn, by the previous century's Ayyubid-Crusader encounter. These connections highlight the extent to which construction was a shared enterprise and dispel oversimplistic readings. In particular, a fresh interpretation of the shift from brick-and-stone to ashlar masonry in the Friday mosque of Bayezid I (r. 1389–1402) suggests the emergence of a distinctive local idiom.

The fourth chapter looks at the layout of the distinctive inverted-T structures introduced in the previous chapter, which prevailed during the Ottoman transition in Bursa, along with their roots and context. These structures served many functions, from prayer to counseling to food distribution. Scholars have assumed that this construction form marked an imitation of Byzantine practices rather than reflecting a process of continuity, and furthermore that the plan came from Central Asia, possibly introduced by the Mongols. But this Mongol thesis relies too heavily on a nationalistic worldview linked to Central Asian origins. To the contrary, this multifunctional structure type was found across the larger eastern Mediterranean in the late Antique Anatolian context, for example, in administrative and palatial structures in Ephesos as well as in the rock-cut reception halls of middle Byzantine Cappadocia. Later, there were similar plans in Abbasid, Tulunid, Fatimid, Norman Sicilian, Ayyubid and Mamluk buildings.

Chapter 5 goes beyond the appearance (façades and decorative details) and plan of these structures to examine how the city expanded past the old city walls a century after the Ottomans took control. While the Ottomans kept major Byzantine buildings and the ceremonial axis of the citadel intact, during Orhan's reign they reoriented the urban center to a new lower city, closer to the plains abutting Mount Olympus, rendering the previous monuments less central to Bursa's economic and social life. For example, the 1862 Cadastral Map displays the Orhan-era imperial socioreligious complex, known as the *külliye*, as an ideal stopping point between the upper city and the tombs of the founders, the palace, and the dynastic mausolea complex below. Thus emerges the notion of "urban choreography," whereby rulers and builders manipulated urban design to direct the gaze of inhabitants (and visitors) so as to give primacy to the current leadership. In particular, under Murad I the focal point moved west of the urban center, where hot springs were plentiful, whereas subsequently Bayezid I built his complex to the east. Such indicators of dynastic succession became landmarks in the evolving cityscape.

In the sixth chapter, I discuss the notion of the (in)visibility of Bursa's fourteenth-century layer today, even though the Ottoman Empire has now been defunct for a century and 165 years have passed since the earthquake leveled much of the city. All such historical turning points, including the very ascendance of the Ottomans, are subject to distortion, appropriation, and neglect when memorialized. Thus, as the empire's first capital city, Bursa's Ottoman/Islamic/Turkish identity has often been emphasized in contemporary Turkish scholarship at the expense of other identities. In works by art and architectural historians, the city has often been portrayed as having an insignificant pre-Ottoman past, as if the Ottomans created the city from scratch. Yet, archaeological sources as well as visual and written sources by travelers weave a richer and more accurate narrative of the city and its Ottoman inhabitation, making clear that the contributions of the past do not threaten the authenticity of the present.

1

Becoming Bursa

The city of Bursa (Map 1), located in the mountains of northwestern Anatolia (Bithynia), stretches along the lower slopes of Mount Olympus, or Ulu Dağ (also known as Keşiş Dağ, or "the mountain of the monks").[1] Between the city and coastal mountains to the north lies a fertile alluvial plain called Yeşilova ("Green Plain," or the ancient Mygdonia). This plain is irrigated by the Nilüfer (Odrysses) River, which originates in the southern foothills of Mount Olympus and flows along a route to the northeast of the Sea of Marmara, west of Mudanya (Apamea Myrlea).[2] The Nilüfer is joined by smaller rivers in the valley. Amid the ravines created by these tributaries, on a bold rock terrace, the city now known as Bursa has stood for over two thousand years.

The foothills and streams that mark the city's topography shaped its growth and gave it a different character from the Anatolian Plateau to the east and from Istanbul, a hundred kilometers to the north. This connection between the built environment and the natural landscape is often overlooked, according to Oya Pancaroğlu.[3] Making Bursa distinctive, Pancaroğlu said, was "its rich soil, healthy climate and idyllic topography."[4] Ravines divide the city into three sections and water sources, both hot and cold, abound.

An Emerging Ottoman Identity

The significance of Bursa far predates the arrival of the Ottomans. The city, then Prousa, was founded in 202 BC by the Bithynian king Prousias I (r. 228–185 BC).[5] It lay near the Byzantine capital, Constantinople, which overshadowed its growth,[6] but the city's location along major trade routes on both land and sea made it an important urban center.

After the Battle of Manzikert in 1071, the defenses of Byzantine Anatolia collapsed in the face of the invasion of seminomadic Turks.[7] Within twenty years, only small pockets of Anatolia remained under Byzantine control, and the Rum Seljuks, a cadet branch of the Great Seljuks of Iran had set up a state based in Nicaea (İznik).[8] Aided by participants in the First Crusade and by astute diplomacy, the Byzantines were able to drive the Rum Seljuks back onto the Anatolian Plateau, where they established a capital at Iconium (Konya). Later, the Mongol threat and the defeat of the Rum Seljuks at the Battle of Köse Dağ in 1243 changed the position completely.[9] By the 1300s, both the Mongols and the Byzantines were in decline. The Byzantine capital was lost to Latin Crusaders in 1204. Although Michael VIII Palaiologos (r. 1259–82) was able to restore Constantinople and some parts of the empire's lands in Anatolia, the overall Byzantine domain had been reduced to an isthmus in western Anatolia. From the end of the thirteenth century into the fourteenth century, a scattering of Aegean islands ruled by the Latins and the Byzantines. The Genoese controlled Chios and Lesbos (Mytilene) and Phokaia; while Venice ruled the islands of Crete, Negroponte, Naxos, Andros, Mykonos, Karpathos, and Santorini; and in 1344, Christian-allied forces captured the harbor in Smyrna and retained control of the port until its fall to Timur in 1402.[10]

Broadly, at the beginning of the fourteenth century, the eastern Mediterranean consisted of a patchwork of small political powers burgeoning and large ones in demise. The ruler of several Turkish principalities had reached the Aegean coastline. The group that had entered Anatolia consisted of not only Turcoman invaders but wandering mystics and townsfolk too.[11] Various petty states emerged, the Ottomans most prominent among them. Ottoman territory enclosed the vestiges of Byzantine territory in Phrygia and Bithynia,[12] and in 1326, the middle of this fluid period, Prousa became the capital of the emerging Ottoman state.[13]

With these changes, and shaped by two centuries of cross-cultural encounters, a new society began to develop within the city. By the late fourteenth century, the city's approximate population was 10,000, a figure calculated by Heath Lowry based on travelers' accounts and archival documents, and included a mix of ethnic, religious, and cultural demographics.[14] In the old city, a new multireligious and multiethnic capital was being built as a part of the earliest efforts toward Ottomanization.[15] People of various ethnic and religious backgrounds, including Turkish and other Muslims, Byzantine Greeks,

Armenians, and Jews, began adopting a new identity as Ottomans. Rather than relinquishing their own religions and cultures, they added a broader identity layer.[16] Indeed, this is what the architectural styles reflect: people from all over Bithynia kept their own artistic or architectural styles even as the Ottomans developed architecture that symbolized their control over the native population.

The inhabitants of early fourteenth-century Prousa/Bursa found themselves in a new society and faced the challenge of forming understandings of the place. The environment and geography, located between the Marmara basin and the Anatolian hinterland, played a central part in this. The historian Rudi Paul Lindner believed that the region's agricultural fertility attracted the Ottomans, and that they realized that Bithynian geography opened up still wider possibilities. In its generally northern and northwestern movement toward areas of greater agricultural and pastoral productivity, important trade routes, and proximity to the sea, the fourteenth-century Ottoman conquest suggests Ottoman interest in urban life, control of trade routes, and easy access to resources.[17] Soon after these conquests, as will be discussed in Chapter 3, the Ottomans shifted their resources in order to sponsor new imperial buildings.

Roman Roots of Byzantine Prousa

Two important written accounts describe urban life in Roman Prousa. The first of these is by a local known as Dio of Prousa or Dio Cocceianus Chrysostom (c. 40–c. 115 AD), a writer, philosopher, and leading figure involved in the city's politics who served as municipal ambassador to Rome. He wrote a series of *Discourses* or *Orations* to share insights on municipal matters such as reimagining the city plan. As discussed further in Chapter 2, he lobbied in particular for the construction of a colonnaded street to beautify the city and keep up with other Anatolian cities, such as Ephesos and Tarsos, and Syrian cities, such as Antioch.[18] The second account is by Pliny the Younger, who was governor of Bithynia from 111 to 113 AD and whose epistolary exchanges with the Roman emperor Trajan (r. 98–117 AD) discuss renewing the bathhouses, the library, and the temple. These letters show that Trajan looked fondly upon the city, which he rebuilt to feature a colonnaded street, along with temples and water mills.[19]

Dio was determined to build not only colonnades and fountains but also "fortifications, harbours, and shipyards."[20] He wanted to make Prousa

> the head of a federation of cities and to bring together in it as great a multitude of inhabitants as I can, and not merely dwellers in this district either, but even, if possible, compelling other cities too to join together with us.[21]

His colonnades and workshops enhanced the city but also created tensions by supplanting the old urban fabric.[22] Despite his many adversaries, Dio managed to complete his colonnade project. The timing corresponded roughly to the reign of the emperor Trajan, predating the wave of remodeling led by his successor, Hadrian (r. 117–38 AD), in the eastern provinces.[23] Dio's ambition to beautify Prousa was complemented by the assignment of Pliny the Younger to the governorship of Bithynia under Trajan.[24]

The correspondence between Pliny the Younger and Trajan gives further insight into urban activities in Prousa. In one letter, for example, Pliny the Younger speaks of a dilapidated bath and his efforts to collect taxes to revitalize it. In another, he describes a different bathhouse "once beautiful but . . . now an unsightly ruin" and recommends abandoning the site. It had been bequeathed by a notable Prousan, Claudius Polyaenus, fifty years prior, with the goal of erecting a shrine to the memory of emperor Claudius (r. 41–54 AD), but nothing had been done and the area was "tumbledown with age." Instead of reviving this area, Pliny the Younger suggested that new baths be constructed "on an open area . . . to enclose with a recess and porticoes the place where the buildings stood" and dedicated to Trajan.[25] In his reply, however, Trajan asked about the state of the shrine to Claudius and did not approve of Pliny's idea to build a new bath complex.[26]

Prousa was renowned for monastic establishments both within the urban walls and on holy Mount Olympus.[27] Menthon claims that the monasteries built in and around Mount Olympus numbered more than a hundred. In the middle Byzantine period, Iconophile patriarchs sought refuge in Prousa from pressure exerted by the Iconoclasts in Constantinople, expanding the town's monastic presence at sites such as Sakkoudion, Medikion,[28] and Horaia Pege.[29] In the thirteenth century, when the Latin Crusaders sacked Constantinople, the Latins also besieged Prousa (1204–5), although they were unsuccessful in the end. The Nicaean emperors-in-exile made donations to enhance Prousa's monastic and civic infrastructure. Byzantine authors such as Gregoras, meanwhile, recorded that in the thirteenth century, Irene, the wife of Emperor John III Vatatzes (r. 1221–54), commissioned the refurbishment of the main church in the monastery dedicated to Saint John Prodromos, which was later reused as mausolea for the early Ottoman sultans.[30]

From Prousa to Bursa

As the city underwent the transition from Prousa to Bursa, the old city's urban legacy was preserved and revitalized, and new residential and commercial areas were developed around it (Figure 2). Three boroughs were founded: one just outside the walls from the time of Orhan, the second to the west and named after Murad I, and the third to the east and named after Bayezid I. The city's inhabitants, its commercial life, and its cultural and military interactions showed a fascinating range of details, as reflected in the writings of travelers in the fourteenth and fifteenth centuries. During its formative period, no other city in Bithynia was comparable. These lesser cities included Nicaea/İznik and Nicomedia/İzmit, conquered shortly thereafter by the Ottomans. The former was the capital of the thirteenth-century Byzantine emperors-in-exile; the latter became an imperial residence under the Tetrarchy of the late antique period. Ottoman conquests in the latter part of the fourteenth century included Adrianople/Edirne in 1361[31] as well as cities in the Balkans, such as Komotini/Gümülcine, Didymoteichon/Dimetoka, and Thessaloniki/Selanik in 1430.[32]

Beyond the Ottoman world, other cities had comparable transformations. The ancient city of Ephesos and its Byzantine counterpart Ayasoluk were conquered by the Aydinids in 1304, a princedom rivaling that of the Ottomans. The Rum Seljuk capital of Konya fell to the Mongol-Ilkhanids in 1243. And Trebizond, on the Byzantine-Caucasian frontier, was the capital city of the Grand Komnenoi, a Byzantine offshoot founded after the fall of Constantinople to the Latin Crusaders in 1204. These cities differed in many ways, but each was a testimony to the changes in Anatolia's urban landscape.

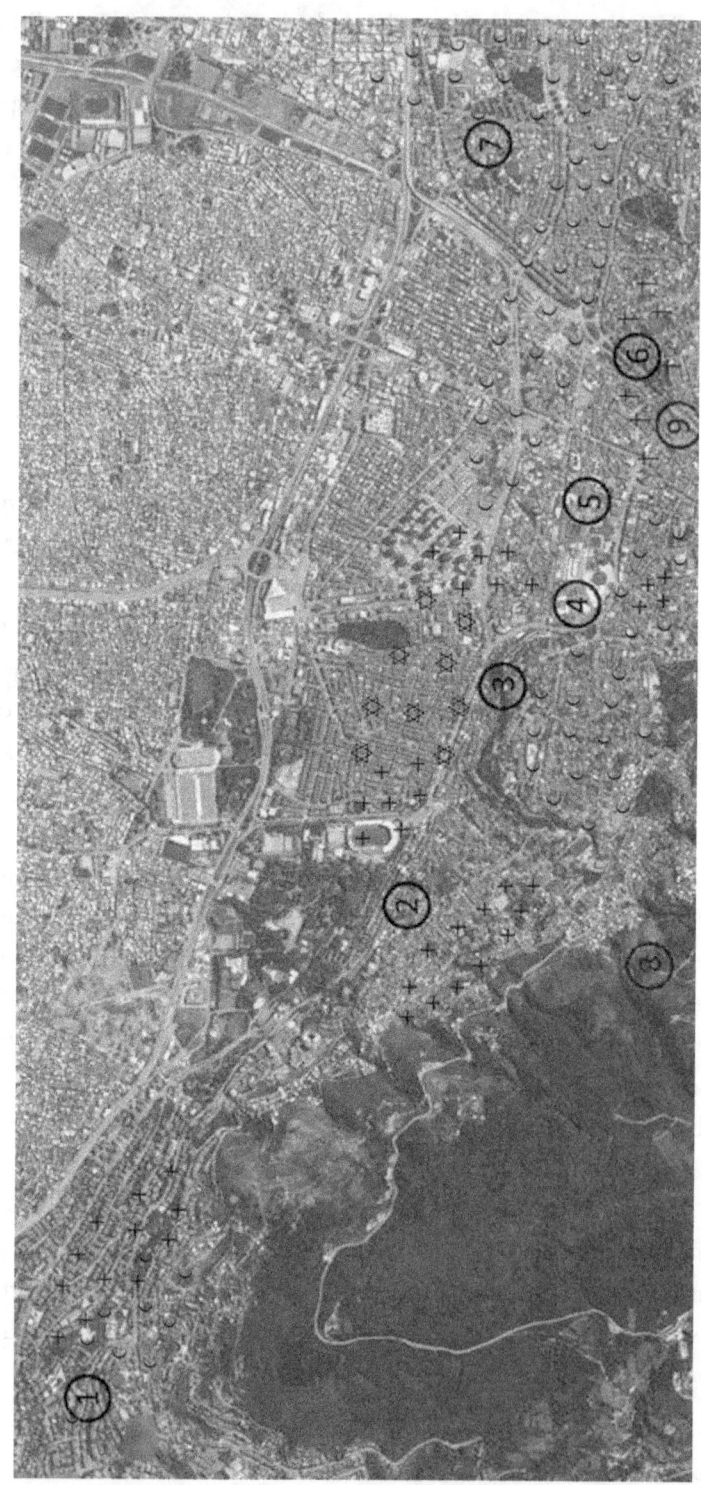

Figure 2 Siting of the socioreligious complexes (*külliyes*), neighborhoods, and landmarks in Bursa. (Google Earth-generated image by Suna Çağaptay).

Defining the Contours of the Islamic City

Orientalist scholars seeking to establish the notion of the Islamic city have focused on the spatial articulation of ethnic, religious, and functional divisions within such cities, as well as the triangulation of a central mosque, marketplace, and the public bath, coupled with social institutions and the emergence of the *umma*, a community of "believers."[33] In those discussions, the case of spontaneous or irregular city planning is often linked with the Islamic city paradigm, in contrast to orthogonal planning, a characteristic of the classical world.[34] However, there has been an overemphasis on the orthogonal planning of classical cities (after all, not all the classical cities had it), and its abandonment in the medieval period in Europe and in Byzantium has often been ignored. In fact, orientalists denigrated the so-called Islamic city by focusing negatively on its mazelike streets and narrow alleys—implying that these attributes did not rise to the level of constituting true cities and, indeed, calling them "non-cities." They thus defined the Islamic cities by what they lacked and not by the richness they offered.[35] Rejecting the orientalist view, scholarship on the Islamic city now acknowledges how such cities borrowed from the classical world, such as in the social role of bathing practices and in *suqs* or bazaars occupying central locations.

Not only has the term "Islamic city" attracted this type of scholarly debate, but the character and context of an Ottoman city[36] has also elicited its own attention. Nowadays, thankfully, a more diversified view of both prevails.[37] On the Ottoman front specifically, I argue for a middle ground to appreciate the continuity from the classical and Christian past to the accommodation of the new religion and its urban constituents. In the case of Bursa, the classical and Byzantine past was acknowledged and reused while at the same time a range of new architectural campaigns were conducted to carry out the transition. My aim herein is to discuss how the Ottoman urban imaginary grew out of Byzantine Prousa, which had itself grown out of Roman-era Prousa. In other words, I intend to attend to each era, rather than eliding the Byzantine one in particular.

Instead of looking backward at how Prousa functioned as a classical or Byzantine city, I engage with the literary and physical evidence for pre-Ottoman Bursa. This approach shows that the inhabitants and rulers of early fourteenth-century Bursa did not turn their backs on their city's past. That city, as we have already seen, was unique in the Ottoman context in that it sat at the crossroads of western and central Anatolia and the Balkans, while reflecting an early Ottoman commercial and cultural context fed by the Persian, Mamluk, and Genoese realms. Further, its cultural, social, and diplomatic makeup borrows from the Rum Seljuks in Anatolia, the Byzantine/Turkic rulership on the western coast of Anatolia, the Slavic and Orthodox princedoms in the Balkans, and its trading partners to the east and west. In sum, Bursa is neither an Arabo-Ottoman nor a Turco-Balkan nor a Persian city.[38]

Bursa: A Quintessential "Ottoman" City

Bursa has been seen as the original Ottoman city and represents one of the richest assemblages of early Ottoman architecture. After all, Bursa was the first capital where the imperial imprint was struck onto the landscape. Indeed, after the 1855 earthquake, Keçecizade Fuad Paşa, the foreign minister to the reigning sultan, Abdülmecid I (r. 1839–61) reportedly said, "Alas, the Ottoman *dîbâce* (lit. the beginning, or the *incipit*) is destroyed."[39] This indicates how Bursa was seen and understood within the development of Ottoman cities.

Historical narratives emphasize the "early Ottoman character" of the city's built environment after its conquest. Yet, such language can obscure a far more dynamic, heterogeneous reality. The early Ottoman capital, evidence shows, was rife with experimentation, wherein the Ottomans sought to establish a new urban language that drew inspiration from, rather than rejecting, preexisting details and forms. Among these forms were those developed by the Christian Greek rulers of the city, led by the Byzantine minister Saroz.[40] Other contributors included the Rum Seljuks, along with Christian Armenians, Crusaders, and Central Asians. After Bursa's fall in 1402 to the Timurids, Ottoman architecture in the city was inflected by this Mongol-Ilkhanid vocabulary.[41]

Under the Ottomans, Bursa became a multifunctional metropolis, presaging the rise of new Ottoman cities in Anatolia[42] and the Balkans.[43] The Ottomanization of the city became the model for many other such fifteenth-century conversions in the Balkans and Anatolia, including Nicaea, Adrianople, and Constantinople. For instance, Nicaea's Saint Sophia was converted into a mosque, and *imarets* and tombs were constructed ex novo. In Adrianople (the second capital of the Ottomans, present-day Edirne), the Church of Saint Sophia was converted into a mosque, and a royal palace was constructed to the east of the old city. In addition, Byzantine commercial areas and dwelling quarters were reused by the Ottomans, as much as what remained of the buildings allowed,[44] beginning in the 1360s, when they first occupied the city, and for the next forty years. Later, in the fifteenth century, the increasing construction of mosques, marketplaces, and soup kitchens was intended to feed the indigent outside the walled city.[45] In Constantinople, Mehmed II constructed his palace in the vicinity of the ruins of the Byzantine palace and converted the Saint Sophia into a mosque, but constructed his *külliye* (begun in 1463) away from the Byzantine areas.[46]

The Ottomanization of cities in the Balkans such as Didymoteichon and Komotini, because of their non-imperial status, largely entailed new construction outside the citadel. Thessaloniki, on the other hand, was enclosed by triangular city walls, and significant Ottomanization took place in the inner fortress on the northern end of the acropolis. In this transformation, the foundations of an early Christian fort were reused to build a new one to accommodate the Ottoman conquerors. Meanwhile, within the city walls, new buildings, mosques, bathhouses, and marketplaces were constructed.[47]

In general, in the fourteenth and fifteenth centuries, development and planning rejuvenated the cities and towns of the Ottoman Empire, whereas previously, more rural settlements had prevailed. As these urban entities became more established, Bursa came into view as the quintessential Ottoman city.

Reconstructing Bursa's Past

Historians often turn to archaeology to tell the stories of abandoned cities, destroyed buildings, or extinct civilizations. Spiro Kostof proposed in 1967 that historians analyze buildings in their "total context,"[48] but the "total context" of Bursa is difficult to assess. A large excavation project is impossible, making the pre-Ottoman layers virtually unknown. It has suffered sieges (1326, 1402, and 1413), fires (1402, 1413, 1518–19, 1521, 1589, 1608, 1743, 1765, 1773, and 1801),[49] and earthquakes (1419, 1508, 1674, 1705, and most notably

1855),⁵⁰ as well as undergone restoration and remodeling after those events. Over the centuries, countless artists and travelers have attempted to capture the "original" appearance of Prousa and the region in paintings, photographs, and sketches.

The changes wrought by restoration and remodeling are best illustrated during the governorship of Ahmed Vefik Paşa (1879–82). Under his leadership, the city underwent a major redevelopment that included the creation of wide, straight, tree-lined avenues, a monumental vista, lines of house façades fronting the avenues, and spacious piazzas.[51] Vefik was mesmerized by Westernization, stirred by fond memories of his time spent in Paris. After the city was struck by an earthquake in the 1860s, Vefik invited French architect Leon Parvillée to restore the dynastic monuments that had been destroyed. Vefik wanted to not only restore the city but also remodel it and give new relevance to the formative period of Ottoman architecture.[52]

Given the then-prevailing ethics of restoration, it is not surprising that the remnants of fourteenth-century Bursa still visible today are almost as much the result of Ahmed Vefik's patronage as of Orhan and Murad I's.[53] That is, the nineteenth-century work masked almost all of the original structural detail. During my last two trips to the region in the summer of 2007, I noted the extent to which the restorers had rebuilt the *Saltanat kapı* (also known as the gate of sovereignty) and the *Yer kapı* (the ground gate) in the upper city. Both gates now look quite different from their appearance in photographs taken in the 1900s. This renovation project, led by the Metropolitan Municipality of Bursa, resulted in the erasure of many significant details, such as the original façade heights, the original stones, and spoliated items, the curvature of arches, and more, as evidenced by the round tower (now located between the *Saltanat kapı* and the *Yer kapı*).[54] Some restoration work, however, revealed interesting details; for instance, the removal of cement in 2007 showed that the corbel table at the Convent-*Masjid* of Murad I was made of bricks forming round arches.

Luckily, in the last two decades several municipality projects have also prompted excavations, with interesting results. These include the partial excavation of Roman or late antique villa mosaics, a sixth-century church with a basilica plan,[55] and remnants of residential complexes in the area of the so-called Byzantine/Ottoman Palace.[56] In my own work, I have sought to peel back the city's Ottoman layers, including through the use of ground-penetrating radar (GPR), which can reveal the remains of fortification walls, towers, chapels, and churches.⁵⁷ To understand the urban nature of the pre-Ottoman city, I conducted a GPR survey in the summer of 2009 on the northern tip of the upper city, focusing on the tombs of Osman and Orhan, the founders of the Ottoman state, and the *Bey Saray* (lit. palace of the rulers), or the Byzantine/Ottoman Palace.⁵⁸ This survey not only revealed important information about the archaeological strata on the northern tip of the castle but also provided a wide range of data, from the impact of the earthquake on the urban infill to water channels, pavements, and street patterns. I complemented the archaeological evidence with visual and verbal depictions of the buildings and cityscape to offer a more complete picture of Bursa. Unfortunately, it is not possible to describe the undocumented urban infill, unstudied original topography, now-vanished skylines, and unrecorded street patterns and water pipes.⁵⁹

In conclusion, Bursa lay at the intersection of many trade and travel routes. It was a crossing point from the Balkans to Anatolia and further east, to Persia. This grand portrait attracted the Ottoman founders to the site, as did its Byzantine and Roman legacy as Prousa. The finer points now attract scholarly attention as well: details such as the prevalence of brick-and-stone masonry show that the "Ottoman city" owed its excellence to the work of so many non-Ottoman hands.

2

The City in Transition

Continuity, Conversion, and Reuse

Bithynia was conquered city by city: Prousa in 1326, Nicaea/İznik in 1331, and Nicomedia/İzmit in 1337, as well as smaller towns such as Kirmasti/Mustafakemalpaşa, Angelokoma/İnegöl, and Miletopolis/Karacabey (Map1). With each conquest, the Ottomans began converting their new urban realms to suit their needs. In his pioneering 1929 study *Christianity and Islam under the Sultans*, F. W. Hasluck used the term "architectural transference" to describe how the idea of sanctity continued from the Byzantine to the Ottoman periods, demonstrated by the conversion of Byzantine buildings into mausolea for the founders of the Ottoman state in fourteenth-century Bursa.[1] Indeed, the architectural conversions were about more than just convenience or opportunism, and their place in Bursa's broader landscape must be understood.

This chapter analyzes both the symbolic and practical conversion of religious and secular buildings, including the citadel gates, city walls, palaces, bathhouses, churches, and mausolea, in order to demonstrate how religious and political sovereignty was made visible. The existing Byzantine architectural forms, the chapter shows, were appropriated for practical purposes, but they were also employed as symbols of conquest and to demonstrate the continuity of earlier beliefs and traditions within the new Muslim context. What was significant about the reuse of the Byzantine buildings is not that "they [were] adopted, but the way they [were] culturally redefined and put to use."[2]

Appropriation and Reuse in Ottoman Construction

The appropriation of ancient sites for the veneration of Islamic figures and the survival of the Christian cults was widespread in the larger Anatolian context.[3] The standard Ottoman practice was to convert a city's main church into a mosque (earning it the moniker *Ulu Cami*—literally the Holy Mosque or Grand Mosque) to lay claim to a newly conquered land.[4] Mosques converted from churches include Saint Sophia in Nicaea/İznik, which became the Ayasofya Mosque in 1331, and the cathedral of Pegea/Biga in Mysia, a region to Bithynia's west, which became Orhan Mosque around the mid-fourteenth century.[5] A later example from Bithynia is the early ninth-century church of Saint Stephanos in Trigleia, which was converted into a mosque in 1560–61.[6]

By the time of Osman's rule, Ottoman construction was prevalent,[7] so it is unlikely that the reuse of Byzantine buildings was a matter of practical necessity. Nor is it likely that Byzantine buildings were necessarily better for Ottomans' various needs than the buildings they might have constructed using their own methods. Instead, appropriation was a preliminary step in the transition from Byzantine to Ottoman control in Bursa. Byzantine construction postdating the city's conquest mainly took place on its outskirts, especially on the southern shore of the Sea of Marmara, in places such as Trigleia.[8] In the case of Bursa, the image of Byzantium was not erased but, rather, Byzantine architectural and decorative details were incorporated into the evolving Ottoman design. This was in contrast to many other Rum-Seljuk and *Beylik* buildings[9] converted from earlier structures or retaining Byzantine spolia,[10] only a few of which displayed antique fragments prominently. In Bursa, complete architectural recycling was the norm, in which all components of a complex were converted. This ethos of conversion broadcast the genealogy of the structure and the inclusion of non-Muslim believers. In the Mausolea of Osman and Orhan, as well as the early Ottoman buildings, continuity in workshop practices is evident, as I will discuss in Chapter 3.

In recognizing continuity rather than trying to eradicate the past, the Ottomans legitimated their ownership. Here, the Byzantine architecture was central to the identity of the Ottomans—rather than focusing on affirming their development as a group, they took power in Bursa with reference to the "authority of the past."[11] Integrating the past into their urban development, the Ottomans created a new visual syntax to identify themselves both to the Byzantines and to themselves.[12] During this period, two cultures coexisted in Bursa, with the dividing line between Ottomans and Byzantines likely blurry.[13] The Ottoman founders and other city occupants acknowledged this blurriness. For example, they likely knew that Osman and Orhan's tombs were originally Byzantine structures but nevertheless identified them collectively as the "Silver Dome."[14]

As the architectural evidence makes clear, the Ottomanization of the city (Figure 2) went beyond the limits of the citadel, in a process that took more than a century. First, outside the old city walls, a new area called the "lower city" developed. Under Orhan (r. 1324–62), the urban center was reoriented toward the lower city. This meant that even though the major Byzantine buildings and the ceremonial axis of the old city were retained, they became less central to the city's economic and social life. Following Orhan, Murad I (r. 1362–89) moved to the west of the urban center, where hot springs were plentiful, and in due course a spa city emerged.[15] Bayezid I (r. 1389–1402) moved to the east of the city, where he built his complex. Each of these moves reconfigured the connection between the citadel, the lower city, and the suburbs.

The axis of Ottomanization can also be observed on the image that adorns the cover of this book. This is a territorial plan of Bursa done by the urban planner Luigi Piccinato in 1958, we note how the early Ottoman urban core is situated within the topography of the city next to a few modern landmarks, giving us a chance to envision how the city might have looked in its medieval setting.

Of the Walls and the Gates: Framing the Old City

Claiming and occupying started with conquering a city and entering through its gates.[16] The 1862 Cadastral Map of Bursa (Figure 3)[17] indicates the outlines of the fortified city walls, the mausolea of the founders, mosques built in the fourteenth century, the layout of the streets, and the palace. The palace, the *Bey Saray*, dates to Byzantine times and roughly corresponds to the military guesthouse in Bursa today.[18] The city's vertiginous natural and man-made acropolis was praised by the fifth-century historian Paulus Orosius. Based on sources from around the time of the Mithridatic wars in the first century BC, he concluded that Prousa was a "heavily fortified city" (*munitissima civitas*).[19]

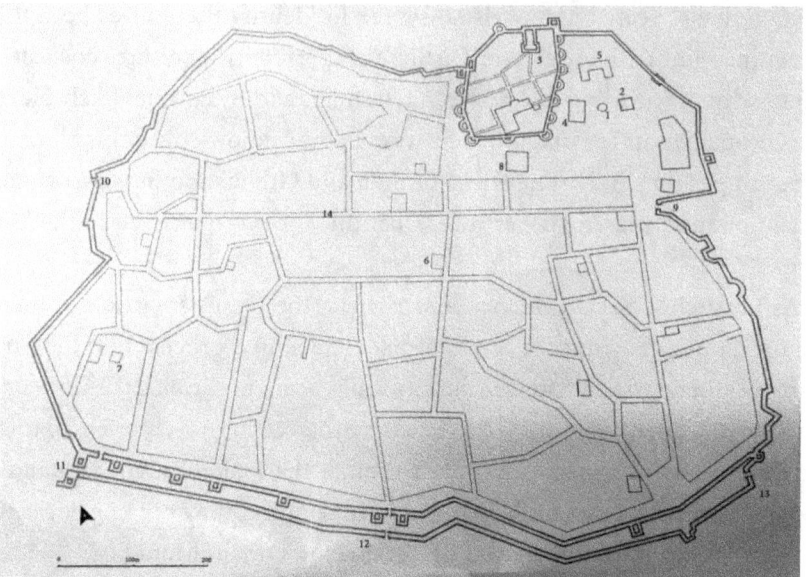

Figure 3 Post-earthquake Cadastral Map of 1862 showing the Old City. (Drawn by Hidayet Softaoğlu based on Ayverdi, *Osmanlı Mimarîsinin*)

The city walls were originally built in the Hellenistic period (late-third–early second century BC) and constantly rebuilt thereafter.[20] In the pre-Ottoman phases, the city walls withstood many attacks.[21] After two centuries of skirmishes between Byzantium and neighboring states, local leaders had erected a well-developed network of fortifications on the city's border and in the interior.[22] But following the city's surrender in 1326, and with the exception of the catastrophic Timurid sack of Bursa after the 1402 Battle of Ankara,[23] the city walls did not face the threat of siege in the Ottoman period.[24]

Unlike the Rum Seljuk urbanism, which involved using fortifications as a major architectural space to claim dynastic legitimacy,[25] in Bursa the fortifications became a physical landmark denoting the perimeters of the city. Once under Orhan's dominion, the fortifications were relieved of their defensive function and went through minor restorations focused on the area of the gates. Then, following the Timurid siege of 1402 and the Karamanid siege of 1413, the walls were strengthened by Mehmed I (r. 1413–21).[26] The walls and gates began to be restored heavily in the early 2000s, so one has to rely on old photos to see the different phases of Ottoman remodelings.

The Cadastral Map of 1862 and the current state of the walls indicate they were appointed with five gates.[27] The steep hills surrounding the city formed a natural defense, reinforced by walls to the west, north, and parts of the east. There was the *Saltanat* (Figure 3.9) on the east (the gate of sovereignty, also known as the *Hisar kapı*, or the fort gate)[28] and the *Kaplıca kapı* (the hot springs gate) (Figure 3.10) on the west. On the south, where a gradual slope offered easier access, an outer wall was added later, possibly in the late Byzantine period. This double line of walls is reminiscent of the double line displayed by the Theodosian Walls of Constantinople, built in the fifth century.[29] The other three gates were located along this outer south line: the *Su kapı* (the water gate) (Figure 3.12) in the middle, the *Yer kapı* (the ground gate) (Figure 3.13) on the east end, and the *Zindan kapı* (the dungeon gate) (Figure 3.11) on the west end.[30]

Overall, the gates display a variety of masonry techniques (alternating brick-and-stone as well as ashlar), structural details (such as segmental, round, and pointed arches), and decorative features (such as spoliated elements comparable to examples in Anatolia and the Balkans). A variety of inscriptions of different dates on these walls were remarked on by John Covel, who visited Bursa in 1675. One such inscription is near the *Saltanat kapı* (the gate of sovereignty) and refers to the reign of Emperor Constantine IV (r. 668–85). The second inscription, from another tower near the *Zindan kapı* (the dungeon gate) is dated to late antiquity and praises a certain John. The third comes from the side wall of the *Yer kapı* (the ground gate) and is dated to first or second century AD; it honors three men, Basilides, Archelaos, and Theogenes. The last inscription refers to the restorations of the walls of the city, commissioned by Theodore I Laskaris (r. 1204–21), and is dated June 9, 1210.[31]

The walls of the old city, as well as the ancient *decumanus maximus* running from east to west (3.14), have survived moderately well to the present day. Under the Ottomans, the walls went through a series of remodelings in the fifteenth, seventeenth, and nineteenth centuries.[32] Remodeling is especially evident in four pentagonal towers situated in the outer line of the double walls described earlier, with three towers between the *Yer kapı* (the ground gate) and the *Zindan kapı* (the dungeon gate) and another to the east of the *Zindan kapı*.[33] Further Ottoman remodelings included strengthening the portals and the towers nearby. After struggling through the Timurid and Karamanid sieges in 1402 and 1413 respectively, a section of the wall on the east side of the city and the *Saltanat* (the gate of sovereignty) were rebuilt by Mehmed I (r. 1413–21) in 1418. This is noted in an inscription that, after sitting in the storage rooms of the Bursa Archaeological Museum for decades, was immured in the entrance of the *Saltanat kapı* in 2007 as a result of restorations conducted by the Metropolitan Municipality of Bursa.

From the Palace of the *Tekfurs* to *Bey Saray*

The palace of the old city (Figure 3.3) is located in the inner citadel. The inner citadel occupied a rectangular plot measuring approximately 150 by 110 meters and was surrounded by fourteen round towers on three sides, with three square towers on the remaining (north) side where it sits on a sheer cliff. It has been described as "das innere Schloss," by Joseph Hammer-Purgstall, the *Seraglio* by John Covel, or *Bey Saray* (lit. palace of the rulers) in Turkish scholarship.[34] It originally dates to the Byzantine era, hence its popular name in the Ottoman period as Palace of the *Tekfurs or Beys* (referring to rulers of the city),[35] but it was expanded under the reigns of a number of Ottoman sultans.

Archaeological studies can help us reconstruct a timeline. Based on a GPR survey, which I briefly introduced in the previous chapter and will discuss in greater detail at the end of this chapter, I argue that the palace appears to have originally been built atop residential units from the late antique period, circa the fifth and early sixth centuries, as well as the early Ottoman periods.[36] Combined with the results of salvage excavations conducted by the Bursa Archaeological Museum in the vicinity of the inner citadel, the results of the GPR survey reveal that the inner citadel and its immediate vicinity to the west are the areas where we note continuity from the Byzantine into the Ottoman period.

Yet, despite this archaeological evidence, it is difficult to construct how the palace looked under the early Ottoman sultans. There are several reasons for this. First, in these formative decades, the Ottoman court was primarily an itinerant one. Ibn Battuta, visiting İznik in 1331 and Bursa in 1333, treated the latter as the capital city of a mobile court. He labels Orhan as the Sultan of Bursa, "as the greatest king of the Turkomans and the richest in wealth, lands, and military forces," and he mentions that Orhan was away at the time conducting raids to conquer fortresses and towns.[37] One might assume that due to the peripatetic nature of the royal figures, the palace lacked durable structures of monumental scale or daring spatial features. The complex was most likely built mainly of timber and brick, with stone to a lesser extent.[38]

But the idea of a palace also went beyond the walls of the citadel in Bursa and extended into Bithynia in the form of pitched tents or movable structures to meet the needs of a court on the move, allowing the sultan to name any location or town as his capital city or palatial ground, while also building residences, such as the one at Yenişehir.[39]

Neither Byzantine sources, such as Pachymeres, nor Ottoman ones, such as Aşıkpaşazade, give us any structural or spatial details about *Bey Saray*. However, one fascinating piece of textual evidence about function comes from the Mamluk world. In 1381, during the reign of Murad I, the wedding ceremony of his son Bayezid I to Devlet (also known as Sultan Hatun), daughter of the Germiyan ruler, took place in Bursa. The guest list included several envoys from the Anatolian principalities as well as representatives from the Mamluk court, who were given the "first seat" in the ceremony.[40] While the sources do not indicate the venue, due to the lavish nature of the event, one expects this to have taken place in the palatial setting of Bursa.[41] In an account by Katib Çelebi he notes that Murad I had built palaces "near Bursa and in Edirne."[42] While this phrase does not identify where in Bursa Murad I built a palatial quarter, it would make sense to think that he had refurbished the palace prior to the royal wedding ceremony. In fact, imperial events such as weddings, circumcisions, and enthronements reportedly took place in Bursa. This includes the circumcisions of Murad I's sons soon after the victory against the Serbs on Maritza river in 1364.[43] Later, in the early fifteenth century, the enthronement of Murad II after the death of his father Mehmed I as well as his marriage took place in Bursa, as reported to us by Aşıkpaşazade.[44]

The palace may well have been in use until 1402, when it was pillaged by Timur's army. It may have lost its importance with the construction of the palatial complexes in Edirne, the second Ottoman capital, especially from the 1420s onward.[45] The Edirne Palace hosted the wedding of Mehmed I to Sitt Hatun of the Dulkadirid dynasty in 1449.[46] After Murad II's marriage to Sultan Hatun, the daughter of the Isfendiyar prince, he decided to take his new bride to Edirne, leaving behind his former wife, Mara Branković, the daughter of the Serbian ruler. Thus, as Amy Singer has discussed, the palace at Bursa came to house the women of the imperial harem who were not demanded by the sultan as well as older women, royal female figures, and their maids. From the 1450s onward, Edirne displaced Bursa as the major venue for imperial events.[47]

Later references to the *Bey Saray* come primarily from western travelers and especially refer to its walled gardens and marble fountains. By 1588, the district was semi-deserted, as described by the German traveler Reinhold Lubenau. The palace had fallen into ruins, and the pleasure garden and artificial lake (most likely a pond) were overgrown and untended. But the building was eventually repurposed: nearly a hundred years later, Covel noted in 1675,

> hard by this monastery are the ruins of a small citadel, about 175 or 180 paces. . . . It was first made *seraglio* (comprising of courtly and administrative offices) after it was taken, but now a bouting house, where they make a sort of fine flour of wheat and rice, for biskot and other bread for the Grand Signor.

George Wheler and Jacob Spon in 1682 similarly described the changed function of the first palace and the addition of a new residential complex, writing, "In this castle are two Seraglios, one old and the other new. The old is almost demolished, and only serves to cleanse Corn and to make fine flour for the Seraglio."[48] The evidence provided to us by the Bursa Court Registers refers to a refurbishment in the reign of Mehmed IV (r. 1642–93) indicating an audience hall, a privy chamber, a bathhouse, and stables and a section for the saddlers.[49]

Just as the Ottomans reused Byzantine religious structures by turning them into mosques and mausolea, they reused their palaces as well. The *Bey Saray*, then, illustrates how the notion of a capital city goes hand in hand with the agglutinatively evolving palatial setting. As the city evolved and the expansionist agendas of the Ottomans became prominent, the palatial grounds, albeit peripatetic, fulfilled the needs of a capital city.

Evolution of the Bathhouses

The earliest Ottoman nonconfessional accommodations claimed the land outside the walls of the old city. The conversion of the bathhouses is a good example of this nonconfessional reconfiguration. The Romans were the first to channel the rivulets flowing from natural hot mineral springs for use as baths. The Byzantines further exploited the thermal hot springs by building an additional bath, establishing Prousa as a resort city in the early Christian period.⁵⁰ Cleanliness is of great importance in Islam, and Muslim residents therefore required, in addition to ablution facilities attached to mosques, bathhouses to serve their urban populations. The insistence on bathing ranged from the ritual to the purely pleasurable. Bathhouse locations were largely dependent on the varying flows of streams and other natural waters. Accordingly, the Ottomans developed this ritual/resort theme on a grand scale with spas just outside the city walls.

Charles Texier and Richard Pullan sum up the pre-Ottoman legacy of the city's hot springs and bathhouses, referring to Pliny and Trajan's exchange of letters on the topic, and they discuss how the baths were later frequented by Byzantine imperial figures, such as Irene and Constantine VI (r. 780–97), Leo VI (r. 886–912), and Constantine VII Porphyrogennetos (r. 913–59), who stopped by the baths after visiting the monks on Mount Olympus.⁵¹

Prousa's Roman baths were mentioned for the first time by Dio, the local political figure we met earlier, when he described his residence within the city and the row of workshops he rented out near the natural hot springs (*epi tôn thermôn*).⁵² Today these are known as the Eski Kaplıca (Old Bath)⁵³ in the Çekirge district, located in the west of the city (Figure 4). These baths are mentioned

Figure 4 A view looking into Çekirge, the western suburbs, the Old Bath on the right, and the siting of the Convent-*Masjid* and *Külliye* of Murad I, nineteenth century. (Photo: Sebah & Joaillier, Personal Collection)

in an inscription dating to the reign of Hadrian in the early second century AD.[54] Additionally, a bronze coin dating to the Severan dynasty (AD 193–235), published by Robert, depicts a tetrastyle portico with two female figures on either side.[55] These figures may be the nymphs of the hot springs. Bekker-Nielsen has claimed that, if Robert's identification is correct, this would indeed represent the façade of the area's Roman baths.[56] The Old Bath, bearing Roman and Byzantine layers, was not the only hot spring complex in this attractive neighborhood in the west of the old city. Nearby was a sulfurous hot spring, the so-called Kükürtlü Bath (lit. the sulfur baths), also known as Kara Mustafa Baths.[57] Both of these bathhouses were praised for their exceedingly hot waters by the fourteenth-century Moroccan traveler Ibn Battuta.[58]

The Old Bath was also labeled by Athenaios of Naukratios, an orator of the early third century AD, as "with hot waters, a *basilika therma* [βασιλικά θερμά, trans. royal hot bath] located in Prousa, towards the Mount Olympos."[59] The scholarship, however, has often mixed up the locations of the Old Bath in Prousa and the one in Pythia. The Byzantine emperor Justinian (r. 527–65), who, along with his wife Theodora, partook of the area's therapeutic sulfur baths, founded a bath complex at Pythia (modern-day Yalova, north of Bursa). Due to the imperial status, scholars have tended to label the Pythian complex a *basilika therma*, creating confusion.[60] When it was founded it bore the name λουτρῶνα εν δημοσίῳ or θερμῶν ὑδάτων (trans. public baths or hot baths), as recorded by Procopius.[61] The bath complex in Pythia is mentioned in several sources, including one indicating their heyday under Justin II (r. 565–74), as indicated by a sixth-century epigram.[62] Not just in the lines of Procopius, but also for Stephen of Byzantium, the sixth-century author of *Ethnika*, a dictionary of geographical names and their etymologies, the meaning of the word θερμά/ *therma* distinguished between the two, describing the one in Prousa as a *basilika therma* and that of Pythia as a mere *therma*.[63] The epithet *basilika therma* given to the baths in Prousa predates that of Pythia, as indicated by the earlier-mentioned writings of Athenaios.

For both bath complexes, a geographical demarcation is given—Mount Olympus. In an epideictic text published in the *Palatine Anthology*, the Prousan bath was ranked above the Pythian one owing to the former's perfect water temperatures, whereas the extremely hot waters of Pythia required mixing with cold water, which was scarce—hence the building of an aqueduct.[64] Such was the conclusion even though Pythia was situated closer to Constantinople, both literally and figuratively (as indicated not only by the Justinianic bathhouse but also by a palace, an aqueduct, a bath, a church, and a hospital).[65] Yet, ultimately, the abovementioned factors dimmed the glory of the *basilika therma* of Prousa.

The baths changed dramatically over time. New wings were added to the Old Bath under the Ottomans, commissioned by Murad I, and they became an important source of income for the *waqfs*.[66] The Old Bath was restored in 1511, 1617, and 1680 and, close to the present day, in the late 1980s.[67] The wooden annexes used for lodging and the adjoining baths were demolished during a recent renovation. The Kükürtlü Bath complex was also enlarged by Murad I, who added a men's section, and later by his son Bayezid I, who added a women's section.[68] The part expanded by Murad I reportedly sat on Byzantine foundations.[69]

Visiting Bursa in 1853, Ubicini noted that the local Muslim population frequented the Old Bath, while the Greeks patronized the one in Kükürtlü. This was due to the complex's sacred spring being associated with Saint Patrikios, Bishop of Prousa, who was martyred by being thrown by either the city's Roman proconsul or the Emperor Julian into a pool of boiling water in a bathhouse complex located near the temples dedicated to Asklepios and Hygea.[70] The core of this complex, surrounded by timber additions, follows the alternating brick-and-stone construction technique on the exterior and demonstrates the exposed masonry of the Old Bath, especially on its west wall. The dome may be an original Byzantine construction with alternating brick-and-stone, banded voussoirs framing round arches, and brick-decorated roundels. The high dome is made of brick and decorated with a corbel table. The rest of the walls are also alternating brick-and-stone but lack any decorative details. Similarly, Byzantine architectural elements were incorporated in the Old Bath, including column capitals and shafts in the octagonal hot and cold rooms. The baths, then, represent an element of functional as well as nonconfessional continuity with the Byzantine past, whether they were restored or replaced.[71]

The Ottoman bathhouse complexes are comparable to the private bathing foundations of the late antique period.[72] They were modest in size and asymmetrical, as opposed to larger *thermae*, as noted in both of the discussed examples. The octagonal hot plunge-bath had recesses used for private bathing and separate wings for men and women. These were features already noted in the Byzantine architectural tradition for baths.[73]

Orhan's (Supposed) Friday mosque and Other Mosques in the Citadel

Moving on from the actual and symbolic claiming of the land, I now discuss ideological claims made through the conversion of religious as well as secular buildings. I also move beyond the Ottoman reuse of municipal spaces to their reuse of Byzantine religious spaces.

In the pre-Ottoman era, the city of Prousa had four monastic establishments: the Prodromos, Hexapytergos, Kabalos, and the grand monastery.[74] Among them, the Prodromos constituted the core of Ottoman reuse of the Byzantine religious complexes, as exemplified by the conversion of the baptistery and the main church in the complex for the tombs of Osman and Orhan (Figures 3.1 and 3.2) the founders of the Ottoman state. Around this urban core, a Friday mosque was reportedly built by Orhan. Although there is no archaeological evidence to support this claim, this converted mosque (Figure 3.4), if it existed, was close to the tombs.[75] Given the Ottoman practice of converting the Byzantine cathedral of a newly conquered city into a Friday mosque, Orhan likely did this in Bursa. The general scholarly consensus is that Orhan built or converted a mosque and a bathhouse in the center of the old city.[76]

Despite the lack of physical evidence for an Orhan-era Friday mosque in the old city, an extant inscription, referred to as the 1337 inscription, is often associated with it. This inscription (Figure 5) is immured in the east entrance of the Şehadet (Martyrdom) Mosque built by Murad I in 1365–66. Its original placement is not known, nor how it came to this mosque, but it was probably moved to the wall during the restorations at Şehadet in 1892, nearly four decades after the earthquake of 1855.[77] The nature of this inscription is discussed in more detail in the next chapter, but here it is important to note that the inscription, written in Arabic, refers to a *masjid* (place of worship) built by Orhan. To avoid confusion in terminology and distinguish it from the convent-*masjids*, I will refer to this building as a Friday mosque instead of a *masjid*. Given that the inscription still resides in the old city, I argue that it originated at Orhan's Friday mosque (Figure 3.4), which he had converted from the Byzantine cathedral. Semavi Eyice, the first scholar to discuss the pre-earthquake state of the founders' tombs in the old city, uses the descriptions of travelers who suggested that Orhan's mosque was built close to the tombs, including Orhan's place of burial in 1362.[78]

Figure 5 The 1337 inscription, now immured within the façade of the Şehadet (Martyrdom) Mosque, mentioning the Friday Mosque of Orhan built in the Old City on the left. (Photo: Suna Çağaptay)

Ibn Battuta, in Bursa shortly after its capture, stated that "Osman's tomb is located within Orhan's masjid and that this structure was formerly a Byzantine church and later converted into a mosque."[79] Ibn Battuta's visit to Bursa coincided with the reign of Orhan.[80] In an Ottoman register of important affairs (*mühimme defteri*) dating to 1576, an approval was given to a request to remodel/enlarge the edifice, which was felt to be too small to accommodate the needs of the increasing congregation.[81] This is telling evidence that despite the new building complexes erected in the lower city and elsewhere, the number of people who wished to use Orhan's Friday mosque was increasing. Evliya Çelebi, writing in 1640, noted that Orhan's mosque was in the old city and was also the place where Orhan was interred: "*içkale camiinde bir kabri pür-nurda medfundur*" ([he] was buried in a tomb surrounded by holy light within the mosque in the old castle).[82]

While visiting the city in 1675, Covel (Figure 6) drew a sketch indicating the locations of the tombs, and possibly "Orhan's Friday mosque." Corroborating

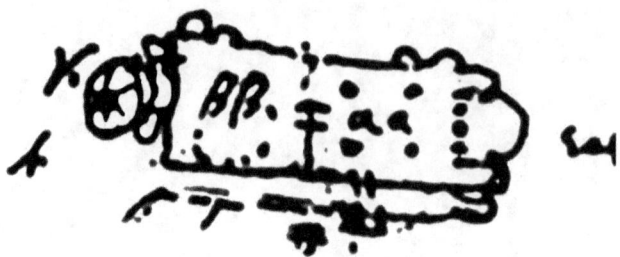

Figure 6 The sketch showing the tombs of Osman and Orhan. (After J.-P. Grélois *Dr John Covel Voyages en Turquie/Texte établi, annoté et traduit*. Paris, 1998, 146, fig. b4)

with Covel, Thomas Smith's observation of the site in the 1680s is also noteworthy, which reports that "Here are the sepulchres of Osman, the founder of the Osmanlee family and his son Urchan, who took the city, near a mosque, formerly a christian church, dedicated to Saint John."[83] This visual and textual evidence can be complemented by a drawing by J. B. Fischer von Erlach (Figure 7) showing a building with a round plan, topped by a dome with round window openings, and two minarets attached on either side. Although Covel and Evliya are known to have visited Bursa, the same cannot be said for Johann Bernhard Fischer von Erlach, who is not known to have traveled outside Europe. His sketches depended on verbal and visual reports by other travelers. It is possible that he shuffled some details that he had read about the mosque in Bursa to come up with a transitional building that was both a mosque and a tomb.[84] The Christian travelers used the word "mosque" for the minaret and *mihrab* (the niche indicating the direction of Mecca) within the complex.[85] Finally, writing just thirteen years before the earthquake, a renowned medical doctor named Charles A. Bernard further corroborated the oral and visual accounts by Covel, Evliya, and Fischer von Erlach,[86] noting that among all the city's mosques, "the oldest one is the one by Orhan, located in a major area within the citadel. Although it is in good condition, it lacks a congregation and hence its doors are always closed. Next to the mosque, a tomb containing the remains of Orhan is located."[87]

There are two other early mosques which are still standing (although heavily restored), both built in the citadel in the fourteenth century. One, in the upper citadel near the southwest gate, was built by Orhan's brother Alaeddin around 1331(Figure 3.7).[88] It is one of the earliest mosques built in this era. Laid out on a single-unit plan, the walls follow Byzantine construction. They are constructed of rubble-stone masonry with bricks placed vertically and

Figure 7 The Friday Mosque of Orhan in the old city by J. Bernard Fischer von Erlach, 1720s. (University of Heidelberg Rare Books Collection)

horizontally between each stone, with a brick-patterned panel. The building is accessed by a front portico adorned with reused sixth-century columns and capitals.

Another mosque (Figure 3.8) was built by Murad I in 1365 and served as a Friday mosque, known as the Şehadet (Martyrdom) Mosque. As mentioned earlier, this is the mosque where the 1337 inscription is now located on its east entrance. It was destroyed by the earthquake of 1855 but restored during a wave of other restorations.[89] In two photographs predating the restoration, alternating brick-and-stone masonry is evident, showing continuity from the late Byzantine workshop practices.[90]

Orhan's Ottomanization process in the old city was not confined to converting monastic and secular buildings into mausolea, a Friday mosque, and a palace. He also engaged in other building enterprises including a *madrasa* (Figure 3.5) and a bathhouse (Figure 3.6). Combined with the mausolea, the Friday mosque, and the palace, the *madrasa* and the bathhouse form the earliest hub of Ottoman urban interventions in the old city before Orhan moved beyond it and established his *külliye* in the lower city. The bathhouse is mentioned in a Bursa court register of 1484 as going through a renovation process and being part of Orhan's tomb and the *madrasa* complex.[91] Little of original details remain as it was destroyed by a fire and rebuilt afterward.

The *madrasa*'s location is a matter of debate as it was destroyed by the 1855 earthquake.[92] Ayverdi mentions that a Bursa court register in 1795 talked about a refurbishment of the side of the Mausoleum of Orhan facing his *madrasa*.[93] This led Ayverdi to situate the madrasa to the north of the mausolea and around the area of the clock tower. The proximity between the Mausoleum of Orhan and the *madrasa* is confirmed by a 1844 court register, which mentions that the *madrasa*, with fifteen cells and a study room covered with a timber roof, was located adjacent to the Mausoleum of Orhan.[94] Neşri mentions that Orhan turned a monastic building into a *madrasa*.[95] Based on this, the Lala Şahin *Madrasa*, also located in the old city, might be a helpful comparison to envision how Orhan's *madrasa* would have looked. Built after 1339 and following an alternating brick-and-stone masonry, this building reused Byzantine columns and capitals and lintel pieces and had seven vaulted rooms. Because of its seemingly Byzantine structural details, it has sometimes been treated as being converted from a monastic building.[96]

While the location and architectural qualities are a matter of debate, one fascinating historic figure known to be associated with the *madrasa* was Davud-i Kayseri (d. 1350). He was the first *madrasa* teacher employed by Orhan in 1336. He wrote a treatise dedicated to Süleyman, Orhan's son, which praised the prince and his ruling father, and he also taught a variety of classes on spiritual and rational matters of Islam. He praises Orhan as the "virtuous and enlightened" sultan.[97] Davud-i Kayseri's presence in Bursa, interacting with the sultan and members of Orhan's family and writing introductory books and treatises, stands as testimony that the *madrasa* existed not just as an architectural unit but also as an institution.

Laid to Rest under Byzantine Domes: The Mausolea of Osman and Orhan

In the early fourteenth century, as we have seen, Byzantine buildings like churches were transformed into mosques and mausolea, the latter to house the remains of the Ottoman rulers Osman and Orhan.[98] In Bursa, the physical transformation was "minimal,"[99] with many decorations kept intact, although tombs and necessary furnishings, such as the Rum-Seljuk regalia,[100] were added. It was thus evident that the buildings had former lives as churches.

Before Prousa fell to the Ottomans, Osman, the empire's founder, died and was buried in Söğüt in 1324.[101] Orhan, his successor, had Osman's remains brought into Prousa shortly after the conquest of the city. Osman was reinterred in a Byzantine religious building in the upper city—the legendary "Silver Dome"[102] of a prominent religious complex, which is called Manastır (Monastery) in Ottoman sources and travelers' accounts.[103] Charles Texier, visiting before the earthquake, attributed the church to Prophitis Elias in Thessaloniki because of its circular layout.[104] On the other hand, Joseph von Hammer-Purgstall and Raymond Janin said that the baptistery in the Monastery of Saint John Prodromos housed the Tomb of Osman.[105]

The layout published by Texier in 1864 shows a building with an octagonal layout accessed through a narthex that suggests several possible origins[106] including a Roman temple or an early Christian mausoleum or baptistery.[107] In 1963, two studies by Eyice that compiled written accounts of travelers from East and West identified the mausolea.[108] Scholarship on this issue has been dormant since then, but interest in the tombs was given new impetus when previously unpublished drawings from the seventeenth and nineteenth centuries came to light in the late 1990s and 2000s, respectively.[109]

The façade drawing indicates that in the main body of the church, a round, domed center room rose from an arcade supported by eight pairs of columns. The *exedrae*, inserted between each set of columns, were echoed on the outside of the building. The interior is comparable to that of the Temple of Portumnus at Porto near Ostia,[110] dated to the mid-third century AD, where the thick walls were modulated on the interior by alternating semicircular and rectangular niches, flanked by a single free-standing column. The interior also resembles the Temple of Minerva Medica in Rome, dated to the fourth century AD.[111] As

Figure 8 The Mausolea of Osman (dome in the forefront) and Orhan (higher-domed structure in the middle) by Catenacci, 1835. (Bibliothèque nationale de France Rare Books Collection)

is typical for a building of this type, such as the Lateran baptistery from the mid-fifth century, the building in Prousa does not have an ambulatory.[112]

While the textual evidence reveals a wide range of architectural activity in Roman Prousa, it does not specify where exactly in the city these efforts took place. Considering the prolific architectural production during the Roman period, one would have to probe further to discover whether the structure housing Osman's remains really dated to this era. Indeed, the octagonal buildings used a structural model common from the Roman period onward.[113]

Orhan died in 1362 and is said to be buried in the main church of the monastic complex where his father and predecessor Osman was interred.[114] Recently published drawings by Cassas in 1786,[115] by Löwenhielm in 1825,[116] and by Catenacci in 1835 (Figure 8)[117] depict the architectural characteristics of the Byzantine church that housed Orhan's tomb. These drawings show a church with a cross-in-square plan whose counterparts in the middle and late Byzantine periods include the Theotokos Church in the Monastery of Hosios Loukas (mid-tenth century) and the Church of the Holy Apostles in Thessaloniki (mid-fourteenth century). Both of these churches have a similar east façade.[118]

The hypothetical plan is further supported by the abovementioned sketch, drawn by Covel in 1675, which indicates a cross-in-square plan defined by the insertion of four columns or piers, with a projecting main apse and two apsidioles on either side.[119] The dome sits on a high drum, recalling the dome structures at several churches on the island of Chios dating to the Laskarid period. One such example is the mid-thirteenth century Church of the Holy Apostles in Phyrghi.[120] In the aforementioned drawings of Orhan's tomb, three registers of windows are inserted on the walls of the main apse. The drawing by Cassas and Catenacci provide more details on the central apse and the sidewalls, which are comparable to several structures of the late Byzantine period, such as the Church 8 on Kahve Asar adası on Lake Latmos (mid-1250s)[121] and the south church of Constantine Lips in Constantinople, built in 1282. Though it is octagon-domed, the Church of Saint Theodore in Mistra, ca. 1290, also offers comparable evidence.[122]

The only elements to survive from the Mausoleum of Orhan are fragments of the *opus sectile* floor(Figure 9).[123] These include parts of five panels and some larger stone plates on the western and southern parts of the building, which are from the original Byzantine pavement of the Mausoleum of Orhan. In the eastern part, components of the first pavement are visible, covered by the catafalques.[124] To the west, about half of the second panel survives. This panel consists of a round medallion surrounded by four other round medallions on the corners, which alternate in the midpoints with triangles and are tied to one another with knots. The third panel, to the south, is also square; only a small part with knots has survived. The fourth panel, to the east of the third, is much smaller than the previous pieces and is a monolithic piece formed by nine interlaced circles. The fifth panel, to the south of the second, is likewise monolithic, bearing large round medallions surrounded by four circles. Between the circles, triangular and trapezoidal pieces of stone are inserted in the panels. The main material of the whole pavement is yellowish marble, joined by green serpentine, orange travertine, red and green porphyry, and red and black calcaire (limestone).

The biggest puzzle is the original state of the floor. Henry Maguire offered several suggestions on categories of design for middle Byzantine opus sectile floors, while setting the medieval floors of the Great Palace in Constantinople within their art-historical context.[125] A similar design and layout can be proposed for the floor in Bursa. The first and second panels seem to bear

Figure 9 General view of the Opus Sectile Panel from the Mausoleum of Orhan. (Photo: Suna Çağaptay)

different designs, repeated on the opposite side of the building. These two panels are also far enough from each other to allow for the insertion of the columns. The smaller two panels are set next to the bigger ones on the west and south. This might be a sign that the two smaller ones were added later as part of a refurbishment process. The bigger panels are on the same axis and bear no similarities in design to the smaller ones, supporting the idea that the floor originally had a cruciform pattern, indicated by the bigger panels, and two separate dates of execution.

The floor drew high praise from travelers for its quality, as did the sculptural pieces and carved column capitals within the building itself.[126] The best comparisons are from the thirteenth and fourteenth centuries, such as the Church of Saint Sophia in Nicaea, the Church of Saint Sophia in Trebizond,[127] and the Church of Saint Sophia in Mistra.[128] Therefore, while Eyice and Demiriz suggest that the floor may date to the eleventh century, using Pinatsi's detailed study on the opus sectile floor in the Churches of Saint Sophia in Nicaea and Trebizond, I suggest an early thirteenth-century dating instead, with the smaller panels being added slightly later.[129]

New Evidence on the Mausolea of Osman and Orhan

The archaeological record often provides clear evidence of the conversion of churches into mosques[130] or mausolea.[131] In the medieval Anatolian context, converting Byzantine structures into mausolea was usually "done to create a visual link between newly sanctified holy figures and historical saints."[132] For example, the mausoleum of Elvan Çelebi near Euchaita in the vicinity of Çorum is believed to have been converted from, or constructed on, the remains of a Byzantine martyrion dedicated to Saint Theodore.[133] This complex, which functioned as a dervish lodge, had a reconstructed martyrion (built in the fourteenth century) and a mosque (added in the sixteenth century). It bore classical and Byzantine spolia that, according to scholars such as Ethel Sara Wolper, linked it with the Christian past and the still-surviving cult of Saint Theodore.[134] Anderson, however, refutes the claims in previous scholarship, citing the lack of archaeological evidence as well as distinguishing features on the spolia, and claims the building represents the consolidation of power by Elvan Çelebi, the earlier-noted important Sufi figure and the son of Aşık Paşa, a historian and poet.[135] Both father and son were renowned and had the economic and spiritual means to rise to prominence.[136]

Despite the wealth of textual and visual evidence from travelers and scholars in the nineteenth century, the Mausolea of Osman and Orhan have been much neglected in present-day scholarship. Among scholars of early Ottoman architecture, both Sedat Çetintaş and Ekrem Hakkı Ayverdi failed to discuss the original forms of these buildings, and Albert Gabriel, in his seminal monograph, dealt with the buildings only hastily and claimed that the evidence provided by travelers was unsatisfactory.[137] In 1963, Eyice became the first scholar to devote an article (in Turkish) to offering a reconstruction of the two buildings and summarizing the evidence gathered from travelers' accounts. Eyice identified the original structure of Osman's tomb as an octagon, while describing Orhan's as a "parekklesion."[138] Annie Pralong and Jean Pierre Grélois, as well as Macit V. Tekinalp on the other hand, provide a long list of alternative structures, while suggesting evolving uses for the buildings throughout the Byzantine era.[139] They do not, however, attempt to derive meaning from the evidence provided by drawings and descriptions.

Thus, moving beyond the drawings by Texier—used too readily by prior scholarship—the drawings by Covel, Cassas, Catenacci, and Löwenhielm stand as important tools to understand perceptions of the structures in the centuries before the earthquake of 1855. Sources like these become especially relevant given that the present-day buildings reveal nothing of the Byzantine versions but instead reflect the nineteenth-century reconstruction, done in such a way that no Byzantine architectural details or clues are visible.[140] However, a problem emerges with travelers' accounts and drawings: they may not always be reliable or even genuine. For example, although such records purport to be original, some are partly or wholly based on works by earlier travelers.[141] Nonetheless, these accounts hold significant details that previous scholarship has neglected.

For these two mausolea, such records suggest that the original buildings were modified several times before the Ottoman intervention. Covel in 1675, for example, provided detailed information on the capitals in Orhan's mausoleum. These were basket capitals, in fashion in the sixth century. They were found across the region, for instance, supporting the domes of the bath complex in Pythia and bearing the monogram of Justin II (r. 565–74).[142] Other sixth-century capitals were reused in the early ninth-century atrium of the Church of Saint Stephanos (present-day Fatih Cami) in Trigleia[143] and in the fourteenth-century Mosque of Alaeddin in Bursa.

According to Covel, the *synthronon*, an architectural element present only in early Byzantine churches, was also intact in the Mausoleum of Orhan.[144] The use of mid-sixth-century basket capitals, the early Byzantine synthronon arrangement, the opus sectile floor with two different phases, and the mosaic program in the main apse that shows an aniconic cross representation, a characteristic design scheme during the Iconoclastic period (in 726–87 and 814–42), are all further evidence that these two buildings experienced centuries of Byzantine use and refurbishment. This body of evidence can be combined with (1) Covel's sketch showing a cross-in-square layout with columns supporting the dome, and (2) visual representations of the façades from different angles to indicate that a cross-in-square church and a round-plan building stood in close proximity to each other.[145] The latter can be seen in the sketch done by Covel and the drawings by Löwenhielm and Catenacci. These two images support the idea that these buildings were not only in close proximity but conjoined.

In many examples of Byzantine architecture, churches were built on the foundations of earlier Christian basilicas, with the basic design transformed only minimally.[146] Thomas Smith, in the 1680s, wrote that the place where the two Ottoman founders were buried formerly served as a Byzantine monastic complex dedicated to Saint John Prodromos and was a "Convent of Religious" built by Constantine Iconomachos (also known as Constantine V Kopronymos, r. 741–75).[147] Gregoras, Pachymeres, and Ephraim of Ainos wrote that Empress Irene, the wife of Emperor John III Vatatzes (r. 1221–54), commissioned the construction of a main church in the monastery dedicated to Saint John Prodromos.[148] In light of the specific evidence regarding the founders' tombs, together with the general patterns of church conversion, the main church in the monastery of Saint John Prodromos in Prousa may have gone through the same transformation prior to its conversion by the Ottomans. It had the form of a basilica with an appended baptistery and was rebuilt as a baptistery on several occasions; moreover, it possibly had original Roman construction. It is also likely that the building that housed Orhan's tomb was a parish church with a baptistery converted to a monastery.

Further Archaeological Discoveries: Results of GPR Survey

A GPR survey was conducted at Tophane Park, which now houses the mausolea, in the summer of 2009. Specifically in the area of Orhan's tomb, it revealed two walls running in an east-west direction and a wall connecting them, possibly hinting at a chapel or church.[149] In the area of the clock tower, our survey revealed a fascinating range of edifices including a small structure with a paved floor, walls running in an east-west direction ending in an apse on the east, and foundation walls.

Even one single grid reading, through a superimposed series of structures, indicates the density of urban activities prior to the Ottomans' arrival.[150] This particular grid also revealed valuable information about the earthquake horizon or debris, which is limited to 0.60–0.90 meters, as confirmed by the remaining profile readings. The building identified at 1.2–1.8 meters is likely a chapel, and at 1.2–2.4 GPR reflections show walls running from east to west. The final feature at 2.1–2.4 meters displays two tightly spaced parallel walls, which, judging from their depth, likely indicate a street pattern or a foundation for a large structure.[151] Compared to the depth of the other reflections around the mausolea, as well as around the military guesthouse (directly atop the palace remains), it can be inferred that structures at 1.2–2.0 meters likely date to the Byzantine period, while those from 2.0–2.4 meters date to the Roman period.

Although it is pure speculation, I wonder if we could attribute the data at 0.9 to 1.2 to the remains of Orhan's *madrasa*[152] built atop of, or reusing the remains of, what appears to be a Byzantine chapel. In the inner citadel, the survey revealed the buried remains of one of the round towers on the east side.[153] In the midpoint of the inner castle, where the parking lot is now, a series of superimposed buildings were identified, including three walls running in east-west and north-south directions at 1.2 and 2.8 meters. Our reading of the profiles revealed wall segments as well as what appear to be walled units with sealed floors buried under a second floor.[154] At this point, only further archaeological excavations can help demystify the nature of the intriguing remains in that area.

A 2014 salvage excavation conducted to the northeast of the mausolea by the Bursa Archaeological Museum, prompted by restorations on the city walls, revealed a basilica dated by the archaeologists running the excavation to the Justinianic period (r. 527–65). They argue that the church was dedicated to the Archangel Michael on the basis of secondary literature by Eyice on the tombs of Osman and Orhan.[155] The excavation team has yet to publish their results, but I believe their current interpretation of the excavated basilica is misleading because the excavation team is misreading Eyice, who corrected a misunderstanding in the writings of Schultze that had claimed that the octagonal structure that housed Osman's tomb might be attributed to the church of the Archangel Michael, or the Michaleion, built by Justinian.[156] Eyice explains that this complex was not built in Prousa, but rather in Pythia (modern-day Yalova, north of Bursa) by Justinian, as discussed in the bathhouse section of this chapter.[157]

While I contradict the conclusion of their findings, this discovery is crucial to understanding Byzantine religious architecture in the city. In sum, the 2014 archaeological discovery in the citadel, combined with the 2009 GPR survey results, in addition to the visual and textual testimonies on the churches, mosques, and bathhouses now destroyed by either the earthquake or human-related activities, alongside the 1337 inscription indicate Bursa as having been born of Prousa. The fourteenth-century rulers and inhabitants of the city not only claimed the city as their own but also accommodated its heterogeneous past through conversion and reuse.

3

Contextualizing the Convent-*Masjids* and Friday Mosques

Local Knowledge and Hybridity

The first step in Ottomanization, as Chapter 2 showed, was the reuse and conversion of classical and Byzantine buildings. The second step, as this chapter will explore, involved the construction of new buildings such as Friday mosques and convent-*masjids*. Their construction techniques and decorative details mixed architectural traditions—some aspects hinted at the continuation of local practices, comparable to Byzantine structures such as the Church of Pantobasilissa on the southern Marmara Sea coast, while others indicated different cultural impacts, such as from the Mamluks and from Latinized Byzantium in the West. Here I will focus on six religious buildings erected by the Ottoman sultans Orhan, Murad I, and Bayezid I: first, three convent-*masjids*, one built by each sultan; second, three Friday mosques, the now-gone Friday mosque by Orhan, the Şehadet (Martyrdom) Mosque by Murad I, and the *Ulu Cami* or Grand Mosque by Bayezid I. This chapter further examines how Bursa gradually acquired an Ottoman character while still retaining many traits of local Byzantine architecture, including brick-and-stone masonry and banded voussoirs. Such a hybrid reality suggests continuity and resilience alongside an Ottoman embrace of a new cultural-urban network including Mamluk and Western elements, all amid the turmoil of leadership changes.

The convent-*masjids* built by Orhan, Murad I, and Bayezid I (Figure 2) were part of the sultans' larger socioreligious complexes known as *külliyes*—a gathering of buildings, including mosques, *imarets*, *madrasas*, other schools, hospitals, *hans* (inns), baths, marketplaces, tombs, and fountains. *Külliyes* functioned as landmarks through which the Ottomans legitimized their power and inhabited Bursa's landscape. The buildings discussed here formed the center of those complexes, were multifunctional, and had an inverted-T plan. A variety of names have been suggested, including *futuwwa* mosques, *iwan* mosques, multifunctional mosques, and convent-*masjid*s.[1] I call them convent-*masjid*s, following Gülru Necipoğlu's categorization, because they combined the functions of lodges, kitchens, and prayer sites.[2] The Friday mosques I will discuss are sultanic mosques, two of which—Orhan's and Murad I's—were in the old city. Today, only that of Bayezid I's survives, located outside the city walls near Orhan's *külliye*. This chapter introduces the six aforementioned buildings from the perspective of their structural and decorative qualities.

The Formation of Neighborhoods and Inhabitants

After the Ottoman arrival, Bursa's old city (Figure 3) was repurposed and revived, both within the citadel and beyond, while new residential and commercial areas were developed on the outskirts.[3] This expansion beyond the citadel began with the reign of Orhan. Accordingly, three boroughs were founded sequentially: one from the time of Orhan, just outside the walls; the second to the west, named after Murad I; and the third to the east, named after Bayezid I. In seeking to understand the Byzantine-Ottoman transition, two sources that stand out are the monastic charters for the former period and the *tahrir* defters for the latter.[4] However, the information from each is limited.[5] *Külliyes* helped to create and promote new lines of boroughs/neighborhoods (or *mahalles* as they are known in the Turkish scholarship). The varying lines found in the sources, some of them arbitrary, some rooted in reality, help elucidate the political, social, and cultural dynamics of the city.

Legitimizing the Ottomans also entailed forming new neighborhoods for the city's non-Muslims. Judging from travelers' accounts as well as Ottoman archival documents, the old city was surrounded by non-Muslim neighborhoods on the hills of the citadel, some new and some old.[6] Even as these different neighborhoods emerged, the boundaries were not as sharp as they were to become a century later.[7] Many Christians had fled to Constantinople during the Ottomans' decade-long siege of the city, but the remaining Christians, including the Christian Orthodox congregation, created new neighborhoods to the east, south, and southwest of the old city.

Despite being under Ottoman rule, the Greek Orthodox inhabitants of Bursa were paying their taxes to Anastasios Kallistos, a representative sent from the Patriarchate in Constantinople in 1382.[8] Armenians occupied a neighborhood to the east,[9] and Jews of Romaniote background lived north and northeast of the citadel,[10] where they were authorized by Orhan to build their synagogue.[11] The synagogue, Etz Ahayim, was constructed to resemble a mosque from the outside.[12]

Moving away from the walled city, wherein the non-Muslim districts were formed, the *külliyes* promoted the rise of commercial areas (for Orhan) or became sites of bathing (Murad I) or religious education (Bayezid I). They also connected neighborhoods, such as the upper city with districts north and south of the central market in the old city. Other Muslim areas of the city east of Gökdere and south of the central district were Yeşil, Yıldırım, Pir Emir, Namazgah, and Emir Sultan, delimited by the Karınca and Namazgah Rivers.

Some non-Muslim neighborhoods also developed on the outskirts (as indicated by pictograms in Figure 2). Directly west of the city, for example, was the Greek neighborhood called Kayabaşı, also known as Philadar. The Church of the Holy Apostles was located here, rebuilt by the Archimandrite Anthemios in 1787. This neighborhood was adjoined by the Muslim/Greek neighborhood known as Demirkapı, with the Church of Taxiarches. Dedicated to the Archangels Michael and Gabriel, this church was originally built during the reign of Orhan (or perhaps carried on functioning as a church under the Ottomans) and was remodeled during the reign of Mahmud II (r. 1808–39), as indicated by its now-lost inscription written in Karamanli Turkish.[13]

The district immediately northeast of the upper city, bordering the market area, was Balıkpazarı. This was a Greek neighborhood from the time of Ottoman conquest until late Ottoman times[14] and it was here that the Metropolitan Church of Saint John the Theologian was located.[15] As mentioned, the Jewish quarter was directly north and northeast of the upper city, and the Armenian quarter, known as Setbaşı, was east of the Gökdere.[16] In this area there were two Armenian churches of Catholic and Gregorian denominations. Now only the former stands, and it is in a dilapidated state.[17]

All these neighborhoods were established in the fourteenth and fifteenth centuries, as verified by sixteenth-century cadastral records.[18] Finally, one institution that brought together Bursans of different ethnic and religious backgrounds was the *bozahane*, where a fermented wheat and barley drink was served. According to İklil Selçuk, by 1482, of the six places selling *boza*, one was in the Armenian quarter of Setbaşı and another was in the Greek neighborhood of Balıkpazarı.[19]

Lowry noted that from the city's conquest in 1326 to the first cadastral register in 1487, references to the non-Muslim population of the city are scarce, except for their presence in the court records of 1478–80 and 1484–86.[20] Using travelers' accounts as evidence, Lowry attempted to account for these residents. Traveling in 1397, Johannes Schiltberger highlighted the presence of eight *imarets* serving food to Muslims as well as to Jews and Christians.[21] Gregory Palamas, the archbishop of Thessaloniki, is another important figure who provided information about the non-Muslim communities. For instance, during his yearlong sojourn with the Ottomans in Bursa and İznik, after being captured by the Ottomans in 1354, he noted the presence of a knowledgeable Christian community in Bursa whose members were eager to talk about issues related to their religious affiliation.[22] In another case, he described his introduction to Orhan in İznik. It seems that Orhan, hearing of his prisoner's intellectual stature, became eager to organize a debate between his own scholars—some of whom were also known as *Chionai* or Islamized Jews—and Palamas.[23]

In examining travelers' accounts over the first hundred years of Ottoman rule, one can find mention of Greek Orthodox Christians, Armenians, Romaniote Jews, and Catholics in addition to Muslims. Lowry suggested that, with the fall of Constantinople to the Turks, the non-Muslim population was forced to move to the new capital.[24] Immediately after this transfer, based on the 1487 cadastral register, and supported by hints and numbers in travelers' accounts, Lowry estimated the population of Bursa to be 33,515 based on an estimate of 6,457 households.[25]

The Convent-*Masjid* of Orhan

The Ottoman chronicler Neşri describes the pre-construction site of Orhan's convent-*masjid* as uninhabited, so barren that the locals did not go there. The sultan aimed to urbanize (*imaret etmek*) the area by commissioning this complex,[26] which was to include a convent-*masjid* as well as subsidiary structures fulfilling public and commercial functions.[27] According to its inscription,[28] it

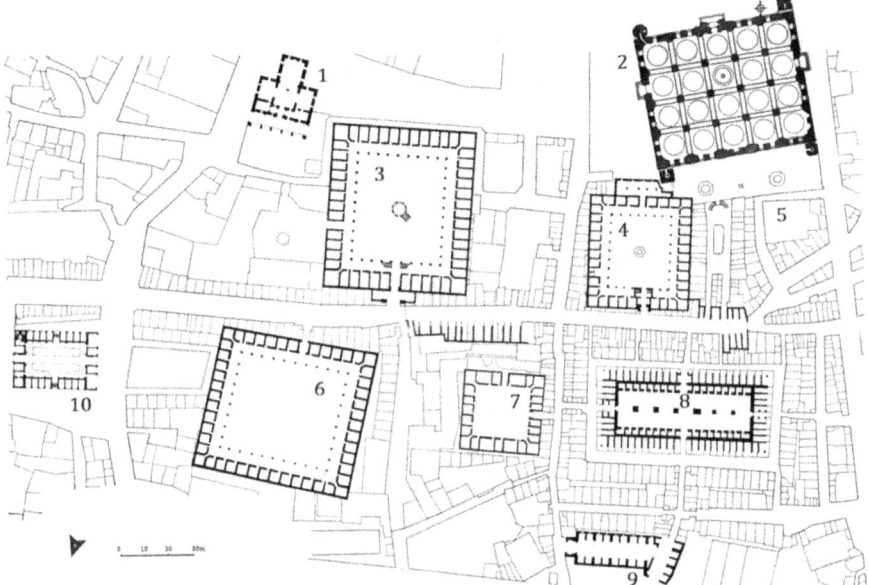

Figure 10 Plan of the lower city, showing the Convent-*Masjid* of Orhan, 1339, Bayezid I's *Ulu Cami*, and the commercial buildings. (Drawn by Hidayet Softaoğlu based on Ayverdi, *Osmanlı Mimarîsinin*)

was constructed in 1339, repaired in 1417, and restored in the 1800s following the massive mid-century earthquake.[29] Most of the wall construction visible today is original, although intricate vaulting was added later.[30]

Orhan's convent-*masjid* follows an inverted-T plan, a common form for early Ottoman Bursa (Figure 10). Along the line of the entrance, two small vaulted side rooms envelop a domed antechamber in the middle. This leads to a second domed space that is raised on a platform with a flight of steps and flanked by two side rooms roofed with domes. Bulky arches placed on both sides separating the domed space from the side rooms produce a sense of symmetry and recall a Byzantine building interior. The entire building is surrounded by walls, which enclose open and closed spaces, gardens, and vineyards.[31]

The façade (Figure 11) is articulated with blind arcades and banded voussoirs of alternating brick-and-stone. Many of the arches are semicircular and outlined in dogtooth. The building also has a decorative roundel with radiating elements of brick-and-stone; an intact example of this feature can

Figure 11 Façade of the Convent-*Masjid* of Orhan. (Photo: Suna Çağaptay)

be seen at the churches at Pantobasilissa in Trigleia and Pammakaristos in Constantinople.[32]

Another striking feature on the façade of the convent-*masjid* of Orhan is the variety of juxtaposed arches, including slightly pointed, ogival, and round arches. For decades, scholars claimed that a characteristic of this period in Bithynia was the common use of slightly pointed arches, ignoring the wide-ranging appearance of round arches on the façades of early Ottoman buildings.[33] These scholars noted that the "Ottoman" builders in this period were not trained to execute round arches. Yet round arches can be found not only on the convent-*masjid* of Orhan façade but also on other early Ottoman buildings in İznik, Yenişehir, and Bilecik.[34] Furthermore, the walls of the convent-*masjid* of Orhan have successive arches: a small pointed arch covered by a slightly larger round arch, both topped by a slightly larger round arch, all framed by a slightly pointed arch lined with a band of dogtooth frieze.

In a study of late medieval arches, Slobodan Ćurčić claimed that the Byzantine round arch in early Ottoman buildings was suppressed. I propose that the round arch form was not suppressed but rather framed and set side by side with other arches, thereby helping strengthen the pedigree for burgeoning

Ottoman architecture.³⁵ The "orderliness" provided by this kind of formal integration in the simultaneous disposition of different types of arches at the convent-*masjid* of Orhan suggests an aesthetic choice not a technical process and experimentation.³⁶ It bears noting that a similar debate persists in the transitional period from Romanesque to Gothic architecture.³⁷ Accordingly, the juxtaposition of different types of arches cannot be taken as signifiers that the buildings were built either by a single group of masons working over a long period of time or by several groups of masons operating at the same time. It is plausible that this juxtaposition was almost endemic in the architecture of Palaiologan Constantinople—the architectural vocabulary in Constantinople included ogival, round, and pointed arches at the fourteenth-century churches of the Pammakaristos and the Chora—and these arches may have been transported to other regions.³⁸

Comparable Byzantine architectural details are not limited to the masonry and use of a variety of arches. The five-bay portico supported by piers is another curious feature of Orhan's convent-*masjid*, recalling the exonartheces of Byzantine churches in its construction, such as the exonarthex of the Chora; otherwise, the brick-patterned panel placed between the arches recalls the twelfth-century brick remodelings at the Church of Santo Stefano in Bologna.³⁹ But some features have no Byzantine comparisons, such as the banded voussoirs with setbacks, sawtooth friezes, and zigzag moldings connected to the arcades on the lateral ends of the façade, where pointed arches have twin openings. Baha Tanman has labeled this the work of Mamluk masons and compared it to the mausoleum of Abu Hurayra, circa 1274, in Yumna in Palestine.⁴⁰

Interestingly, Greek participation is evident principally in walls and masonry and in elevation compositions—not in plan and layout. When the discussion is extended to include plan and layout, we note the impact of the Mamluk masons. Mamluk participation appears to have been limited to the front portico, as in Orhan's convent-*masjid* in Bursa, and decorative details, as in Bayezid I's Great Mosque in Bursa and the Mosque of Mehmed I in Dimetoka (ca. 1420).⁴¹ Whatever the limitations of the Mamluks' work, it demonstrates that not just Byzantine but also other masons and builders added their efforts to Ottoman buildings through elevation and plan, decoration, and construction techniques. Indeed, a wide range of Mamluk, Timurid, and local Anatolian-Balkan elements also appear in the early fifteenth-century architecture of Bursa in the aftermath of the Timurid sack and during the interregnum period.

The Convent-*Masjid* of Murad I

Murad I's convent-*masjid* (Figure 12) is part of a complex three kilometers to the west of the city. It was commissioned in 1365 and completed twenty years later.[42] The overall plan is unique: a two-story structure houses the mosque (*iwan*) on the first floor, while a *madrasa* occupies the second floor. The first floor is symmetric, two sequential antechambers lead to a domed space. While, two lateral rooms connected to the first antechamber, the rest of the rooms are accessed through the central space. This space ends with a pentagonal niche functioning as *mihrab* and has four more rooms to each side. On the upper floor, a corridor envelops the domed space and the *iwan* below. There are cells for the students in the *madrasa* arranged

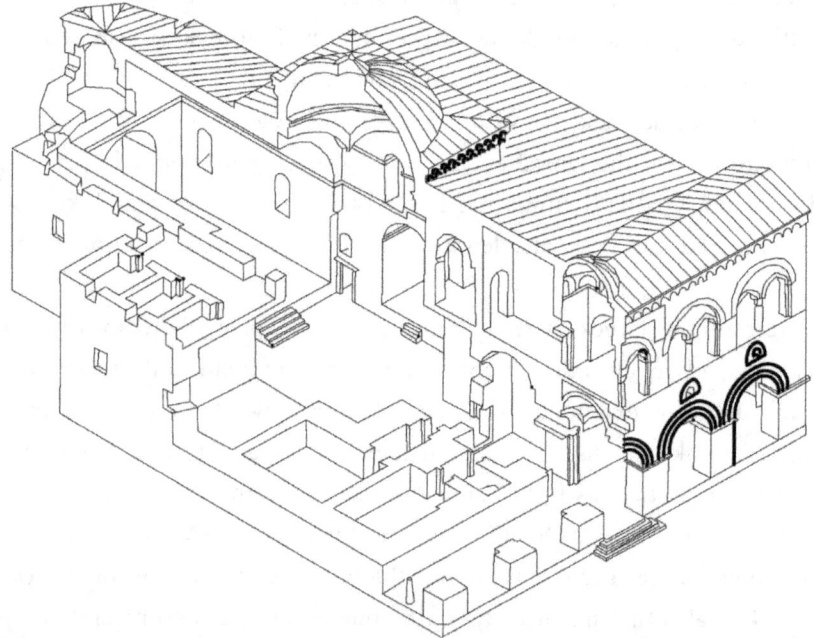

Figure 12 Isometric view of the double-storied Convent-*Masjid* of Murad I, 1363–85. (Drawn by Hidayet Softaoğlu based on Orbay, *Bursa*, after Kuzucular, for the *Aga Khan Award*.)

symmetrically on both sides, with one on each side of the stairs and another over the *mihrab*.

The two-story layout and the alternating brick-and-stone masonry (Figure 13) resemble those of the Church of Saint Sophia at Ohrid (1313–14) (Figure 14), with particular similarities in the execution of the "multitiered arcade."[43] The structure has also been compared to the two-story church of Panagia Paregoritissa (1283–96) in Arta.[44] Another Byzantine feature is the twin windows found on the second story of the façade, comparable to the fourteenth-century refectory from the Monastery of Docheiariou on Mount Athos. The twin window openings and double-storied elevation are among several decorative and construction details in the vocabulary of medieval Dalmatian architecture, which had long been exposed to Apulian and Lombard influence.[45] Illustrative cases for comparison are found in the mid-thirteenth-century Canon's House in Poreč in Dalmatia.[46] The

Figure 13 Façade of the Convent-*Masjid* of Murad I, 1363–85. (Photo: Suna Çağaptay)

Figure 14 The Church of Saint Sophia, Ohrid, Macedonia, 1313–14. (Photo: Suna Çağaptay)

last distinctive feature is the so-called Lombard frieze, a detail originating in the eponymous region and spreading into Balkan architecture under the Serbian, Bulgarian, and Byzantine kings. At the Murad I convent-*masjid*, this detail is visible running on the eave line all the way around the building.[47]

While the masonry follows Byzantine practice and the comparisons given are all to Christian buildings, no clear allusion to Christianity is apparent. Part of the uniqueness and originality of Murad I's convent-*masjid* derives from this visual puzzle—Byzantine masonry and decorative elements exist and hint at the presence of an "other" but do not openly betray any associations with Christian practice or identity. Interestingly, the elevation is transformed with an artistic vocabulary unique to the Islamic architecture in Anatolia. The combination of a convent-*masjid* and *madrasa* in one building and the architectural form heralds a design and façade decoration that seems logically conceivable as Byzantine alone, although with Latin flavor from the Balkan territories and beyond, stretching from Albania to Dalmatia, where Murad I conducted his campaigns.[48]

The building utilizes marble architectural pieces such as capitals, columns, and post and lintel fragments dating to the Byzantine period. When we look at the marble stringcourses on the façade, we encounter another type of visual puzzle. Scholars have often miscategorized these as spolia because they were used for the same purpose that they would have served in their original context before spoliation.[49] However, judging from the carving style and thickness of the pieces, I have argued elsewhere that the marble stringcourses at Murad I's convent-*masjid* are likely pseudo-spolia.[50] Evidence that they are not spolia includes their crudeness and rough execution; indeed, only one small piece in the lower-level, mid-left arch is likely to be a Byzantine original. This suggests these pieces were not simply surviving fragments or remnants of past styles. On the contrary, they demonstrate the continuity of workshop practices and traditions. Accordingly, the use of pseudo-spolia is another indication of how the builders were limited in their knowledge of building materials and their use in the building. Whether true or pseudo, the spoliation of Byzantine pieces suggests that Ottoman-era masons and builders valued the aesthetic qualities of each piece, perceived its Christian connotations, and embraced its stated antiquity and affiliations with the region.[51]

To scholars' knowledge, the unique plan of the building housing the convent-*masjid* of Murad I was never repeated in its entirety in any later-Ottoman buildings, with the exception of the Ak *Madrasa* in Niğde built in 1409 by Karamanid Ali Bey, whose wife was an Ottoman princess.[52] Descriptions of this convent-*masjid* are speckled with references to other centers of production as follows: "a curious mosque built in a semi-Byzantine style"; "a beautiful Byzantine church";[53] "recalls the Venetian palaces";[54] "Eastern like Cypriot or Western like Italian";[55] and "Mamluk in origin combined with features from Crusader-Ayyubid style."[56] With the exception of the nineteenth-century *Usul*, all sources attribute a non-Byzantine pedigree to the building. In delineating the routes by which architectural forms found their way to Bithynia from Italy, Latinized western Byzantium, or Syria and Palestine, these scholars still fail to account for the transfer of specific details. Stated differently, "Architectural forms do not float freely across the regions, they require a human agent to effect the passage."[57]

A portrait of the cultural interactions of the period would, therefore, be aided by identifying the ethnicities and places of origin of the masons who worked on Bursa's frontier beyond those already known, such as, perhaps, the Latinized Byzantines and Mamluks. Given the Genoese alliance forged by Murad I, and Bayezid I's use of a Genoese architect for fortifications, Genoese were likely present on the Bursan frontier as well.[58] Still, I do not mean to advocate the "creation of taxonomies and classifications of monuments into different microstyles or manners attributable to masons" from different backgrounds. This approach leads to a focus on the details at the expense of considering the building as a whole.[59] Instead, I see the convent-*masjid* of Murad I, as hybrid, "unrepeatable" outcomes of the techniques of masons and builders from many backgrounds working together. This permits the convent-*masjid* of Murad I to be conceived as a whole, rather than the sum of disparate parts.[60]

The Convent-*Masjid* of Bayezid I

Just like Orhan and Murad I, Bayezid I (Figure 15) commissioned the construction of a convent-*masjid* in a complex that now bears his name.[61] The plan contains three side rooms, with diamond vaults and mirror vaults on either side of the two elevated domed spaces. The heavy hipped arch in the prayer hall, meeting with the *muqarnas* niches at each end, is known as the "Bursa-style arch"[62] in the scholarship. The side rooms are two-storied, with the upper floor reserved for lodging and accompanied by hearths and storage spaces.[63] Unlike the structures for Orhan and Murad I, Bayezid I's convent-*masjid* is constructed solely of ashlar stone blocks. As a result, it conforms to a guiding construction principle of the period, similar to the *Ulu Cami* (Grand Mosque) in the lower town.

Art historians claim that Bayezid I's shift from alternating brick-and-stone to ashlar masonry was a conscious choice. It has been suggested that this new shift gave him the chance to claim broader architectural traditions and move beyond the local traditions of Bithynia. The legacy of ashlar masonry was in part associated with the preexisting architectural cultures in Anatolia, represented by the Rum Seljuks and Mongol–Ilkhanids, as well

Figure 15 Façade of the Convent-*Masjid* of Bayezid I. (Photo: Suna Çağaptay)

as the contemporaneous construction techniques and details of the Timurid and Mamluk builders and artists.[64]

From Convent-*Masjid*s to Friday mosques

Despite being constructed through sultanic endowments, the convent-*masjids* of Orhan, Murad I, and Bayezid I were not Friday mosques. They were not meant for Friday prayer congregation but, rather, as spaces for dining, education, and lodging, as well as for prayer.[65] Using Ottoman sources, Gülru Necipoğlu concludes that the construction of the Friday mosques was related to the conquest over the infidels.[66] As described in Chapter 2, the moniker *Ulu Cami* or Grand Mosque (or Friday mosque) was given to buildings converted from Byzantine cathedrals or mosques built anew. While convent-*masjids* were built in the suburbs and other areas of previously sparse habitation, the Friday mosques went up in the center of Bursa. The former constituted part of a larger socioreligious complex, the *külliye*, whereas the latter stood on their own. The function of a Friday mosque or *Ulu Cami* was to celebrate the sultan's victory and claim ownership of the lands. As Gülru Necipoğlu has discussed, while the reigning sultan's name was cited during the Friday *khutba*, the Friday mosques in Bursa and Edirne were not named after the sultans who commissioned them, a practice we begin to see starting from the reign of Mehmed II (r. 1444–46; 1451–81) in Istanbul.[67]

The Friday Mosque of Orhan

If these convent-*masjid*s were not built for Friday *khutbas* and prayer, where then did fourteenth-century inhabitants of Bursa go to pray? Likely in the Byzantine cathedral, echoing the Ottoman practice in other cities.[68] The first mosque (Figure 3.4) was likely part of a broader conversion process in the old city during the reign of Orhan. Any discussion of the likelihood of having a Friday mosque converted from a Byzantine church in the old city brings to mind the 1337 inscription discussed in Chapter 2. Now immured in the east entrance of the Şehadet (Martyrdom) Mosque built by Murad I in 1365–66, it is labeled by Paul Wittek as "the oldest Ottoman epigraphic document."[69] It was written eleven years after the conquest, and in later scholarship it is simply called the "1337 inscription." The inscription (Figure 5) includes titular embellishments such as "The Exalted Great Emir, Warrior on Behalf of God, Sultan of the Gazis, Gazi son of the Gazi, Champion of the State and Religion, and of the Horizons, Hero of the Age."[70]

The inscription also includes an image of the much-disputed *Gazi*, about which historians spilled much ink following Wittek's *Gazi* thesis.[71] For Wittek and scholars who followed his vision, this ideology established grounds for Ottoman religious and political legitimization.[72] According to earlier scholarship led by Wittek,[73] references to the term *gaza* in medieval treatises suggested "an irregular raiding activity whose ultimate goal was the expansion of the power of Islam."[74] As a result, they discussed the notion of this ideology as being deeply rooted in the notion of jihad. However, an alternative interpretation of the *gaza* has emerged in newer scholarship involving a "predatory raid" or "an excursion into foreign country."[75]

The 1337 inscription does not describe Orhan as a *gazi* or a warlord only. In a recently published work, Hüseyin Yılmaz underlines the phrase "Champion of State" (shuja' al-dawla) in the inscription. He explains how this harks back to the Rum Seljuk practice of emulating the Abbasid rulership and links it with the use of the same phrase in coins struck during Orhan's time. Yılmaz reads this as a sign of Orhan's attempt to legitimize himself as the rightful heir to the pre-Ottoman Islamic past in Anatolia and beyond.[76] Given this, the 1337 inscription combined with the fourteenth-century Ottoman architectural interventions helps us identify more of an ethos than an ideology, wherein a conquest was inevitable but moderated by a dialogue with Bursa's past and present, its urban fabric and its inhabitants.

The 1337 inscription also refers to a *masjid* built by Orhan. In light of its location in the old city, it may have originated in Orhan's Friday mosque, the one converted from the Byzantine cathedral of Bursa. As discussed in Chapter 2, relying on travelers' accounts and secondary scholarship, being the first Friday mosque in Bursa, it was likely built close to prominent tombs or even within the tomb in which Orhan was buried.[77] Here it helps to recall Evliya's description of Orhan's tomb in 1640 as being surrounded by holy light and found within the mosque in the old castle. Evliya also elaborated on the size of the Orhan's Friday mosque, its dome and its dimensions, and said Orhan is buried inside.[78]

Andreas Mordtmann, a contemporary witness to the catastrophic effects of the 1855 earthquake, noted that the Orhan's Friday mosque was completely destroyed with no remains standing, making reconstruction from the ruins impossible.[79] The depiction by von Erlach done in the 1720s suggests the likelihood that several units from a Byzantine complex, the main church, and a baptistery were converted into a Friday mosque and the mausolea for Osman and Orhan. This was the case in the Saint Sophia in Istanbul; upon the city's conquest, it was turned into a mosque and its baptistery became the mausoleum where two Ottoman sultans, Mustafa I (d. 1623) and İbrahim I (d. 1648), were interred.

The Friday Mosque of Murad I

Orhan's *masjid* was not the only Friday mosque built by the Ottoman sultans. Murad I also built a Friday mosque in the old city,[80] which is known as the *Şehadet Cami* (Martyrdom Mosque) (Figure 3.8). As it stands today, the mosque bears a plan with two domed units of equal size ranged along the axis of the *mihrab*; it was heavily damaged in the earthquake of 1855 and subsequently restored during the governorship of Celaleddin Paşa in 1892. The pre-earthquake plan of the building is a matter of debate. Gabriel, for example, argued that it may have been a basilical or an inverted T-type.[81] Ayverdi also opted for a basilical scheme.⁸² Baykal, however, without any evidence, claimed that it had a nine-domed plan.⁸³ Robert Anhegger pointed to older photographs and drawings to suggest that it was a multiunit mosque, with a central aisle covered by three successive domes and side bays narrower than the width of the domed central spaces, recalling the mosque in Bursa's lower city and the *Ulu Cami* in Plovdiv built in 1389. Sedad Hakkı Eldem, corroborating Anhegger, argued that it had a squarish interior, having two, not three, domed units. ⁸⁴

In light of recently published drawings, especially travelers' depictions and photographs, the building is certain to have been a mosque covered with two domes.⁸⁵ For example, the abovementioned drawing done by Cassas in 1786⁸⁶ depicts the eastern façade of Orhan's mausoleum and includes the eastern side of the *Şehadet* (Martyrdom) Mosque, showing two domes and a minaret.⁸⁷ In two different city panoramas done by Löwenhielm, which I use as the first and last visuals of this book (Figures 1 and 20), further clues emerge: the first indicates a multi-domed plan with two domes and pointed blind arches on the façade, and the second suggests a triple-domed roofing system recalling the inverted-T plan and a minaret. Later on, the photos taken after the 1855 earthquake conform to these details.⁸⁸ Based on these images, I suggest that an inverted-T plan would likely form the original ground plan of this building.

The Friday Mosque of Bayezid I

Like Murad I, who built his *külliye*⁸⁹ following his victories in the Balkans in 1364, Bayezid I built a *külliye* to commemorate his victory in the Battle of Nikopolis (Niğbolu) in 1396. The Battle of Nikopolis came on the heels of Ottoman expansion in Anatolia against the Karamanids in the 1390s, the conquest of Adrianople in 1361 (and its gradual transformation into becoming the second capital city of the Ottomans), and the siege of Constantinople initiated by Bayezid I in 1394. These victories allowed Bayezid I to portray himself as *Sultan-ı Rum*, and he wanted to have his reign mimic that of Alexander the Great.⁹⁰ His great maneuvering skills on the battlefield led to his being nicknamed Thunderbolt/Lightning (Turkish Yıldırım). Bayezid I also built the Grand Mosque in Bursa, known as the *Ulu Cami* (1396–1400) (Figure 10.8). Hoca Sadeddin noted that the mosque was begun by Bayezid

I using the spoils of battle taken by the Ottoman army.[91] Located just to the north of Orhan's *külliye*, for several centuries it has been regarded as the most important religious monument in the city, and it is referred to locally as the *Makam-ı Hamis* (fifth sanctuary), ranked after Mecca, Medina, Jerusalem, and Damascus.

The *Ulu Cami* (Grand Mosque) is made of cut stone and marble blocks, punctuated by arches with setbacks and windows. The rectangular structure is accessed via three entrances. The main portal in the middle of the north façade is more monumental and ornate than the other portals on the east and the west. Adjoining the northern corners are minarets that were heavily restored in the nineteenth century. The inside of the mosque differs from a typical inverted-T plan. The large prayer hall is organized into twenty bays, separated by twelve gigantic piers in three rows of four, supporting twenty domes of equal size with varying height. The plan is a variation on the Rum Seljuk mosque type, where the bays are defined by the insertion of columns; here at the *Ulu Cami*, the huge piers break up the continuity of the space.

The *Ulu Cami* is particularly of note because, as with the convent-*masjid* of Bayezid I, it was built completely out of ashlar masonry. This represented a shift in the architecture of Bursa, as well as Bithynia, from brick-and-stone to the more expensive stone and marble masonry and from juxtaposed arches to unified arch forms, implying "a shift in taste and identity."[92] Several other details suggest borrowings from broader geographical horizons. For example, the inscription on the *minbar* hints at an artist originating from Ayntab (a city in southeast Anatolia, then under the control of the Mamluks), who also worked for the *Ulu Cami* of Saruhanid princedom in Manisa.[93] The lamp patterns incised into the blind arches on the façade of the building are also attributed to Mamluk workmanship, with the globular feet and flared necks recalling the Mamluk glass lamps.[94] The lamp incisions seen on the blind arches are also similar in notion to the depictions of hanging lamps suspended from arches found on seventeenth-century Ottoman mosque carpets and prayer rugs. Indeed, the image of a lamp suspended from an arch is a curious feature evident in Islamic art. Margaret S. Graves has discussed the appearance of the lamps as objects in glass and ceramic that bring light to the inner space and on carpets to indicate the *mihrab* niche and its symbolic connotations.[95] At the *Ulu Cami* in Bursa, each arch with an individual lamp incised in the middle creates an axis for the prayer space within the multi-domed ground layout of the mosque. Carved on the facade of the building, the image of the "blind" lamp form is far from illuminating the inner space, but it may well stand symbolically for the notion of light. Bayezid I's *Ulu Cami*, then, indicates the following: first, the façade articulation transforms alternating brick-and-stone prototypes into elaborately decorated surfaces in stone without exploiting its sculptural massing possibilities. Second, the images of the "blind" lamp on the façade replace physical illumination offering a new aesthetic on the creation of the praying space.

Within the context of medieval Anatolia, the use of ashlar masonry and marble finds an earlier comparison at the *Ulu Cami* of İsa Bey at Ayasoluk, built in 1374–5. Built by a Damascene builder by the name of Ali ibn Musheimesh al-Dimishqi, the İsa Bey Mosque at Ayasoluk draws stylistic parallels from still earlier periods such as the Umayyad and Ayyubid Syria, as well as more contemporaneous examples in Mamluk Syria and Egypt.[96] Bayezid I conquered Ayasoluk and put an end to the rise of the Aydinids in 1390, just before the construction of his külliye and *Ulu Cami*.

The period of Bayezid I—the late fourteenth century—also witnessed apparently intensifying Aydinid and Ottoman connections with the Mamluk realm controlling the regions of Syria, Palestine, and Egypt. While it is difficult to locate a Mamluk builder in the epigraphic evidence in the examples commissioned by Bayezid I (with the exception of the abovementioned woodwork artist from Ayntab—the modern-day city of Antep in southeastern Turkey bordering Syria—working on the *minbar* of the *Ulu Cami*), one can trace the Mamluk architectural impact by their construction and decorative techniques. One such example is noted at the Rum Seljuk mosque of Alaeddin in Konya, which was completed in 1235. Under an arch with moldings decorated with zigzags ending in loop patterns, we read the name of Mohammed ibn Hawlan al-Dimishqi, "of Damascus," referring to the storied city, then under Ayyubid rule, dated to 1219–20.[97] This suggests Syrian itinerant artists and builders working in Anatolia a century earlier.

According to Michael Meinecke, the design of the İsa Bey Mosque at Ayasoluk as well as the *Ulu Cami* in Manisa, built in 1366–7 in the Saruhanid domain (a neighboring principality), came from a group of itinerant Mamluk architects and artisans who were likely active in construction in Fustat and subsequently came to Anatolia.[98] Baha Tanman asserts that the Aydinid mosque of İsa Bey stood as clear testimony that "the Mamluk world was omnipresent in Anatolia during the *Beylik* period."⁹⁹ It is within this climate, as argued in previous scholarship, that the Mamluks inevitably rendered their impact on the emerging architectural styles in Anatolia. These buildings, the *Ulu Cami*s of the Saruhanids and Aydinids as well as Bayezid I *Ulu Cami* and his convent-*masjid*, bespeak a genuine Syrian or Egyptian implant via Mamluk hands, as exemplified by features from walls to portals and decoration to the choice of materials.

In a broader context, Bayezid I *Ulu Cami* combined with his convent-*masjid* is a standing testimony to his attempt at earning a more prestigious royal claim by blending in material and symbolic borrowings from architectural traditions of the eastern Mediterranean.¹⁰⁰ The architectural vocabulary seen at Bayezid I's *Ulu Cami*, as well as the rest of his architectural patronage, is in line with his expansionist aspirations, which led him to conquer most of western and central Anatolia in the 1390s.

Creating an Architectural Idiom: Reuse, Translation, and Innovation

In sum, investigating indigenous and nonindigenous forms reveals the emergence of a hybrid and synthetic style that incorporates the masonry techniques and decorative vocabulary of late Byzantine architecture. The evidence strongly suggests that local former Byzantine builders helped nourish a shared visual vocabulary in constructing the convent-*masjids* of Orhan and Murad I. While following the designs put forth by their Ottoman patrons, the builders used their traditional workshop practices, for example, when constructing walls.

On the one hand, this shared vocabulary of construction methods, forms, and decorative details served as the visual vehicle for the Ottomans to lay claim to their newly conquered land. On the other, Byzantine masons continued producing buildings for inhabitants of both faiths. The Pantobasilissa at Trigleia was a Byzantine church built by Greek masons for the Greek community. Textual evidence shows that Trigleia was still in Byzantine hands in 1337 when the church was constructed, although the date of the town's ultimate conquest is unknown.¹⁰¹ The ground layout of the building is an elongated cross-in-square, a variation of the type seen frequently in the ninth-century monastic context of Bithynia.[102] The construction of buildings like the Pantobasilissa hints at the fluidity of the Bithynian frontier in the early fourteenth century. Perceived borders expanded and contracted, and the area was more porous than hedge-like, with trade, cultural interactions, and intermarriages and conversions occurring between the Byzantines and Ottomans.[103]

"Hybridity" in architectural vocabulary, in the structures discussed thus far, suggests more than an agglomeration of details from bordering religious and cultural spheres. Rather, it implies a deeper commonality held by people of different backgrounds in the frontier culture. The inclusion of Byzantine subjects, details, and architectural elements within the wider perspective of Ottoman architectural representations presages an overarching system of shared visual vocabulary, with Muslims and Christians serving as participants in, and inhabitants of, the same visual world. As a result, it is possible to perceive the architectural production of this period as something beyond the "overlap" suggested by "hybridity," and rising to the level of autonomous works of architecture rooted deeply in the rich architectural heritage of the region and receptive to new developments brought by mobile masons. The spread of architectural features from one cultural-historical setting to another has often been ascribed to "utilitarian opportunism" or "triumphalist impulse."[104] This, however, is a narrow view.

Although the Ottomans had a well-developed architecture prior to their capture of what would become Bursa, they looked to the Byzantines for inspiration as they gradually took control of the region. Predating 1326, Ottoman construction focused on building mosques in Söğüt, Bilecik, and Yenişehir. Whereas the late thirteenth-/early fourteenth-century mosque complex at Söğüt was renovated in the nineteenth century at the behest of Abdülaziz (r. 1861–76), the Orhan Mosque in Bilecik was built and rebuilt by Orhan after the first iteration was destroyed by the 1855 earthquake. The later mosque had alternating brick-and-stone masonry and blind arches on the wall plane. Although the plan conforms to a church plan known as the atrophied Greek cross, as identified by Ousterhout, the dome is supported on deep recesses under arches, suggesting an Ottoman structural system.[105]

The six architectural projects described in this chapter—the convent-*masjids* by Orhan, Murad I, and Bayezid I, as well as the Friday mosques of Orhan, Murad I (*Şehadet*) and Bayezid I (*Ulu*)—show the ways in which architectural practices developed over the fourteenth century. They were the material expressions of the early Ottoman civilization and were mixed in character. For example, while the wall construction and decorative features resemble and reference Byzantine techniques, the period also witnessed a conscious choice to omit these techniques and details. But another way to read this is that the buildings constructed in the period between 1300 and 1402 became independent proclamations of the architectural culture of Bursa, constituting a group without parallel. In displaying the aspirations of builders and patrons, the architectural culture in Bursa became distinctly "transitional," a process that entailed the transmission of several themes, such as alternating brick-and-stone masonry, spoliated items, and brick patterning, over the course of a century. This also reflected the limited economic and organizational means of the Ottomans at the time.

While the use of alternating brick-and-stone masonry is a distinguishing feature in the early religious as well as nonreligious Ottoman buildings of Bursa, during the reign of Bayezid I the architectural culture shifted to stone-marble ashlar masonry. I would like to argue that the Timurid sack of 1402 did not disrupt the Ottoman empire-building project so much as herald a continuation carried out with similar materials but an evolving vocabulary. The Ottoman project was resumed in full when Timur left Anatolia about a decade later in 1413 to pursue his longtime ambition of conquering Asia itself.[106] The new architectural style included many borrowings from the Mamluk, Timurid, and local Anatolian-Balkan elements, as showcased by the Green (*Yeşil*) Convent-*Masjid* (1419–21) established by Mehmed I (r. 1413–21).[107]

During the Ottoman rule of Bursa, a set of new design ideas evolved and were utilized, such as the porticoed entrances with twin openings as well as double-storied elevations and multi-domed roofing systems. Ashlar masonry also came to replace alternating brick-and-stone masonry. These details show how reuse, translation, and innovation were the products of a dynamic encounter among rulers and builders from multiple cultures, all allowing the architectural idiom in Bursa to be "appropriated, translated, rehistoricized and read anew."[108]

4

The Roots and Context of the Inverted-T Plan

In terms of masonry techniques and decorative details, the convent-*masjid*s built by Orhan, Murad I, and Bayezid I suggest a continuity in local construction practices, as Chapter 3 explored. But there is something curious in their plans, on which this chapter focuses: the impact of non-Ottoman or nonlocal (i.e., non-Bithynian) concepts, as exemplified by the inverted-T plan. Bursa's inverted-T's demonstrate an early Ottoman structural hybridity through which masons worked in a gradually evolving masonry tradition for patrons. The residential and utilitarian functions of these buildings, not simply their religious uses, also merit highlighting. Instead of linking the reappearance of this plan with the convents and lodges built a century before in post-Kösedağ central Anatolian towns, as previous scholarship has done, I situate it within a common Islamic building plan prevalent in the Mediterranean basin beginning in the eighth century under different dynasties and rulerships. In doing this, I seek to provide context for the roots of these building plans in early Ottoman Bursa.

My stance is an alternative to two prevalent scholarly assumptions on the inverted-T: one, that the wall construction in the inverted-T was simply an imitation of Byzantine practices and not a process of continuity, which I refuted in the previous chapter; and, two, that the plan came from Central Asia and was possibly introduced by the Mongols. The limitations of this second assumption are made evident with examples from Byzantium and the Islamic domains of the broader Mediterranean and Middle East.

What is an Inverted-T Plan?: Identity, Origin, and Function

Considered in terms of form and space, the inverted-T plan (Figure 10.1, as indicated by the plan of the Convent-*Masjid* of Orhan) is one of the most interesting and original types of early Ottoman architecture. A typical inverted-T building consists primarily of a domed space that leads into an *iwan* (a rectangular vaulted space walled on three sides and open on the fourth) and another domed space on an axis, with two smaller domed or vaulted chambers flanking the *iwan*. In most cases, the buildings are fronted by five-bay porticoes and usually include side rooms reserved for lodging.

One of the main hurdles in understanding inverted-T buildings involves terminology and usage.[1] Indeed, because the side rooms were referred to by many names (e.g., *zaviye*, *hankah*, *imaret*, and *tekke*) and occupied by mystic figures and sufi saints,[2] scholars such as Semavi Eyice have claimed that they provided temporary lodging for the *ahis*, sufi sheikhs, and the other members of heterodox groups.[3] Others, however, such as Ahmet Doğan, have argued that the robust architectural elements in the side rooms, such as their high elevation and domical design, as well as their lack of amenities like bathrooms and kitchens, signal that these rooms were not used as lodging places but, rather, as meeting halls known as *mahfil* or *majlis* for the *ahis* and dervishes.[4]

In early Ottoman Bursa, several references to dervishes appear, including Geyikli Baba, a heterodox dervish, and Ebu Ishak Kazeruni, a sufi dervish of Persian origin who lived in the mid-eleventh century and in whose memory Bayezid I built an inverted-T convent.[5] An *ahi* (lit. being young, also spelled *akhī*) is a group of young men organized based on occupation—a kind of fellowship.[6] *Ahi*, further, was a name given to the groups in Anatolia to separate them from other *futuwwa* groups.[7] In the tenth-century Persian and Arab tradition,[8] *futuwwa* groups followed a moral code and functioned like a fraternity. The *ahis* appropriated the codes of the *futuwwa* groups and rose to prominence in the aftermath of the collapse of the Great Seljuks of Iran and the rise of the Rum Seljuks in the thirteenth century, but they gradually diminished in size with the rise of the Ottomans and the making of Bursa as the Ottoman capital city.[9] According to Ahmet Yaşar Ocak, the *ahis* combined three qualities: "mysticism, chivalry and craftsmanship."[10] In an oft-quoted detail in the fourteenth-century travelogues of Ibn Battuta, he described their garb as "long cloaks and boots on their feet," while they carried "a long knife

[and] attached to a girdle and on their heads were white bonnets of wool."[11] Ibn Battuta also expresses his approval of their banquet of fruits and sweetmeats, followed by dancing and song.[12]

The *ahis* and dervishes frequented the convent-*masjid*s in Bursa. In the context of thirteenth- and fourteenth-century Anatolia, the *ahis* were always urban-based and *ahi* and sufi or dervish group identity was often linked to the construction of an *ahi* lodge or a dervish convent.[13] As in post-Kösedağ central Anatolia, these complexes played into the developing scene in early Ottoman cities.[14] Studying the patterns of land grants in the 1487 cadastral registers by the early Ottoman sultans, İklil Selçuk has identified three groups who were granted lands: *sheikhs*, *fakihs* (possibly Islamic jurist or imam), and *ahis*. Ahis got the smallest portion of the lands, leading Selçuk to assume that they lost their power amid the centralization of the Ottoman state.[15]

Accordingly, one scholarly quibble is to locate these figures in a spatial setting. Where did those figures live and how did they make use of the buildings? In the previous scholarship, occupying a central position within the *külliyes*, the inverted-T convent-*masjid*s were often regarded as having a principally religious function.[16] Eyice, as well as other Turkish scholars, focused their attention on the domed space, leading to an overemphasis on the religious function of these buildings. A new wave of scholarship, however, has included the side rooms, which may have functioned as guest and service rooms. The side rooms have been identified by Doğan and others as congregational halls for *ahis*, *fakihs*, sufi dervishes, and state officials who were establishing the new society in Bursa.[17] Overemphasizing the religious function of the inverted-T convent-*masjid*s at the expense of other uses and simply calling these complexes mosques fails to fully account for their functional range. Supporting this, Sedat Çetintaş has noted that these buildings were not built as mosques but, rather, were "multifunctional."[18] But this thesis never gained traction due to overwhelming scholarly objections, especially from Ekrem Hakkı Ayverdi, who always argued for the pure Muslim origins of Ottoman architecture. He claimed that Çetintaş's argument is ungrounded and employs crippled reasoning in making his case.[19]

Interestingly, this building type often lacked the architectural details necessary for a mosque or a *masjid*, such as a *mihrab*, *minbar* (pulpit for Friday *khutbas*), and *minaret*.[20] In the case of Bursa, the minarets were an afterthought, including at the convent-*masjid*s of Orhan[21] and Murad I,[22] although some have argued in the latter case that the minaret, on the northwest corner of the second story, was original to the construction.²³ In sum, these details, or lack thereof, signal the multifunctionality of such structures. Reinforcing this notion, the categorical division suggested by Gülru Necipoğlu suggests that some of these buildings served primary functions other than as mosques for Friday prayer. In addition to lacking a minaret, some lacked large areas for congregational prayer—instead, they had rooms of varying functions, and even interior pools of water. This explains Necipoğlu's notation of these convents, lodges (*zaviyes*), or hospices (*imarets*) as convent-*masjids*.²⁴

The problem with overemphasizing the religious function and identity of the inverted-T leads to a complementary discussion: their residential and utilitarian nature. Eyice, and later Kuran, trace the origins of this plan back to the Central Asian house or four-*iwan* plan form that was brought to Anatolia by the Turks.²⁵ But there is no clear precedent for this plan in Central Asia.²⁶ An earlier type of this plan may have been introduced to Anatolia by the Mongol-Ilkhanids with the dissolution of the Rum Seljuk power in the post-Kösedağ context, as with the Çifte Minareli *Madrasa* in Erzurum (1280/90–1300) and Gök *Madrasa* in Sivas (1271–2).²⁷ Its origins have been attributed to the *madrasas* built during the reigns of Nizam-al Mulk (d. 1042), the vizier of the Rum Seljuk sultans Alp Arslan (1063–72), and Malik Shah (1072–92).²⁸ However, this was a building type also known to have existed before Nizam-al Mulk.²⁹ For instance, there were four *madrasas* in Nishapur, in northeastern Iran, during the reign of Sultan Mahmud of Gazna (997–1030).³⁰

Yet, until recently, the Central Asian house plan has been upheld as the most likely forerunner of its counterpart in Bursa. Sedat Emir, author of the latest scholarship on the "Bursa incarnation" of this type, claims this was not the case. He discusses a group of *zaviyes* in Tokat in central Anatolia built in the late thirteenth and early fourteenth centuries, concluding that the characteristic feature of the Tokat buildings was the consistent use of an axial volumetric core comprising the domed sofa and vaulted *iwan* in various spatial organizations. Then a new scheme was created within a short period of thirty years. This was the scheme used in the first Ottoman buildings in Bithynia.

While Emir's argument speaks to a continuity in the individual units of the inverted-T between the buildings in central Anatolia and Bithynia, it does not elucidate the formal relationship. Emir has argued that the initial plan came from Mongol–Ilkhanid planning principles, not those of the Central Asian Turks,³¹ and although Emir designates the plan as coming from the

Mongol–Ilkhanids, he does not establish how this connection would be reconstructed. Ousterhout, however, following the historical details outlined by Lindner, suggests that the plan may have been created by a Muslim master who came from inner Anatolia in the 1320s and 1330s along with other immigrants, including schoolmasters and elites fleeing the disorder of Mongol rule.[32]

Indeed, the Mongols facilitated the large-scale migration of craftsmen, administrators, and scholars across different parts of Asia. This began under Genghis Khan in the 1220s, when Muslim artisans from the western regions of the empire were transferred to China to engage in building projects there. This was an unprecedented level of human circulation and cross-cultural contact, which only increased with the widening reach of Mongol rule.[33] The Mongol influence is evident in the evolution of Rum-Seljuk architecture in thirteenth-century Anatolia, as described by Sara E. Wolper in her book *Cities and Saints*.[34] I do not refute the possibility of Mongol origins[35] for early inverted-T Ottoman structures, or the overlaps between the ones built in the post-Kösedağ context of Anatolia and those of Bursa and Bithynia, but focusing solely on this contribution can be misleading if it acts as a distraction from the regional dynamics between the Byzantine and Islamic centers in the Middle East and the Mediterranean. Understanding the inverted-T structures as institutions of devotion and hospitality in the diachronic dynastic succession of medieval Anatolia has recently been argued by Oya Pancaroğlu who offers a fresh way looking into the concepts of multi-functionality of these buildings. Following a larger geographical realm and pursuing the inverted-T as a spatial concept serving to the collective, ceremonial and spiritual needs of the Islamic dynasties, I would like to discuss what this form might mean in the fourteenth-century Bursa.[36]

Furthermore, the emphasis on Mongol origins does not do justice to the function and needs that the inverted-T plan served in Bursa. Focusing on Mongol origins also has a distinctly nationalistic cast, suggesting that if the wall construction or decorative details are not of Central Asian or Mongol–Ilkhanid origins, then the "Ottoman authenticity" of Bursa architecture could be in question.

Locally Grown

From the arrival of the Ottomans at the dawn of the 1300s until 1402, the inverted-T's gave impetus to the creation of a new built reality in Bursa. By 1380, Bursa, as well as other Bithynian cities such as Nicaea/İznik and Yenişehir (the latter, as implied by its name, a "new city" with no urban past), were defined dramatically by these rising edifices. As previously discussed, the inverted-T's share certain features with earlier regional Byzantine structures, such as alternating brick-and-stone construction.[37] These features indicate the deep roots of local architectural practices and the ways builders contributed to continuity along the Byzantine-Ottoman frontier in Bursa and in Bithynia more generally.

The continuity in the architectural style of these structures has been identified as both "hybrid" and "semi-Byzantine."[38] But a more convincing interpretation is that the early Ottoman builders borrowed from their forerunners and translated the previous styles within a new context. In addition, whether or not the early Ottoman buildings bore superficial details from the Byzantine era or followed Byzantine workshop practices, they represented a "dual heritage" that allowed masons to work in an unchanged masonry tradition but for Ottoman patrons. While the layout of the buildings proclaimed Muslim decorum and ritual, their "skin" was Byzantine and reflected the mixed ethnicity of the groups in Bursa as well as Bithynia under Ottoman rule.[39]

Ottoman inverted-T buildings of this period are therefore similar to their predecessors on the surface, but their function and design ideals differ. Put another way, "Ottomans did not simply look and copy."[40] The use of different components in buildings, whether imported by the conquerors or continuing local traditions, became the driving force of a new, distinct, homegrown entity—a hybrid architecture. This hybrid architecture maintained the legacies of the builders and culture of Bursa at the time, while also enacting a significant cultural change. The continuation of style is less important here since "style . . . can be learned through observation."[41] By contrast, construction techniques are "learned through active participation in the construction process,"[42] so studying them helps us see the direct routes of the relationships among buildings, regions, and cultures in fourteenth-century Bursa. In particular, masonry and decorative details are the signatures of a given workshop. However, the extent to which masons preserved their own local knowledge—that is, how Byzantine construction techniques, decorative details, and forms were transmitted or translated into their new works—is not yet known. Further study of the buildings of the Islamic Mediterranean courts will work to elucidate these pathways.

The inevitable question now arises: Who was in charge of producing and reproducing the Ottoman inverted-T buildings? Often Christian builders turned slaves are credited with this role. Yet would "Nikomedianus," "Christodoulos," and "Stephanos"[43]—names mentioned in textual records—in fact have been the master builders working for the Ottoman sultans? And, if so, why was their work limited to the construction of walls and the insertion of spoliated pieces, while excluding other activities such as the execution of the vaulting systems and other decorative details?[44] One prospect is that the Christian or multiethnic builders took credit for these limited tasks to evoke particular meanings through the architectural forms they were creating—by deconstructing the prototypes into individual elements and then reassembling them, so that they bore different relationships to one another, and hence building completely new structures.[45]

Globally Known

Not only the wall plane, but also the plan of the inverted-T evinces continuity. My focus is therefore on a larger Mediterranean scheme, in both Christian and Islamic settings, involving continuous use of the inverted-T. The earliest examples have been found in the eighth-century garden palace at Ukhaidir, in present-day Iraq, wherein modular courtyard units are accompanied by a long portico connecting to a central hall.[46] The tenth-century examples from Fustat, in Egypt, are also noteworthy.[47] Scholars working on these two types of evidence have claimed that the origins of this plan can be linked to Mesopotamia, from where it was introduced into Egypt during the governorship of Ibn Tulun, who was sent by the Abbasid court in 868.[48] In the tenth century, the inverted-T's gained a new name: *al-Hiri* (a central large room flanked by side rooms).[49] This is, for example, how al-Masudi (d. 956) referred to the building created by al-Mutawakkil (r. 847–61):

> And in his days al-Mutawakkil created a building that the people had not known, and it was the one known as "the *ḥīrī* and two sleeves and porticoes" [*al-ḥīrī wa kummayn wa arwiqa*]; and that is to say, one of his companions in nightly entertainment related to him one night that a king of al-Ḥīrā of the Nu'maniyya [line] of the Bani Nasr created a building in his permanent residence, which is to say al-Ḥīrā, in the image of war and its form. . . . And the portico had in it the seat [*majlis*] of the king, which is the chest [*ṣadr*], and the two sleeves [*kummayn*] to the right and left.[50]

The plan, with two sleeves and two side porticoes, was often seen as the spatial manifestation of al-Mutawakkil's military tactic of attacking his enemy by forming a central column with flanks of guards on either side.[51] The important structural details to note here are that the main room functioned as the reception area and the side rooms were used as cloakrooms and for food storage.[52]

Across the region, the typological references to the inverted-T show the interchanges throughout the Middle East and Mediterranean, such as their use as meeting or audience halls. For example, there are also more modest *al-majlis* sites, sitting or meeting places, in Fustat, dating to the Tulunid and Fatimid periods. These houses follow a particular spatial layout, with an emphasis on symmetry, underscored by a rectangular courtyard. An inverted-T layout known as the *majlis* or a *qa'a* (raised sitting area) was typical, with a large space in the middle surrounded by slightly smaller, usually narrower, spaces on either side.[53] This open-courtyard house type in Fustat evolved into use in Ayyubid palatial complexes[54] as well as in the standard Mamluk *durqa'a-iwan*.[55] The Mamluk *durqa'a-iwan*, formed by a four-*iwan* composition or cruciform-shaped plan, is an example of the residential use of this layout, both for private and group housing (known as the *rab'*).[56] In the Mamluk period, this building type was fronted by a gallery (*riwaq*), which was separated from the main area by a set of doors. The main area was either an open court or roofed central square. When roofed, it was known as a *durqa'a* and was often complemented by a lantern and a pool in the *iwan*. Similarly in the Ottoman context, *majlis* or *mahfil* rooms were the places where the formal ceremonies took place.[57]

The inverted-T plan was common in the Mediterranean for several centuries.[58] For example, it recurred in the residential architecture of middle Byzantine Cappadocia (tenth–twelfth centuries).[59] Mathews and Daskalakis-Mathews associated the Cappadocian houses with those of the Islamic world based on the common elements of the broadly defined inverted-T plan and the arcaded façades. However, Ousterhout[60] has argued that Byzantine and Islamic cultures share a Roman heritage that includes architectural elements such as porticoed façades and ceremonial halls.

The impact of the inverted-T and its variations was not confined to the eastern Mediterranean. Overlapping typological and functional similarities also appear in Ayyubid and Norman Sicily, especially in the context of a building's internal waterworks. For example, at the Ayyubid palaces in Aleppo and Shawbak, as well as the Norman-Sicilian examples of La Cuba and Lo Scibene, pools are dug into the courtyard, as discussed by Dana Katz.[61] A similar arrangement appears in the convent-*masjids* of Orhan and Murad I, the latter of these being the only example still standing.[62]

These examples show a regional interconnectedness in the continuous use of the inverted-T plan for residential or palacelike structures under different Islamic and Byzantine rulers. The implications of a shared architectural tradition are interesting, but the question of how to provide a model for the transmission of the inverted-T into Bursa remains. The existing methodology focuses on a geographic transmission system for placing buildings and their plans in the flow of time. Such an approach might focus on the builder's creative process and the specific moment when a plan emerges. This is what George Alexander Kubler calls a "prime object," or in this case, a "prime building." Following Kubler's concept, the inverted-T is an important component showing "an abrupt change" in historical sequences of construction styles, "when an entire language of form suddenly falls into disuse, being replaced by new language of different components and unfamiliar grammar."[63]

In Bursa, the abrupt change is represented by the shift from one ruling group to another: Byzantine to Ottoman, previously Tulunid to Fatimid, and others. And the historical change is enacted through the transmission of the inverted-T from one place to the next, traveling from one center of Islamic rule (or "signal," in Kubler's words) to another. Following this model, there is an accidental or coincidental way that a building's core plan and units occur and reoccur through time. The transmission of an architectural form as a conveyance of information and ideas is thus not linear or based on a chronological sequence but rather based on the communicative relationships through time.

New historical knowledge of the inverted-T's in Bursa affects the analysis of the earlier Ukhaidir *majlis* type, "as if history moved not forward but backward and then forward again." These are "reproduced reproductions"— that is the buildings in the region are reproductions, or *non*originals. My alternative reading of the inverted-T plan suggests a dynamic model of continuous change and adaptation, a model that has proven productive for other scholars, too, as a lens through which to view architectural production.[64]

5

Memory and Monuments

The *Külliyes* of the Sultans

A visitor to Bursa today sees quite a bit of urban sprawl: the present-day city extends beyond the linear axis that existed in Roman, Byzantine, and Ottoman times. Continuing its role as a major commercial town, the city encompasses dwelling areas, private and state-owned factories producing automobiles, wool, and silk, as well as lands reserved for agricultural production and areas promoting winter and summer tourism. But photographs, travelers' depictions, and maps provide evidence that from the nineteenth century until the 1950s, the land around Bursa was vast and relatively unoccupied. It was arranged in several concentric rings.[1] The most important land, used to produce labor-intensive crops such as vegetables and fruits, was closest to the urban center. The outermost ring served as animal pasture for meat and dairy production. Osman gave cheese, dried yogurt, animal fat, and clotted cream as gifts to the Byzantine rulers of Belekoma (modern-day Bilecik, a hundred kilometers west of Bursa)[2] in return for protecting the property left behind every year by Ottoman tribes migrating in summertime to pasture their herds.[3]

The city is set on the foothills of Mount Olympus. To the west and the east, it levels into plain, the preferred building site for the Ottoman sultans. Both old city and new complexes alike backed onto the mountain, facing the fullness of the plain. Indeed, the complexes dominated the plainscape. Topographical reality required promoting urban development on an east-west axis; each sultan exploited topography to leave his sultanic and dynastic legacy on the landscape, while also emphasizing the historical connection between the old city, Orhan's lower city, and the plain. The old city provided vistas of the newly emerging neighborhoods as well as both cultivated and uncultivated plains.

The urban fabric outside the old city (Figure 2) was developed based on the sultans' preferences for their *külliye* sites. The rings of different agrarian and land-use activities helped these rulers carry out their architectural and urban programs. After the conquest, starting with the reign of Orhan, the city began to expand beyond its walls and suburbs. For example, Orhan occupied and revitalized the ring closest to the urban center for his architectural patronage. Murad I moved west of the urban center, where hot springs abounded, famed since the classical period. Bayezid I moved east of the city to make his personal and dynastic imprint on Bursa's landscape. All three inaugural sultans, Orhan, Murad I, and Bayezid I, demonstrated an awareness of using architecture to link the city with their structures and the pastoral lands.

Expanding Control of the Land: A New Architectural and Social Order

With the Ottoman territorial expansion into Bithynia in the early 1300s, a fundamental change took place between the people and their environment. As the capital city at the center of an expanding territory, Bursa had a crucial role to play. The Ottomans' "urban process," as already pointed out, was twofold.[4] In the first stage, as discussed in Chapter 2, construction was applied to sites of former Byzantine splendor, restoring an ancient urban order to transform the existing one. In this chapter, I turn to the ways Ottomans optimized the geographical context of Bursa and its outlying lands to visually substantiate their presence. Thus, previously uncultivated areas came to be settled, a marker of civilization under the Ottomans and the signaling of a new order.

Expansion of the city and control of the land entailed a rapid urban enterprise dictated in large part by landscape elements. As the population increased, neighborhoods in the old city became surrounded by attractive, expanding suburbs with farmlands and gardens on the perimeters. The sheep breeding that occurred around Mount Olympus sustained an industry based on wool, as described by the German traveler Reinhold Lubenau, visiting in 1588.[5] The region produced grains and legumes,[6] and gardens were complemented by olive trees, vineyards, and forest lands.[7] Long thought to be a luxury item in the Ottoman realms, fresh vegetables actually flourished in small urban plots, improved by crop rotation, which helped to feed residents.[8] Pero Tafur, visiting the city in 1437, reported that Bursa functioned as a "half-way port" exporting foodstuffs, silk, and cotton.[9]

The farmlands and gardens attracted the attention of nearly all visitors to the city. Perhaps the most striking account is from Evliya Çelebi in 1640, in which he noted the mulberry trees in the plain north of the city.[10] In 1675, George Wheler, Jacob Spon, and John Covel visited Bursa. As Wheler put it:

> The City hath one of the pleasantest Comings to imaginable; the Country on the side of it, being a large Plain near the city, shaded by Mulberry, Walnut, and Chestnut Trees, planted with Gardens on each side of the high way, which is plain, and with an easie ascent bringeth you to the City.[11]

This language suggests how the plains and mountains alike shaped the lives of Bursa's farmers, merchants, and city dwellers.[12]

The Shrine of Abdal Murad: Claiming and Commemorating the Land

The uninhabited areas around the city were also claimed through the construction of convents and shrines to saintly figures. These figures were originally nomadic raiders who assisted Osman and Orhan in conquering Bursa as well as the cities in Bithynia. Once the conquest took place, these figures gained a new status by having shrines and convents built for them by the Ottoman sultans. Thus, we may note an overlap between sultanic aspirations and the need to commemorate the ethos of the frontier society[13] established in Bursa.

These shrines were located at former sacred locations, such as monasteries, in the foothills of Mount Olympus. As most of the travelers' accounts discuss, and looming large in the modern Turkish imagination, Mount Olympus, which was once the home of many monastic establishments, shifted from a mountain of *keşiş* (Christian monks) to one of *derviş* (Muslim Sufi saints). In the sixteenth century, both monasteries and dervish convents were side by side on the mountains, as Lubenau noted in 1588.[14] He attended a service with Greek monks in a monastic church located on Mount Olympus, although he mentions that the monks did not live in the monastery due to security concerns and, instead, climbed the mountain daily for services. This particular account is testimony of a Greek Orthodox religious practice on the holy mountains of Bursa. Later, in 1853, Ubicini emphasized the shift from it being the mountain of monks to the mountain of dervishes, as is evidenced by the transformation of Christian sacred edifices into dervish convents on Mount Olympus.[15]

One such shrine (Figure 2.8), executed in the 1330s–40s, is the Dervish Convent of Abdal Murad, a Sufi saint originating from Horasan. Abdal Murad was one of the frontier figures who accompanied Orhan in the conquest of Bursa.[16] His shrine was situated on the slope of Mount Olympus above the lime kilns (known as the Alacahırka district), next to a single standing cypress tree, and it bore a spectacular view of Bursa. According to Evliya, it was frequented by Muslims and Christians alike, who donated pots and pans and made their wishes.[17] Today, nothing of the complex survives except for the cenotaph of the saint, which, according to travelers' accounts, originally had a convent and the tomb of Abdal Murad.

The tomb contained a large wooden sword with which Abdal fought the infidels and a mace given to him by Sultan Orhan, who then commissioned the construction of the complex to bless the memory of Abdal. The sword is often mentioned in the accounts of Western travelers and refers to the sword of Roland, an eleventh-century legendary hero mentioned in the French epic *La Chanson de Roland*.[18] Lowry has more recently elaborated on how the sword itself demonstrates the transformation of a Christian relic into an Islamic one.[19] The case of Abdal Murad is an often forgotten yet important facet in showing how Bursa became a physical and symbolic site of contrasting visions and transformations.

The Ottoman Urban Enterprise: Changing Functions, Changing Audiences

In the cases of all the early Ottoman urban interventions, the citadel remained the focal point as the new city expanded beyond its walls. In 1339–40, as introduced in Chapter 3, Orhan ordered the building of a *külliye* on the sloping terrain northeast of the citadel (Figures 2 and 10).[20] Most of the buildings in this complex were lost to a succession of fires and the devastating 1855 earthquake that leveled Bursa. Only the convent-*masjid*, an *imaret*, and a *han* known as the Emir Han survive today.[21] But Orhan's *külliye* remains significant for establishing the concept of site planning and for its role as a residence and a node of urbanization.

The model of Ottoman spatial configuration exemplified in the Bursa *külliyes* has been compared to the Rum Seljuk practice of constructing dervish convents and mausolea in peripheral areas[22] away from the urban core. In an article by Grigor Boykov, he revisits this Rum Seljuk model, arguing that the Ottomans similarly aspired to move away from the old city, while transforming the urban scene through the construction of complexes including inverted-T's.[23] Offering a larger reading on Ottoman cities, but also referring specifically to Bursa, Boykov contends that the aim was to establish new neighborhoods.[24] But the Ottomans' reasons for building on outlying lands differed from those of the Rum Seljuks.

First, the *külliyes* were not always constructed in uninhabited areas. For example, Murad I's complex was hardly in an untouched place—there were still bathing complexes and colonnaded road systems in the area from Roman and Byzantine times. Those built in previously uninhabited spots, such as Orhan's complex, were commissioned not just to civilize an area considered "unsafe" but rather, and mainly, to stimulate commercial and economic activity.

Second, in the *külliyes* sponsored by Orhan, Murad I, and Bayezid I, the architectural-spatial references point more toward the aspirations of classical cities than to the Rum Seljuk model. As discussed earlier, the siting of each complex exploited the landscape in a way that recalls the siting strategies of classical and late antique cities. Being perched on hilltops, both the Murad I and Bayezid I complexes (Figures 2, 4 and 16) offered panoramic views overlooking the city and the plains. In a way, each created a version of Prousa's acropolis with its siting and urban framework. Orhan's complex, just outside the acropolis, functioned as the heart of the lower city. Here, an imperial core was promoted, mimicking that of the Hellenistic cities; it is perhaps even comparable to a Roman imperial forum, serving as the nucleus for commercial, social, and judicial activity.

Third, each of these complexes functioned almost as a city within the larger urban framework of Bursa. This radically differed from the Rum Seljuks model wherein the dervish convents did not constitute discrete "cities." Orhan's complex was the first Ottoman urban intervention beyond the city walls, and the projects in the lower city helped him symbolically frame the old city. During the reign of Bayezid I, as explored earlier, the area inhabited by Orhan's

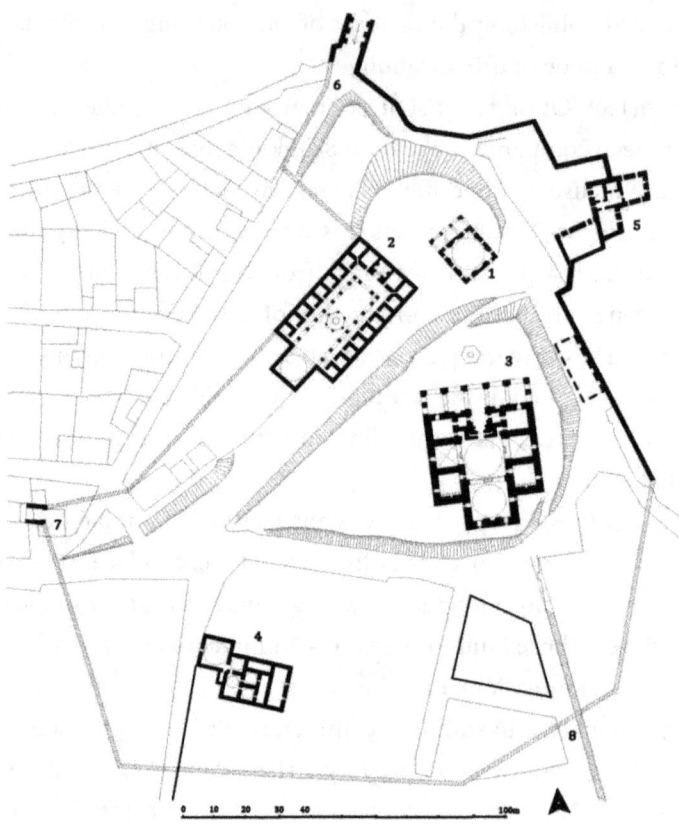

Figure 16 Plan of Bayezid I's *külliye*. (Drawn by Hidayet Softaoğlu based on Arapi, *Archnet*)

külliye became a new center for establishing the *Ulu Cami* (Grand Mosque), or Friday mosque. In other words, while previously a place for locals to live and get their various needs met, it became, under Bayezid I, a site of sovereignty, where the Friday *khutbas* were offered.

The old city, the original central node, was developed mainly by Orhan. It comprised the conversion of a Byzantine complex to function as a Friday mosque and as the eternal resting place for him and his father Osman. It also encompassed the palace and a *madrasa*, a bathhouse, and new mosques, such as the one his brother Alaeddin built in 1331. To this urban construct, the Friday mosque known as *Şehadet* (Martyrdom) was added in 1365–6 by Murad I. In doing this, Murad I asserted his sovereignty over the upper city, but he also prevented his *külliye* from turning into a new city proper, maintaining its character as an emerging neighborhood intended to make use of the abundant water resources. Murad I's urban strategy substantiated the importance of the upper city as a focal and sacred point.

Overall, the focal point of these sultanic complexes was their inverted-T type convent-*masjid*s, surrounded by subsidiary structures into which the posthumously built mausolea of the Ottoman sultans were incorporated.[25] An important detail to highlight is the funerary function acquired by Ottoman *külliye*s beginning from the time of Murad I onward.[26] Orhan had two urban nodes, the aforementioned one in the old city and a second in the lower city, the site of his *külliye* and convent-*masjid*. According to Gülru Necipoğlu, these socioreligious complexes, with convent-*masjid*s accompanied by subsidiary buildings, were humbler or smaller versions of the Mongol-Ilkhanid complexes in Tabriz and Sultaniya.[27]

Besides these efforts toward urbanization, each sultan, in different parts of the city, engaged in another important Ottoman undertaking known as colonization.[28] Discussed by Ömer Lütfi Barkan in 1942, the theory of colonization encompasses how the Ottomans deliberately intervened in the spatial and urban fabric of Byzantine cities and the role of dervishes in this transformation. Barkan's theory has been revisited by a series of scholars, but suffice to say that Ottoman colonization transcended the work of dervishes alone. A more intricate reading is necessary to appreciate the emergence of different audiences and alliances in the Ottoman urban context, including examining references to the traveling dervishes or sheikhs, scholars known as *baba*s, converts, *akıncı*s (warlords), and *ahi*s (fraternities).

In the thirteenth century, Aflaki, a learned man whose travels led him to Anatolia, said:

> A madrasa is appropriate for imams, a khanaqah for shaykhs, a palace for commanders, a caravanserai for merchants, lodges for the rogues, and the mastaba for foreigners.[29]

The many subcultures and their places of congregation were clearly designated in this urban context. One such example outside Bursa surfaces in the 1324 endowment deed of a hospice or *tekke*, established by Orhan in Mekece (east of İznik) and entrusted to his freed eunuch slave, Şerefeddin Mükbil. The deed stipulates that upon the former slave's death, he would be succeeded by the children of the slaves attached to the building.[30] The identity of the entrustee as a former eunuch is fascinating, and it suggests the Ottoman rulers may have employed eunuchs to be in charge of public buildings, drawing on Rum Seljuk and Byzantine precedents. The building was later equipped to feed the local Christian population. Covel, visiting in 1675, wrote that "every Friday is made ready a good store of churba (or porridge) and pelaw and the like for all sorts of poor that will come thither."[31] A further reference showing congregation patterns comes from the Bavarian captive turned Janissary soldier Johannes Schilberger, who reported the types of religious buildings in Bursa as the *masjid*s, *imaret*s, and *madrasa*s. Regarding the *imaret*s, he notes eight in all, saying they are open to everyone irrespective of faith, "whether they be Christian, idolaters (Muslims), or Jews."[32]

As discussed in Chapter 4, the vocabulary utilized for the buildings in the Ottoman urban enterprise is contested, with descriptive monikers such as *tekke*, *zaviye*, or *imaret* employed interchangeably. Each of these building types hosted an array of guests, with people of different ethnic and religious backgrounds often intermixing. Moreover, the Ottoman urban enterprise relied not just on the imperial complexes built by the rulers but also on various alliances among different groups, their contexts,[33] and the corresponding ways structures were claimed.

Orhan's Complex: *Zaviye* (Convent) and *İmara* (Imaret)

The 1862 Cadastral Map (Figures 2 and 3) displays Orhan's *külliye* as an ideal starting point leading to the old city, which included a route passing through the tombs of the founders, Orhan's Friday mosque, Murad I's Friday mosque, as well as the *Bey Saray*, and ending at Murad II's dynastic mausolea complex below. In examining such a route, both overlapping and diverging layers of architectural expression are evident, an interplay with both ideological and visual implications.[34]

The location of his *külliye* (Figure 10) reflects Orhan's attempt to reorient the urban center to the lower city. The role of Orhan's *külliye* in the constantly evolving urban landscape of Bursa is elucidated by the foundation charter and the epigraphic evidence. Each labels the complex's major function differently, emphasizing the multifaceted needs of the community around it. The endowment deed, for example, dated to 1359–60, describes the building as a *zaviye*, or a convent, and it also mentions a religious school, a guesthouse, a soup kitchen, and several inns, or *hans*.[35] The inscription now adorning the main entrance identifies the structure as an *imara* (*imaret*) and refers to the building's commissioning by Orhan in 1339–40, its burning by the Karamanids in the year the inscription was put up, and its restoration by Mehmed I in 1417.[36]

The choice of terminology—*zaviye* in the endowment deed, *imaret* in the inscription—indicates how the building fulfilled different functions simultaneously and accommodated different constituents. As Oya Pancaroğlu has discussed, *imaret*, especially, does not stand for an individual building type but, rather, for a complex complemented by a series of buildings bearing different functions. The deed indicates that the people allowed to stay there included itinerant sheikhs, descendants of the Prophet, the poor, as well as scholars, and they could stay for a maximum of three days, with extensions given with the trustee's consent.[37] Not only did this complex provide food and a place to stay and worship, but the addition of the *han* and the rise of the *ahi* class also helped situate it as a center of commercial life.[38] Thus the functions were not only religious but also civic and, along with promoting commercial life, these formed the raison d'être of this complex.

The *han* that was included in the foundation charter of Orhan's *külliye* was the Emir (lit. the ruler) Han. Located to the north of the *Ulu Cami*, it is identified as the Sultan Han in the accounts of Neşri, replacing what was once the horse market in the area. Later, when it was replaced by a new *han* structure built by Bayezid I, it is referred to as the Old *Bezasistan* (lit. a covered market).[39] Just like the rest of the buildings in the complex, the *han* suffered fires and sieges and was heavily restored in later centuries. The building today follows a typical *han* plan, having a square framework and a large open courtyard in the middle. It has alternating brick-and-stone masonry and has thirty-six rooms on the ground floor and thirty-seven on the second floor. Each room is identified by an arch in the modular system of the building; the ones on the south and east are round, while the ones on the north and west are pointed. The rooms on the ground floor open up to the courtyard and do not have windows on the rear wall, while the ones on the upper floor have windows and fireplaces. As is the usual practice, the rooms on the ground floor were likely used for storage and animals, while those on the upper floor were reserved for travelers and commerce people.

The other buildings mentioned in the *waqf* registers are the bathhouse, the *madrasa*, and the school buildings, of which we have either very few or no physical remains. The bathhouse is located in front of the convent-*masjid* and next to the school and has been heavily restored.⁴⁰ The female section of the bathhouse was restored by Sedat Çetintaş,⁴¹ and the male section was adjoined to a *han* in 1957. Unfortunately, the school and the *madrasa* buildings did not fare as well, with the former totally gone and the latter replaced by an early twentieth-century administrative building.⁴² Although not supported by physical remains, Ayverdi, using archival materials, argues that this was an area known as the *aşağı hisar* (lit. lower walled city). Thus Orhan's complex in the lower city was walled, stretching from outside the *Yer kapı* (the ground gate) on the west, extending to *Demirkapı* to the north, and circling the area of Orhan's *külliye* to the south.⁴³ If this was the case, it shows how in the reign of Orhan there was a need to use the walls to demarcate the area between the habited and uninhabited.

Murad I's Complex: *İmaret-i Kapluca* (The Bathhouse Imaret)

Murad I continued the pattern of forming a new neighborhood by commissioning a *külliye* initiated by his father, founding his *külliye* (Figures 2 and 4) some kilometers west of Bursa, on a terrace just north of the village of Çekirge. As discussed, this part of the town housed many spas, the water sourced from the same thermal springs as those used for the Roman- and Byzantine-period bathing complexes. Murad I's complex included a two-story mosque and *madrasa* complex as well as an *imaret*, a bathhouse, latrines, and what would later be his own tomb.⁴⁴ Zeynep Oğuz Kursar, in a recent piece, discusses the architectural references at Murad I's tomb and how Murad I evolved from being just a sultan into becoming a saintly figure. Following his murder in Kosovo in 1389, Murad I became a martyr and was labeled a holy warrior and saintly figure. He became known for his miracles, and the hot waters in his bath complex were praised for their generative and therapeutic qualities.⁴⁵

The endowment deed for Murad I's complex refers to it as an *İmaret-i Kapluca*. It identifies the main building as a *zaviye* (convent) and lists subsidiary structures such as kitchens, bathhouses, a school, and other buildings. It describes how the complex was meant to accommodate religious men of different ranks as well as the needy. The deed does not list a *müezzin* but speaks of an *imam*, as well as the members of *ulema, sheikhs, seyyids,*

Quran reciters, complemented by the *fukara* and *mesakin*. It has been argued that the terms used for the latter two may stand not just for the needy but also for the itinerant Sufi dervishes.⁴⁶ The endowment deed also reveals how the building's function transformed over the years: a postscript added to the deed in 1400 noted that a new didactic mission was added to help generate income for the complex.⁴⁷ This is further evidence of how these buildings changed functions over time amid a shifting urban and social framework.

On the west side of the complex there was a school and kitchen; the tomb of Murad I was located to the northwest of the complex. All three of these buildings were heavily restored after the 1855 earthquake. In Chapter 2, I discussed the evidence for the evolution of the Old Bath and the Kükürtlü as nonconfessional loci in the Ottomanization process. In fact, these two complexes were part of Murad I's *külliye*, although both were not situated within the immediate grounds of the complex.⁴⁸ Another bathhouse, designed on a much smaller scale was constructed as part of the *külliye* and located to the east of the convent-*masjid*. This small bathhouse was designed for the pupils attending the *madrasa*. It had a squarish main bathing room (approximately 6.3 x 6.5 meters), two smaller individual bathing units, and five toilets. This design scheme is comparable to the Mamluk examples, such as the latrines at the Suq al-Manadil in Aleppo, 1356–7, with private and small baths adjoining mosque complexes.⁴⁹

Murad I's *külliye* dramatically expanded the city limits by linking Çekirge in the western suburbs to central Bursa.⁵⁰ Signaling Murad I's authority, the architectural units in this complex allowed him to display ownership over a piece of valuable land and its resources. The complex is a visual testimony to Murad I as a royal personality, known also as an *ahi*, a saint, and Hüdavendigar.⁵¹ As Yılmaz discusses, the title of Hüdavendigar (lit. the master teacher, devotee of God) is evocative of Rumi, a thirteenth-century Sufi mystic based in Konya who was known as Hüdavendigar by his followers. Murad I was the first Ottoman sultan to use this title, which presented Ottoman sultans as the leaders of the frontier and countered and accommodated competing claims by Sufi figures.⁵² Murad I's conquests in the Balkans led him to be perceived as a *Gazi* and a saint, and his multifaceted identities, in turn, enabled him to commission a complex that, in a way, brought back to life the classical-era efforts of Dio and Pliny the Younger in the first and second centuries AD to beautify this suburb renowned for its flowing waters. Murad I's complex elevated the status of the bathing complexes while also fulfilling the functions of a sultanic complex, providing a venue for education and ritual practices.

Bayezid I's Complex: *Zaviyetü'ş-şerife ve'l-'İmaretü'l latife* (The Noble Lodge and Pleasant İmaret)

Following Murad I was his son and successor, Bayezid I. He, too, followed the two-tiered strategy for expanding and controlling the land that I addressed earlier. As I described in Chapter 3, he built a congregational mosque, the *Ulu Cami*, next to Orhan's *külliye* complex in the lower city in the 1390s. Constructed as a free-standing building, it was meant to house a growing congregation. To strengthen commercial activity in this part of the city, he also commissioned the construction of the Old *Bezasistan* or the *Bedesten* (marketplace). He built his *külliye* (Figures 2 and 16) some kilometers to the east of the old city between 1390 and 1395. It was destroyed by the 1855 earthquake and remodeled in the 1870s, undergoing further restorations in the 1950s. The complex, just like that of his father's in Çekirge, made an impressive use of the topography, taking advantage of the uneven ground. The convent-*masjid* is located in the center of the *külliye* with enjoyable vistas of the city in many directions. This complex included structures far surpassing those of his predecessors in architectural scope due to the use of ashlar masonry in the inverted-T convent-*masjid*.

Referred to in the endowment deed as the "Noble Lodge and Pleasant İmaret,"[53] Bayezid's *külliye* consisted of a mosque, a *madrasa*, a garden palace, a hospital, a *han*, a bathhouse, stables, a fountain supplied by an aqueduct, kitchens, service rooms, and the sultan's eventual tomb. The deed also lists the various occupants and associated figures—bakers, janitors, builders, cooks, *müezzin*s, teaching assistants, and students—acknowledging and remembering these actors in early Ottoman society. It notes that special prayers were to be recited for stately figures as well as the *ahis*. Thus, the presence of *ahis* is remembered within another imperial-architectural context; after all, Bayezid I's father, Murad I, viewed himself as an *ahi*. The complex does not have an obvious, overarching site plan, and individual building units are scattered with no optical or geometric pattern. It is encircled by a wall with monumental gateways marking the entrance.

The building's endowment deed[54] makes clear who would—or, rather, who would not—be lodged in this complex: "'infidels' or 'those subscribing to one of the six sins,' a stipulation reflecting this particular convent-*masjid*'s function as the center of a new Muslim quarter on the outskirts of Bursa."[55] The structure, fronted by a portico, encompasses a hospital, a hospice, a *madrasa*, and lodging quarters built of alternating brick-and-stone. This complex also had Bayezid I's mausoleum, built by one of his sons, Süleyman.[56]

With this *külliye*, Bayezid I extended his architectural tradition into the lands outlying the capital. The *külliyes* of Murad I and Bayezid I, situated at the western and eastern ends of the city, respectively, were material pronouncements of the imperial desire to expand and control the land while acknowledging the upper city and the first *külliye* established by Orhan. The *külliyes*, as we have seen, became landmarks in the evolving cityscape, representing a chain of complexes from one sultan to the next and implying a dynastic succession. As opposed to the Byzantine practice of building the aristocratic or monastic *oikos*, as described by Paul Magdalino,[57] these establishments cannot be seen as the formalization of an existing pattern of neighborhood development. Bayezid I, for example, chose the Küşteri or Şüşteri *bağçe* (garden) listed in Orhan's *waqfiyya* as the site of his *külliye*. As compensation, he bequeathed a larger agricultural land to Orhan's *waqf*. With their charitable and educational aims, the *külliyes* had largely public functions, including a "commemorative" celebration of the patron sultan's reign.[58] The *külliyes*, then, marked a significant change in urban planning, a new "urban order." Furthermore, they heralded the formation of neighborhood centers and amenities laid out at the same time.

The *külliyes* exemplified a kind of urban "choreography" wherein builders created irregularly designed complexes for the sultans not because they lacked training in geometric order but, rather, because they sought to favor certain perspectives by manipulating the spectator's visual field[59] or to avoid sacrificing "overall visibility."[60] In other words, the builders wanted to ensure visitors to the city would not miss these prominently placed landmarks. Organic urban patterns in the formation of cities in the medieval and early modern period, and their lack of geometric order, have been discussed by both Spiro Kostof and Marvin Trachtenberg.[61] The former studied a wide range of cities and periods, from medieval Siena to the birth of New Delhi, and the latter focused on fourteenth-century Florence. Each scholar has discussed how the cities assumed their eventual spatial forms. Refuting earlier claims that pre-Renaissance city planners lacked an understanding of geometric order and focused, instead, on random planning, they contend that city builders sought to create an urban and spatial layout that emerged organically but also as the result of deliberate planning.[62]

In Bursa, these *külliyes* emphasized the connection between the city and its suburbs by monumentally acknowledging the landscape. As Diane Favro has argued in the case of the Roman *fora*, the organic construction of the *külliyes* and their prominence in the landscape suggest that the builders were "familiar with optical theory."[63] The *külliyes* established the Ottoman presence but also promoted new and different neighborhoods and attributes of commercial life. Thus, visibility and monumentalization[64] were key to the urban morphogenesis in Bursa.[65]

Forming the "Ancestral" Capital: The *Külliyes* of Mehmed I and Murad II

Notably, two more *külliye* complexes were built in the aftermath of the Timurid sack, when the city was revived under Mehmed I (r. 1413–21) and Murad II (r. 1421–44; 1446–51). Each of these complexes conveyed a series of ideological and cultural implications. Mehmed I built his *külliye* (also known as the *Yeşil* Complex) in 1419–24 to commemorate his success in putting sibling rivalry to an end and claiming the throne. Located on a hilltop between the old city and Bayezid I's complex, this complex created a new neighborhood between two urban zones.

On the one hand, Mehmed I's *Yeşil* Complex (Figure 2.6) preserved and revived the pre-interregnum architectural idiom that had already been established in Bursa by the former sultans. Just like the previous *külliye*s, it included a convent-*masjid*, a *madrasa*, a bathhouse, and the eventual tomb of the sultan, which emphasizes a sense of continuity.[66] But this is not a simple continuity—it also took Ottoman architectural production to a new level. Just like Bayezid I's convent-*masjid*, Mehmed I's convent-*masjid* was built in ashlar masonry, while his tomb was built of ashlar and revetted with turquoise tiles. The subsidiary buildings, however, were built in alternating brick-and-stone masonry. Mehmed I's dialogue with the pre-interregnum Ottoman past was multi-layered: he completed the Old Mosque in Edirne (1414) commissioned by his brothers in Edirne. He was also keen to claim his legitimacy by rebuilding a mosque in Söğüt (1414–20) which was reportedly rose upon the foundations dating to the reign of Orhan.[67]

As discussed, the change in "identity" reflects growing "sultanic" ambitions under Bayezid I, who adopted ashlar stone masonry. This technique was a sign of high-status construction in Rum Seljuk architecture, contemporaneous princedoms in Anatolia, and the Mamluk construction in Syria, Palestine, and Egypt.⁶⁸ Thus Mehmed I's *külliye* sits at the intersection of the old and the new. In the aftermath of the interregnum, the previous *külliyes* seemed old-fashioned. For the Yeşil Complex, innovative construction and decorative materials were celebrated; for example, the use of exquisite ashlar masonry combined with the turquoise tiles for which the complex was named, ensuring the new *külliye* would rival the architectural culture of neighboring areas.

Completed in 1430, the complex (Figure 2.2) built by Murad II, known as the Muradiye,⁶⁹ emphasized a continued connection to previous *külliye* construction. It included a convent-*masjid*, a *madrasa*, an imaret, a school, a bathhouse, and twelve mausolea belonging to members of the Ottoman family. Situated on a low plain like Orhan's *külliye*, this complex used alternating brick-and-stone masonry on the façade of every building. However, the inside displays examples of tiles. In other words, the buildings of the complex intentionally remained archaic on the outside, recalling the buildings constructed in the reigns of Orhan and Murad I, but on the inside the contemporary decorative details brought the complex up to date again.

One further archaic detail of Murad II's complex is the inverted-T plan noted in the convent-*masjid*. Along with the one he built in 1435 in Edirne, this is the last example of a sultan-commissioned inverted-T. From this point on, the type was built only by non-royals. I argue that the hybrid appearance of the building can be linked to the dual function of the complex: on the one hand it commemorated the reign of Murad II, and on the other it aimed to create a dynastic loci in Bursa, as evidenced by the abundance of mausolea in the complex. With the addition of these mausolea at the Muradiye, Bursa became, in the words of Dimitri Kastritsis, the "ancestral" capital.⁷⁰

There is also another layer to note here. In a forthcoming book chapter, Aslı Akışık succinctly reexamines Ἀπόδειξις Ἱστοριῶν, a universal history text written by Laonikos Chalkokondyles sometime after 1464. This text situates Orhan as the first Ottoman sultan to practice fratricide, killing two of his older brothers upon his father's death, and discusses his claim to the throne. Contemporaries of Chalkokondyles offered the reign of Bayezid I as the *terminus post quem* for Ottoman fratricide.⁷¹ Chalkokondyles contradicts this and attributes the start of the practice to Orhan in Bursa. He discusses cases of familial murder for each sultan until the time of Mehmed II, when fratricide was made official by an imperial decree. Going against the Ottoman chronicles depicting the period pre-Bayezid I as peaceful between the sultan and his brothers, this account—bearing in mind the question of its credibility—aims to find legitimate grounds for the origin of fratricide as well as creating room for the authorization of this practice,[72] which was first put into practice in Bursa. The complex of Murad II offers a snapshot of the Ottoman imperial family, housing the tombs of princes who died untimely deaths, or in exile, or were killed by their reigning brothers or fathers, as well as those of princesses, the sultans' wives and favorite consorts, and midwives.[73] The location of the complex, immediately to the west of the old city, situates it between the tombs of Osman and Orhan in the old city and the *külliye* of Murad I in the western suburbs. These burial sites also included the tombs of their immediate family members, such as their sons, grandsons, wives, and mothers. This helps us to understand how the notion of dynastic mausolea was transformed from being a familial to an "ancestral" one.

Support for viewing Bursa as the "ancestral" capital city can be found in the endowment deeds of both Bayezid I and Mehmed I. Bursa was mentioned as the main Ottoman capital, referred to as *dar al-mulk*, "abode of sovereignty."[74] Although Adrianople/Edirne was conquered in 1361, its transformation into the second capital of the Ottomans was gradual. From 1402 to 1422, both Bursa and Edirne functioned as capital cities, largely because the Ottoman sultans were campaigning and needed to hold administrative offices in both locations.[75] Throughout this period, Bursa remained the center, while Edirne became a frontier town from where the campaigns into the Balkans were controlled, including the conquests of towns along the line from Constantinople to Adrianople as well as towns located to the west of the latter, such as Pythion/Kuleliburgaz, Didymoteichon/Dimetoka, and Komotini/Gümülcine. For this reason, it was often called the *dar al-ghuzat*, "abode of the gazi raiders."[76]

Thus, Bursa can be seen as the "ancestral" capital and Edirne as the frontier capital or the center of diplomatic affairs. The ruler of the Germiyanid principality in western Anatolia visited Murad II in Edirne in 1420. On his way to his hometown of Kütahya, he wanted to make a pilgrimage to the mausolea of the Ottoman sultans in Bursa. For Amy Singer, visiting Murad II in Edirne cements it as the imperial capital and visiting the mausolea shows how Bursa was regarded as the imperial dynastic city.[77] Edirne never fulfilled the function of having any sultanic funerary grounds; despite having sultanic mosques built in the fifteenth and sixteenth centuries, none of the complexes contained tombs.[78] The sultanic mausolea seen in Bursa's *külliyes*, which are centered on the convent-*masjids* and surrounded by subsidiary structures scattered throughout luscious landscapes and gardens, are simply absent in Edirne. The gardens in the *külliyes*, in addition to their role in demonstrating godly bounty and abundance, also became eternal settings where the members of the imperial family were laid to rest, as well illustrated in the case of the Muradiye.[79] They were not revived again until the construction of sultanic complexes in the classical Ottoman buildings of Istanbul, which feature a Friday mosque fronted by a portico with tombs situated in a garden at the back.

As the discussion makes clear, it is difficult to conclude that the Ottomans moved the imperial power from one city to another following the succession of Bursa, Edirne, and Istanbul. Rather than seeing clean breaks and attributing numbers to the capitals of the Ottomans, we need to appreciate how each fulfilled the different functions we often attribute to imperial or capital cities. Through this lens, Bursa remained the eternal capital, where the dynastic power and ideology were formed and put into display with the help of the built environment.

Controlling the Land: Commercial Networks and *Hans*

The capital city's rapid expansion outward took place over nearly two centuries. It was dictated not only by the establishment of the *külliyes* but also by the structuring of an economic system. Hence, the political impact of the Ottomans generated a substantial economic base which grew along the routes linking the Marmara basin to the other regional economies, inland Bithynia being the most prominent. In Ottoman chronicles, references appear concerning exchanges between the Ottomans and their Christian neighbors. For example, according to Aşıkpaşazade, the Ottomans presented carpets, cheese, and clotted cream as gifts to the local Byzantine rulers.[80] Mustafa Akdağ proposed a fascinating theory to discuss the emergence of a "Marmara-basin economy" that has its roots in the times of Ertuğrul and Osman.[81] Akdağ strongly emphasized commerce, symbiosis, and fruitful relations between the Ottomans and Byzantines across Bithynia. Laiou corroborates this argument, suggesting that a peaceful time allowed for the relative prosperity of Turkish-occupied Anatolia.[82]

If the *külliyes* are the ultimate symbols of Bursa's Ottomanization, an even deeper sense of this role emerges from seeing how they shaped commercial activities, namely transportation and the sale and exchange of goods. Here, a focus on their formal characteristics becomes secondary. In commerce, the *hans* (Figure 10) were instrumental. They provided accommodation for the traveling merchants on whose transcontinental activities much of the state economy depended.[83] The *hans* as commercial institutions in Bursa are inextricably linked to geographical position;[84] the city was a major trade node, a role carved out via strategic rerouting through the plains and mountains as well as by its proximity to the sea. Municipal leaders protected this role by expanding the city outward. One such example demonstrating the sultanic complexes functioning as the shaper of trade activities is the 1455 land register (known as the *mufassal defter*), listing fifty villages as tax payers to the Murad I's *külliye*. Each village's agricultural and pastoral capacity is noted and terms of taxation for businesses and produces were compiled and commercial activities were carried out at the Oil-Scale/Measurement (aka Kapan Han) located in the lower city.[85] Unlike their Rum Seljuk counterparts, many of these later buildings were in urban locations.[86] Trade partners, beginning in the 1300s, consisted prominently of Westerners such as the Venetians and Genoese;[87] for the latter, Orhan granted special trade privileges within Ottoman lands. Orhan granted special trade privileges within Ottoman lands. This made the Ottomans an integral element of the Mediterranean economy.[88] In the words of Kate Fleet, the Ottomans "apparently in contrast to the emirs of Menteshe and Aydin, controlled and manipulated the markets, actively seeking to use their economic muscle to improve their relations with western states."[89] In the 1300s and into the next century, the construction of *hans*—begun in the 1200s under the Rum Seljuks[90]—proliferated, with these structures assuming more varied forms and functions. This created a more dynamic economic framework than the other Anatolian principalities, allowing the Ottomans to become a major trade power in Anatolia.

In Bursa, *hans* served functions beyond accommodation for merchants, pilgrims, and other travelers, acting also as depots, warehouses, and markets, and selling items such as produce. The *hans* were not merely meant to provide hospitality, but also separated travelers from existing city inhabitants, largely for the visitors' benefit. In Bursa, the construction, expansion, and placement of the *han* compound (*han*, chapel, bath, and perhaps oven) helped constitute a

Figure 17 Irgandı Bridge, the current state of the bridge after the restorations. (Photo: Suna Çağaptay)

lively commercial scene among merchants and the local population. *Hans* often catered to guests from a common ethnicity or speaking a common language, such as Genoese or Venetian merchants.[91] Thus, the presence of a home within a foreign land where visitors might speak their native language, practice their religion, and indulge their cultural practices offered an infrastructure stable enough to sustain trade.

Benedetto Dei, a traveler and merchant from Florence visiting in 1470, described the city as a hub of Florentine moneylenders, merchants, stores, consulate buildings, and churches.[92] Indeed, fifteenth-century published court records indicate a well-established system of trade carried out by Genoese, Venetian, and Florentine merchants.[93] They were subject simultaneously to their own autonomous rules and to the authority of the Ottoman state.[94] Evliya Çelebi's notes on Bursa's Irgandı Bridge (Figures 17 and 2.9), at Gökdere in the valley of Olympus, elaborate on how non-Muslim merchants functioned in the city:

> At both ends of the bridge are metal doors like castle gates with openings on top of them. If the gates were to close, it would be impossible to enter from any other place. One end of the bridge is empty. It is a guest-house like a *han*, and one's horses can be tied up there.[95]

He adds that the covered bridge is lined with shops and populated especially by weavers, a reference to the flourishing silk trade conducted there. Evliya generally labels Bursa the "emporium of silk," discussing how the city's wealth derives from the "manufacture of velvets, and the cultivation of silk."[96]

One can conclude from Evliya's account, and those of several other travelers,[97] that the bridge itself was used for lodging by non-Muslim tradesmen, especially of Genoese and Venetian descent, while also serving as a weaving workshop. Functionally linking the two sides of the Gökdere River, the bridge thus became a commercial and residential center. Structurally, the bridge was made of stone, its upper level constructed with vaulted arches and covered with lead; the rooms reserved for workshops and accommodations protruded outward from the façade. In nineteenth-century photos and prints, such as those by Texier, one can discern a band of corbel frieze on the façade identical to that on the convent-*masjid* of Murad I, and resembling that on the mausoleum of Lala Şahin at Kirmastı/Mustafakemalpaşa.[98] The bridge, restored in the early 2000s,[99] was likely built sometime toward the end of the fourteenth or beginning of the fifteenth century. Its overall visual effect echoes the Ponte Vecchio in Florence, as indicated by the nineteenth-century photos published by Engin Özendes.[100]

The Ottoman *hans* and caravanserais, as indicated earlier, emerged as a type independent from their Rum Seljuk predecessors, and they became widespread. Whereas the Rum Seljuk-period *hans* were usually in rural and suburban areas, especially on roads between cities, during the Ottoman period they were slowly overtaken by urban *hans* linked to the immediate hinterland. One example of this network linking urban and semi-urban areas in Bursa was the emergence of a series of seven village towns ending with the suffix "Kızık" (lit. the tribal name given to a nomadic tribe located in that area). These Turcoman villages located 10–15 kilometers west of Bursa were situated along the trade route provisioning Bursa and were home to *ahis* who were actively participating in craft production and securing the route of the caravans.[101]

Following the caravan routes, the items to be traded arrived in one of the specialized *hans* located in the center of Bursa. The generic layout for the urban *hans* consisted of two stories, featuring a series of rooms neatly organized around a central courtyard, surrounded by porticoes, with open arcades serving as corridors leading to the individual rooms. Many *hans* that survive in good condition today date from the fourteenth and fifteenth centuries,

Figure 18 General view into the Cocoon Han. (Photo: Suna Çağaptay)

reaffirming the city's role as an important commercial center of the time. Some *hans* built in Bursa's commercial center (Figure 10) were given names to match the commodity traded therein, such as the Salt (*Tuzpazarı*) *Han*, Silk (*İpek*) *Han*, Cocoon (*Koza*) *Han*, Rice (*Pirinç*) *Han*, and Copper (*Bakırcılar*) *Han*. These *hans* all bear alternating brick-and-stone construction with arcaded porticoes of varying forms of construction—either brick and stone or solely brick—and are surrounded by a colonnade with round and pointed arches. Each of the specific *hans* just mentioned is similar in plan, except that the Cocoon *Han* has a small, elevated octagonal *masjid* (Figure 18) at the center of its courtyard, in the manner of the Sultan *Han* near Kayseri, which was built by the Rum Seljuk Sultan Alaeddin Keykubat I *c.* 1232–36.[102]

The market buildings and *hans* of Bursa were significant not only for the trade in silk, fabrics, salt, dyes, and other wholesale items but also for their endowments of mosques and other social services. In Bursa, these *hans* functioned similarly to *funduqs* in the larger eastern Mediterranean context (where travelers lived, stored and traded their goods, and often were taxed)[103] and *wakalas* (buildings designed for lodging that arose as alternatives to *funduqs*).[104] Like *funduqs* and *wakalas*, *hans* could be owned by individuals or the state, or tied up in *waqf* endowments. For example, some *hans*, such as the Oil-Scale/Measurement (aka *Kapan*) *Han*, were built to defray the costs of

Murad I's convent-*masjid/madrasa* complex in Çekirge. The Rice *Han*, built in 1507, was constructed by Bayezid II to generate money for his *külliye* project in Istanbul. The Cocoon *Han* and the Silk *Han* were built to finance the *külliye* of Mehmed I in Bursa.[105]

The formation of new architectural complexes, commercial areas, and neighborhoods indicated the value ascribed to populating the land.[106] Both imperial and civic structures became vehicles for Ottoman expansion. Beyond the imperially promoted areas, uninhabited and uncultivated terrain was also sought. These lands were regarded as possessing social and cultural cachet beyond economics; this paradigm eventually linked what was cultivated and currently valuable with what was uncultivated and imbued with potential.

In the fourteenth century, when most of the population was mixed, the residents continued to need basic services, such as *hans*, roads and bridges, and bathhouses. There was no particular reason to replace or even convert such structures. One can then surmise that whereas new political rulers asserted their power through studied transformation of religious structures, the changes needed for the utilitarian buildings were far less momentous. Secular, sacred, commercial, and utilitarian buildings were the important vehicles used by the Ottomans to negotiate the rise of an imperial city against the background of expressing an ideology and the values of a frontier society.

6

Concluding Remarks on "Invisible Prousa/Bursa"

> A description of Zaira as it is today should contain all Zaira's past. The city, however, does not tell its past, but contains it like the lines of a hand....
>
> Italo Calvino, *Invisible Cities*, "Cities & Memory," 3

Bursa has inspired numerous works of history, literature, music, and theory. For the twentieth-century scholar Albert Gabriel, Bursa's early Ottoman architecture represented the "multiple attestations of the Seljuk persistence... where Ottoman art was born and evolved and reigned... and expanded."[1] For the art historian Howard Crane, the sultanic mosques of Bursa were "icons of imperial legitimacy,"[2] and for Saygın Salgırlı, an architectural historian, Bursa was "as a town networked to the larger Mediterranean world."[3]

The city endured fires, earthquakes, and military sacks, all of which left immeasurable damage on its urban fabric and material culture. Moving beyond the scholarly writings that label Bursa's architecture as iconic or as the progenitor of Ottoman art, I would now like to look at how the city and its fourteenth-century actors were perceived and imagined in the context of catastrophic events. To begin, the first act of Handel's *Tamerlano* (Timur), which debuted onstage in 1724, takes place in an enclosed garden and palace rooms in Bursa. The play narrates Bayezid I's captivity and suffering, as well as a passionate love triangle involving Timur, emperor of the Timurids; Bayezid I's daughter, Asteria; and Andronikos, a Greek prince from Trebizond.[4] This differs strikingly from a visual depiction drawn (Figure 19) by the Polish painter Stanislaw Chelebowski in 1878, now on display at the Lviv National Art Gallery in Ukraine,[5] which portrays an imprisoned and enfeebled Bayezid I

Figure 19 Stanislaw Chelebowski's 1878 depiction of the 1402 event when Bayezid I was taken captive by Timur. (Lviv National Art Gallery in Ukraine) (Photo: Suna Çağaptay)

lying supine in a timber alcove, visited by Timur. Notably, the structural details are anachronistic, displaying *cuerda seca* blue-green tiles and inscribed panels and wooden furniture, recalling the Green Mosque in Bursa built by Mehmed I (r. 1413–21). This mosque was built almost two decades after the battle scene, during the interregnum period under Sultan Mehmed I.

The Timurid sack in 1402, which marks the end point of this book's chronology, is undoubtedly an important moment in Bursa's history and image of rulership. It certainly was in the minds of renowned observers from the baroque and Orientalist periods, such as Handel and Chelebowski. Another significant date was 1396, when Bayezid I defeated the Crusade armies at the Battle of Nikopolis and took the son of the Duke of Burgundy as a prisoner of war. According to a French chronicle written in 1405, Bayezid I gave a speech in which he said he wished to reign like Alexander the Great of Macedonia. As ransom for the return of the duke's son, he asked for luxurious textiles as well as metal goods. Among the items presented to Bayezid I was a tapestry bearing lifelike figural representations, which was later seized as booty and transferred to Samarkand when Timur sacked Bursa.[6] Notably, the Timurid sack divided an Ottoman realm that had been consolidated culturally and politically over the course of a century.

A twentieth-century observer, the writer Ahmed Hamdi Tanpınar, describes Bursa almost inimitably as a city "with the untouched dreams of the past that it has preserved up till [sic] now."[7] In 1946, Tanpınar's *Beş Şehir* (Five Cities) was published, which claimed that Bursa "preserved the spirit of its formative age and breathes its poetry."[8] The section on Bursa is complemented by travelogues on Ankara, Erzurum, Konya, and Istanbul. Within the descriptions of these five cities, Tanpınar narrates social and political transformations and confronts the Western-minded Turks, urging them to reconcile with the Ottoman, Islamic, and Anatolian past. Although the prose very much reflects the post–Second World War scene when it was written, Tanpınar's book, especially the section on Bursa, intricately explores the urban fabric, the prose inflected with details on architecture including descriptions of fountains, or *sebils*, and references to neighborhoods and the sound of flowing water.

From Past to Present

Natural events and human interventions alike complicate the task of piecing together Bursa's past. For historians, producing an image of the city, especially in its earlier periods, requires both addition and subtraction. Unexpected elements can appear in unexpected places. For example, a late antique villa might turn up in a basement, the floors decorated with the image of Helios.[9] In the Bursa Archaeological Museum, statues of noted figures from Roman Prousa leave further mysteries to unravel. Perhaps one of these statues represents Dio Chyrsostom, a leading figure in the city's second-century civic life—or, alternatively, one of his nemeses. On such matters, further clues may emerge from archaeological excavations, for example, the 2014 salvage excavations conducted on the terrace at the northern tip of the old city, close to the tombs of Osman and Orhan. As described in the introduction and Chapter 2, these excavations revealed an early Christian basilica, likely part of the Prodromos, the monastic complex with the mausolea of the Ottoman sultans.[10]

Scrutiny of the Byzantine and Ottoman periods and their ethno-religious communities requires similar creativity in observation. For insights into the Genoese merchant class, one must pause, as we saw, at the recently restored Irgandı Bridge. Another bridge, Setbaşı, offers a portal into the Armenian class, where a *boza* seller was once located.[11] Stepping forward in time, what does a 1687 tombstone for the daughter of a certain Isaac Ashkenazi say about the Jewish community in the city?[12] Does it indicate the existence of earlier Romaniote Jews in Prousa?

Early Ottoman Bursa's (in)visibility also finds some resolution in an "urban armature" formed by the old city and the complexes built in the suburbs. It is the armature effect of these early architectural campaigns involving both repurposed and new buildings that helped Bursa's inhabitants claim their distinctive identity. Developed by William MacDonald in 1986, the term "urban armature" implies "a clearly delineated, path-like core of thoroughfares and plazas" and, more aptly, "an architecture of connection."[13] It helps us to visualize Bursa's architectural axis and its overall design in the early Ottoman period.

The most infamous earthquake, that of 1855, occurred during the governorship of Ahmed Vefik Paşa. He had served previously as an ambassador of the Ottoman court to Paris, where he encountered Haussmann's urban design ideals.[14] Hence, the buildings constructed in the aftermath of the earthquake have a Parisian ethos.[15] About a century later, Bursa saw another intervention when Luigi Piccinato,[16] an Italian, was invited to offer planning advice following a fire that destroyed the city center in 1958. After the fire, Piccinato saw the city's historical fabric divided in two, the first group less durable and residential, the second more durable and public. He demonstrated an appreciation for the city's architectural legacy, including the classical, Byzantine, and early Ottoman layers. He saw the richness of its urban and rural landscape, and in turn included the bathhouses, industrial districts, and undeveloped areas in his master plan.[17] Piccinato recognized problems created by past planning efforts, including those imposed by nineteenth-century urban planning attempts.[18] For instance, complications had emerged when a Frenchman, Henri Prost, had attempted in 1938–44 to adapt Bursa's roads for motor traffic, as well as to create open areas circled by axial roads around historic monuments such as the Green Mausoleum.[19]

Piccinato was hopeful that, aided by his planning regime, the *yeşil Bursa* (lit. green Bursa), would maintain its historical cohesion and architectural legacy.[20] Although it was approved by the Turkish Ministry of Development and Housing in 1960, Piccinato's master plan was never realized. Anyone familiar with Bursa today might wonder what this Italian planner would make of the state-sponsored construction of concrete residential blocks sprouting up in the heart of the city, buildings that obstruct nearly every vista. Yet, even as the population approaches two and a half million and the city becomes a major industrial hub second only to Istanbul, Bursa retains a mystical and inspiring air. As one traveler has recently stated: "Bursa is Turkey's fourth largest city, is surprisingly beautiful, is authentically Turkish, and is historically significant, yet it remains disproportionately underrepresented in Turkey travel literature."[21]

Spaces of Power, Spaces of Memory

In these closing pages, I seek to provide some resolution to the following questions: What factors lead to the establishment of a monument? Does a monument always unite memory and identity, both on personal and collective levels? What impact does the monument have on the society? A preliminary answer for Bursa is that the architectural culture shows how the idea of space can be materialized. Recognizing where particular events occur—such as the Grand Mosque (*Ulu Cami*) as the locus of the Friday *khutba*; the convent-*masjid* of Murad I as a place for education; the Irgandı bridge as the site where Latin merchants conducted their business; or the convent-*masjids* of Orhan and Bayezid I as places for serving food to the needy regardless of their religious beliefs—shows why and how these monuments came into being, and therefore to what extent the cultural landscape shapes the conceptual usages of space.[22]

The transformation of urban forms, combined with the development of uninhabited land, offers historical evidence of human interactions with the landscape. Bursa's landscapes, as this book has sought to show, are expressive of the culture that produced them. For example, *külliyes*, palatial gardens in the upper city, and cemeteries can be examined as sites for recollection of material presence and urban memory linked to social interrelationships and statecraft. Hence, Bursa acted as a social and cultural testing base for the formulation of the Ottoman state. To trace the patterns of connections, historians must consider the politics of state formation, economic development, trade ties, material production (e.g., of alum, silk, wine, and pottery), and the social structure of the urban aristocracy whose architectural commissions proclaimed Ottoman control over land in remote places of the region, such as Nicaea/İznik and Kirmasti/Mustafakemalpaşa.

Accordingly, the understanding of Bursa's landscape is chorographic. For Cosgrove, "chorography... concerned specific regions and locales understood without necessary relation to any larger spatial (geographical) frame."[23] In other words, chorography is a useful tool in imagining and reflecting the distinctive characteristics and complexities of a unique locale such as Bursa. Often scholars give individual locations for Bursa's *külliyes* so as to create a "national" picture, but one sensitive to regional variation. This results in a scenic and pictorial use of the term "landscape."[24] But what is missing in those discussions is the territorial idea of landscape and the fact that the urban process was formed not only by the *külliyes* but also by the old castle, buildings in the plain, and buildings with nonreligious loci, such as *hans*, baths, and bridges. For example, the 1862 cadastral plan displays the imperial socioreligious complexes linking the upper city with the tombs of the founders, the palace, and Murad II's dynastic mausolea complex below. This reading allows an ideological and visual perception of the route made of overlapping and diverging layers that are architecturally defined.[25] A "national" reading of the city, setting such elements in a larger context, glosses over such meanings and their potentially rewarding interpretations.

The distance created by the monumentality and visibility of the early Ottoman buildings is by no means an actual gap between the observer and the observed. The "distanciated gaze" is a form of seeing which involves claiming and commanding. Specifically, the monumental building programs of Orhan, Murad I, and Bayezid I represent the "distanciated gaze" of the Ottoman sultan, whose sovereignty was reflected through the land he ruled and controlled. In these complexes, the convent-*masjids* occupy the focal points from which the other buildings are visible. In each area of Ottoman urban enterprise forming these socioreligious complexes, the landscape is constructed as a bounded and measured plot. When Bursa's landscape becomes the object of a "gaze," it stands for the rights and power of the ruler, here implying the sovereign.[26]

Pierre Nora, the well-known scholar of the intersections of history and memory, emphasizes the potential of actual places and conjectures, as well as moments and concepts, to establish themselves as *lieux de mémoire*.[27]

Here, architectural culture in fourteenth-century Bursa offers a solid foundation on which to explore the spatiovisual construction of power and the emergence of urban memory. Constructed as sites of memory, the early fourteenth-century buildings of Bursa—as well as İznik and other places, with their Byzantine forerunners in the fortified town—fashion a memory of architectural enterprise, a palpable construct closely tied to physical locale and fabric.

Conclusion

In the early fourteenth century, Bursa became a site of cultural-religious transformation, a node in the ascent of the Ottomans and the demise of the centuries-old Byzantine state. But, as this book has argued, the Ottoman claim to Bursa beginning in 1326 constituted more of a transition or reconstruction than a forceful, bloody takeover. This challenges the view with which both medieval and modern historians have regarded the period—as a triumphalist appropriation. Such discussions emphasize the proclamation of power by the new arrivals, seeing them as wholesale rulers of the recently acquired territory. But the Ottoman conquest of the city was gradual, and the local population and its institutions were assimilated into the emerging state. Among those institutions were the workshops of builders who maintained their established construction practices despite the changes in patronage and architectural forms.

I have attempted herein to holistically analyze Bursa's vibrant architectural activity. Looking at how buildings blend different construction and decorative components, whether from the conquerors' home regions or based on local Byzantine construction practices, brings to light the hybridity of the region's architecture.[28] This approach also sets the pre-Ottoman histories of Bursa's residents alongside the era's significant cultural and urban transformations. For example, while some wall construction and decorative features resemble and refer to Byzantine techniques, evidence also exists of conscious choices to omit these techniques and details. Over time, some common features, such as alternating brick-and-stone construction and juxtaposed arches, were replaced by stone masonry and pointed arches. This may seem like little more than a change in workshop practices, but there is an alternative way of looking at the issue: the buildings constructed in the 1300–1402 period became proclamations of an independent architectural culture in Bursa.

Even with this emerging visual independence, features endured from the Byzantine past. These included alternating brick-and-stone wall construction throughout the region, decorative brick panels in the convent-*masjids* of Orhan and Murad I, and the underlying structures for mausolea (Osman's and Orhan's) and the Friday mosque (Orhan's). This hybrid architectural identity, forged during the transitional fourteenth century, became crucial in defining the parameters of the city. If the sultans, other leaders, sponsors, and builders were seeking to create this complex reality, visitors and settlers no doubt perceived it as well. How did this rising, transforming city look to rulers versus relative commoners? For the rulers, of course, the anointing of a new capital was imbued with significance and symbolism.[29] The new complexes loomed over the emerging residential neighborhoods, signifying the power of the Ottomans. A Muslim silk-maker might have perceived the changing city by observing the permacultural activities of the local Christians and Genoese merchants passing through the city buying and selling goods.[30] The newcomers and existing residents alike would have had a range of sociocultural experiences that would inform their reception of the changing city.[31]

Norman Bryson coined the term "visuality" to define the experience of seeing as culturally-produced.[32] He addresses visuality not only in the sense of culture but also as psychology, implying an unbridgeable distance between viewer and object. In this construct, a given viewer is always incapable of seeing through another's eyes. The fourteenth-century Ottoman cultural-historical scene, by this reasoning, is well out of bounds for us today. Even through our own eyes, according to Bryson, we cannot fully recognize what we see. Building on Bryson's view is Michael Baxandall's theory of the "period eye,"[33] which points to the role of cultural and moral ideas in the Ottomans' understanding of visual systems. This conception also assumes that we cannot entirely know what fourteenth-century inhabitants saw when they looked at Bursa.

Recognizing the constraints suggested by this theory, we can turn once again to the many artists who have portrayed Byzantine buildings in the context of Ottoman urban environments, and the images they provided of the built environment in its fourteenth-century state. Among them were scholars and travelers such as Ibn Battuta, Covel, Cassas, Catenacci, Wheler and Spon,

Figure 20 A view looking into the old city, *Şehadet* (Martyrdom) Mosque on the upper left and the tombs of Osman and Orhan, as well as the *Bey Saray* situated to its right, drawn from the east, possibly from the area of the *Külliyes* of Bayezid I and Mehmed I, by Löwenhielm, 1827. (Uppsala Library Rare Books Collection)

Fischer von Erlach, Evliya Çelebi, Smith, Löwenhielm, and Texier, as well as photographers such as the Abdullah brothers (a group of three Armenian brothers) and Jean Pascal Sebah and Polycarpe Joaillier (owners of the first photography studio in Istanbul).[34] All rendered popular urban representations that implied an approved context for viewing the cultural landscape.[35]

Numerous written and visual depictions of the city and its region emphasize it as a place of natural attractions. Visiting in 1825, Löwenhielm (Figure 20) portrayed the cityscape impressionistically, set within its natural environment. His images convey the broad urban panorama from actual vistas, but they also reflect choices and interpretations by the artist, demonstrating the city's chorographic reality. And even though Löwenhielm's work is perceived as offering a "snapshot" of the cityscape almost four hundred years after the transition, his images also show an exchange between the observer and his subject, as well as with the broader Bithynian urban vista, with evidence of urban planning, architecture, and city life. Löwenhielm's views give a sense of the "hybrid" nature of the city and the region—a mix of Byzantine and Ottoman forms—that is much like its fourteenth-century appearance.

In sum, Bursa's modern urban fabric is inextricable from the multifaceted milieu of its fourteenth-century dynamics, which encouraged the exchange of skills, ideas, and forms. This may be the ultimate tribute to the city and its region characterized by continuity, diversity, and multiplicity in architectural production. Early Ottoman Bursa can also be viewed through a more poetic lens. A visitor today will not quickly perceive signs of the fourteenth-century past, or of Prousa's before it. Instead, the observer must look for this past, as in the "lines of a hand" metaphor in Calvino's Zaira with which I opened this chapter. One has to analyze the opus sectile floors in the tomb, examine the stringcourse frieze on a mosque, descend to the basements of later-Ottoman houses located in the old city to stare at the mosaic floors or bathing quarters with hypocaust tiles. Or pause at the museum's coin displays, stop to interpret the graffiti on the *hans*' walls, or read the many fascinating descriptions by European travelers. Bursa's landscape and natural resources also shaped the visual appearance of the early Ottoman city. Graced with abundant water, protected by hills, and surrounded by rich agricultural lands, including fruit trees planted in rows, the city appeared to fourteenth-century inhabitants as a manifestation of order fashioned from the chaos of the Byzantine-Ottoman transition.

Notes

Preface

1 S. Papaioannou, *Michael Psellos: Rhetoric and Authorship in Byzantium* (Cambridge, Cambridge University Press: 2013), 176.
2 Christie, R., R. McKane, and T. S. Halman, *Beyond the Walls: Selected Poems of Nazım Hikmet* (London: Anvil Press Poetry, 2002), 82.

Introduction

1 Aşıkpaşazade, *Osmanoğulları'nın Tarihi*, 9–10. Translation is by C. Kafadar, *Between Two Worlds. The Construction of Ottoman State* (Berkeley: University of California, 1995), 8. P. R. Lindner, *Nomads and Ottomans in Medieval Anatolia* (Bloomington: University of Indiana Press, 1983), 37 for the full narrative of the dream. For the impact of the dream on the creation of a dynastic myth, C. Imber, "The Ottoman Dynastic Myth." *Turcica* 19 (1987): 7–27 and more recently, E. Kermeli, "Osman I," *Encyclopedia of the Ottoman Empire*. Edited by G. Ágoston and B. Masters (New York: Facts on File, 2009), 444–45.
2 S. Çağaptay, "Visualizing the Cultural Transition in Bithynia (ca. 1300–1402): Architecture, Landscape, and Urbanism" (University of Illinois at Urbana-Champaign, 2007); Chapter 1; H. Lowry, *The Nature of the Early Ottoman State* (Albany, State University of New York Press, 2003), 18–19, gives a succinct analysis of these conquests.
3 C. Foss, "Prusa," *The Oxford Dictionary of Byzantium* (New York and Oxford), 1991 (3): 1750; H. İnalcık, "Bursa," *The Encyclopedia of Islam* TWO (1990) 1: 1333–86; Giorgiali and Loumakis, "Prousa (Byzantium)," *The Encyclopaedia of the Hellenic World, Asia Minor* (published online, September 1, 2018, and accessed online October 15, 2018). The city's name is spelled variously as Prousa, Prussia, Prusa, Bursa, Brussia, Burtzia, and Wursa. For consistency throughout this work, I use Prousa when I refer to the city in the Byzantine period and Bursa to refer to it in the Ottoman and Republican periods.

4 Some scholars claim that Karacahisar (near ancient Dorylaion) and Söğüt (near ancient Belekoma), northwest of Bursa, were the first places that the Ottomans conquered (the first in 1288, the second less than ten years later), hence they were the first capitals. But Bursa's legacy from this period is more significant. For recent archaeological expeditions in Karacahisar castle, E. Altınsapan, Z. Demirel Gökalp, H. Yılmazyaşar, A. Gerengi, "2010–2014 Kazıları Işığında Eskişehir Karacahisar Kalesi." (The Karacahisar Castle in the Light of 2010–2014 Excavations). *ASOS* 10. 3 (2015): 621–33.

5 In terms of Ottoman capitals, Bursa was briefly succeeded by Adrianople (Edirne) in 1361, followed by the rise of Constantinople (Istanbul) in 1453. The exact year of the conquest of Edirne is a matter of debate. I follow İnalcık's argument in which he argued, in two different publications almost thirty years apart, that despite the fact that Edirne was made the capital in 1361, the transfer of imperial power from Bursa to Edirne was gradual and was finalized during the reign of Murad II (r. 1421–51), see H. İnalcık, "The Conquest of Edirne (1361)," *Archivum Ottomanicum* 3 (1971): 185–210; idem, "Edirne'nin Fethi (1361)." (The Conquest of Edirne, 1361). In *Edirne: Edirne'nin 600. Fetih Yıldönümü Armağan Kitabı*, edited by O. N. Peremeci (Ankara: Türk Tarih Kurumu Yayınları, 1993), 137–59. For alternative dates attributing the conquest of the city to the years extending from 1365 to 1380, claiming that the *akıncıs* (warlords) led by Hacı İlbeyi were acting on their own and conquered the city about 1369, see Beldicenau-Steinherr, "*La conquête d'Andrinople par les Turcs: la pénétration turque en Thrace et la valeur des chroniques ottomans*," *Travaux et Mémoires* 1 (1965): 439–61; E. Zachariadou, "The Conquest of Adrianople by the Turks," *Studii Veneziani* 12 (1970): 211–17. Zachariadou agrees with Beldicenau-Steinherr on 1369 as the year of the conquest and references a laudatory poem written in 1368/1369 that was commissioned by Polykarpos, the Metropolitan of Adrianople to John V Palaiologos (r. 1341–91). This poem emphasizes how Polykarpos prays day and night to prevent the Ottoman Turks from putting an end to the Byzantine Empire. A. Heisenberg, "Kaiser Johannes Batatzes der Barmherzige," *Byzantinische Zeitschrift*, 14 (1905): 197–201 also finds that the thirteenth-century Laskarid urban interventions were in ruins around the time of the Ottoman conquest. Rhoads Murphey discusses in "Exploring Ottoman Sovereignty," 42 how Bursa and Edirne co-functioned as capitals between 1361 and 1453. More recently, Amy Singer, "Enter, Riding on an Elephant: How to Approach Early Ottoman Edirne," *Journal of the Ottoman and Turkish Studies Association* 3, no. 1 (2016): 89–109 eloquently summarizes the gradual transition to Edirne amid the presence of multiple and mobile capital "spaces" in the Ottoman realm.

6   H. A. R. Gibb, *The Travels of Ibn Battuta, A.D. 1325-1354*. 2 Vols. (Cambridge: Hakluyt Society, 1958-1962), 449-50.
7   J. P. de Tournefort, *Voyage d'un botaniste*. Edited by S. Yerasimos. (Paris: F. Maspero, 1982), 300, also cited by O. Pancaroğlu, "Architecture, Landscape, and the Patronage in Bursa: The Making of an Ottoman Capital City," *Turkish Studies Association Bulletin* 20.1 (1995): 40-55.
8   Bertrandon de la Broquière, *The Voyage d'outremer*. Translated and edited by G.R. Kline (New York: Peter Lang, 1988), 82-6.
9   Sericulture was an important industry in Byzantine times as well, as discussed by D. Jacoby, "Silk in Western Byzantium Before the Fourth Crusade," *Byzantinische Zeitschrift* 84-85 (1991-1992): 452-500 who claims that the evidence is superficial and at times apocryphal. For Prousa's role in silk production and the imperial silk production in Nicaea (which ended in the 1290s, idem,"Silk Economics and Cross-Cultural Artistic Interaction: Byzantium, the Muslim World, and the Christian West," *Dumbarton Oaks Papers* 58 (2004): 197-240. Another leading expert on Byzantine silk, Anna Muthesius, argues that the sophistication in sericulture under the Ottomans is often linked to the idea that it had originated in the Byzantine period, A. Muthesius, "Constantinople and Its Hinterland: Raw Silk Supply," in *Studies in Byzantine and Islamic Silk Weaving*, edited by A. Muthesius, (London: The Pindar Press, 1995), 315-35, especially 328. For an analysis of travelers' descriptions of Bursa's silk products, see H. Lowry, *Ottoman Bursa in Travel Accounts* (Bloomington: Indiana University Press, 2003), 39-70.
10 U. Schlemmer, *Johannes Schiltberger: Als Sklave im Osmanischen Reich und bei den Tataren: 1394-1427*. (Stuttgart: Thienemann, 1983), 106. He also mentions that the Persian silk was shipped from Bursa to Lucca and Venice.
11 J. Thevénot, *The Travels of Monsieur de Thevénot into the Levant*. Edited by A. Lowell. (London: H. Clark, 1687), 1:88-9.
12 Evliya Çelebi, *Seyahatnâme*, 2: 20.
13 C. Imber, "The Ottoman Dynastic Myth," 7; for elaboration on the concept of the "black hole" and actual usage, idem, "The Legend of Osman Gazi," In *The Ottoman Emirate, 1300-1389*, edited by E. Zacharidou (Rethymnon: Crete University Press, 1993), 75.
14 For a recent and succinct overview of the scholarship on medieval Anatolia, P. Blessing and R. Goshgarian, *Architecture and Landscape in Medieval Anatolia, 1100-1500* (Edinburgh: Edinburgh University Press, 2017), Chapter 1, "Introduction—Space and Place: Applications to Medieval Anatolia."
15 P. Wittek, *The Rise of the Ottoman Empire* (London: Royal Asiatic Society, 1938), 14.

16　H. Lowry, *The Nature of the Early Ottoman State*, 33.
17　As I discuss in Chapters 2 and 3 in detail.
18　Lowry, *The Nature of the Early Ottoman State*, 7, 33–4; Kafadar, *Between Two Worlds*, 42–50 and 162–4.
19　S. Vryonis, *The Decline of Medieval Hellenism in Asia Minor and Process of Islamization from 11th –15th Centuries* (Berkeley, London: University of California Press, 1971), *passim*.
20　For a review of Lindner's methodology, Kafadar, *Between Two Worlds*, 50–1.
21　Lindner, *Nomads and Ottomans in Medieval Anatolia*; R. P. Lindner, *Explorations in Ottoman Prehistory* (Ann Arbor: University of Michigan Press, 2007).
22　C. Heywood, "Boundless Dreams of the Levant: Paul Wittek, the George Kreis, and the Writing of Ottoman History," *Journal of the Royal Asiatic Society* 1 (1988): 7–25; C. Imber, "Canon and Apocrypha in Early Ottoman History," in *Studies in Ottoman History in Honour of Professor V. L. Ménage*. Edited by C. Heywood and C. Imber (Istanbul: Isis Press, 1994), 117–37.
23　Kafadar, *Between Two Worlds*, 47–60.
24　Lowry, *The Nature of the Early Ottoman State*, 69–71. For a survey of the term, C. Finkel, *Osman's Dream: The Story of the Ottoman Empire, 1300-1923*. (New York: Basic Books, 2005), 6–10.
25　F. W. Hasluck, *Cyzicus* (Cambridge: The University Press, 1910), 59–61.
26　C. Mango, and I. Ševčenko, "Some Churches on the South Shore of the Sea of Marmara," *Dumbarton Oaks Papers* 18 (1973): 235–40.
27　S. Ćurčić, "Architecture in the Byzantine Sphere of Influence Around the Middle of the Fourteenth Century," in *Dečani i Vizantijska umetmost sredinom XIV veka*. Edited by V. Djurić, 55–69 (Belgrade: Serbian Academy of Sciences and Arts, 1989), 66; R. Ousterhout, "Constantinople, Bithynia and Regional Developments in Later Byzantine Architecture," in *The Twilight of Byzantium*, eds. D. Mouriki and S. Ćurčić. (Princeton: Princeton University Press, 1991), 75–110; idem, "Ethnic Identity and Cultural Appropriation in Early Ottoman Architecture," *Muqarnas* 1995 (12): 48–62; idem, "The East, the West, and the Appropriation of the Past in Early Ottoman Architecture," *Gesta* 43.2 (2004): 165–76; G. Necipoğlu, "Anatolia and the Ottoman Legacy," in *The Mosque: History, Architectural Development and Regional Diversity*, eds. M. Frischman and H. Uddin-Khan (London: Thames and Hudson, 1994) 150; S. Çağaptay, "Frontierscape: Reconsidering Bithynian Structures and Their Builders on the Byzantine-Ottoman Cusp," *Muqarnas* 28 (2011): 155–60.
28　A. Gabriel, *Une capitale turque, Brousse-Bursa*, 2 Vols. (Paris: E. de Boccard, 1958), 56–60 and plate XV.

29 E. H. Ayverdi, *Osmanlı Mimarisinde Fatih Devri 855-886 (1451-1481)* (Ottoman Architecture During the Reign of Mehmed II 855–86 (1451-1481)) Vol. 3 (Istanbul: Istanbul Fetih Cemiyeti, 1973), 58–60.
30 B. Anderson, *Imagined Communities: Reflections on the Origins and Spread of Nationalism* (London, New York: Verso, 1983), 11.
31 Ibid.; N. Necipoğlu, "State and Future of Byzantine Studies in Turkey," in *Aptullah Kuran için Yazılar—Essays in Honor of Aptullah Kuran*, eds. Ç. Kafescioğlu and L. Thys-Şenocak (Istanbul, Yapı Kredi Yayınları, 1999), 23–6; Kafadar, *Between Two Worlds*, 20 and 80–2.
32 A. H. Tanpınar, *Beş Şehir* (Ankara: Ülkü Matbaası, 1946), 93.
33 Ibid., 93. Translation is by I. Orbay, *Bursa* (MIT: Aga Khan Awards Ceremony Local Office, 1983), 35.
34 D. F. Ruggles, *Gardens, Landscape, and Vision in the Palaces of Islamic Spain* (Pennsylvania: Pennsylvania State University Press, 2000), 9.
35 Lowry, *The Nature of the Early Ottoman State*, 56–7, 77, 195–6.
36 R. Janin, *Les églises et les Monastéres des grands centres byzantins* (Paris: Institut Français d'études byzantines, 1975),127–91; Foss, "Prusa," 3: 1750.
37 In a recent analysis, Z. Yürekli, *Architecture and Hagiography in the Ottoman Empire: The Politics of Bektashi Shrines in the Classical Age* (Farnham: Ashgate, 2012), 140 and ft. 14, revisits the theme of tearing down churches and monasteries to construct mosques and *madrasas* in their place and how those attempts were read in later accounts as triumphalist messages using the display of spolia collected from those buildings. Also, Z. Yürekli-Görkay, "Osmanlı Mimarisinde Aleni Devşirme Malzeme: Gazilerin Alamet-i Farikası," in *Gelenek, Kimlik, Bireşim: Kültürel Kesişmeler ve Sanat; Günsel Renda'ya Armağan = Tradition, Identity, Synthesis: Cultural Crossings and Art; Essays in Honor of Günsel Renda*, eds. Z. Yasa Yaman and S. Bağcı (Ankara: Hacettepe Üniversitesi Yayınları, 2011), 275.
38 I. Melikoff, *La Geste de Melik Danishmend 1: Etude critique du Danishmendname.* (Paris: Maisonneuve, 1960), II: 270; S. E. Wolper, *Cities and Saints Sufism and the Transformation of Urban Space in Medieval Anatolia* (University Park, PA: Pennsylvania State University Press, 2003), 93–6. On the symbolic and ideological dimensions of dismantling and architectural reuse, Yürekli, "Osmanlı Mimarisinde Aleni Devşirme Malzeme," 273–82; M. Kiprovska, "Plunder and Appropriation at the Borderland: Representation, Legitimacy and Ideological Use of Spolia by Members of the Ottoman Frontier Nobility," *Spolia Reincarnated: Second Life of Spaces, Materials, Objects in Anatolia from Antiquity to the Ottoman Period*, eds. I. Jevtić and S. Yalman (Koç University Publications, Istanbul, 2018), 51–69.

39 I. Melikoff-Sayar, *La Destan d'Umur Pasha (Düstürname-i Enveri)*. (Paris: Bibliothèque byzantine, 1954), 47; B. Kitapçı Bayrı, *Warriors, Martyrs, and Dervishes Moving Frontiers, Shifting Identities in the Land of Rome (13th–15th Centuries)*. (Leiden: Brill, 2019), 182–3.

40 Wittek, *Rise of the Ottoman Empire*, 2; Kafadar, *Between Two Worlds*, 69–70.

41 Lowry, *Ottoman Bursa*, 79–84. C. Hamlin, *Among the Turks* (London: Robert Carter & Brothers, 1878), 248 was an American missionary and eyewitness to the earthquake in 1855, which he described as follows: "All the solid stone and brick buildings were either ruined or injured. The twenty-four domes of Ooloo Djami [Ulu Cami] fell in. Every minaret but one was decapitated, and that the one highest up the side of Mount Olympus; the bazaars were destroyed and burned. Well-built wooden houses of course escaped, but the adobes were wrecked. It was reported that six thousand persons perished. The whole population spent a fearful night in the cold open air. . . . The great solid structures, the churches, the mosques, the baths, the bazaars, were all unoccupied at the time. The houses were empty. Those that fell, the adobes, mainly in the Jewish quarter, fell every way, leaning against each other, presenting a scene of wild confusion, and yet few fell so as to bury their owners if within."

Chapter 1

1 The climate, natural and cultural landscapes, land use, vegetation, and soils have been examined in detail: J. Sölch, "Historisch-geographische Studien über bithynische Siedlunge," *Byzantinische-Neugriechische Jahrbücher* 1 (1920): 263–83; C. L. Stotz, "The Bursa Region of Turkey," *The Geographical Review* 29 (1939): 81–100; B. Geyer, "Physical Factors in the Evolution of the Landscape and Land Use," in *The Economic History of Byzantium*, ed. A. E. Laiou, Vol. 1 (Washington DC: Dumbarton Oaks Research Library and Collection, 2002), 32–45; B. Geyer, "Donnés Géographiques," in *La Bithynie au Moyen Âge*, eds. B. Geyer and J. Lefort (Paris: E. Lethielleux, 2003), 23–40; V. Kandes, *Προύσα ετη αρχαιολογικα ιστορικη γεωγραφικη και εκκλησιαστικα περιγραφη αυτες* (Athens: Asmodaios, 1883), 163–76.

2 Apamea Myrlea (Mudanya) was the port city that gave Prousa access to the Sea of Marmara (to the northwest).

3 Pancaroğlu, "Architecture, Landscape and the Patronage," especially 40, 41–2, and 45. She argues that scholars working on the early Ottoman architecture overemphasize Bursa's architecture as a progenitor of Ottoman architectural practices (which developed further in Edirne and Istanbul); A. Kuran, "A Spatial

Study of Three Ottoman Capitals: Bursa, Edirne and Istanbul," *Muqarnas* 13 (1996): 114–31, especially 114–18.

4   Pancaroğlu, "Architecture, Landscape, and the Patronage," 40.

5   See L. Robert, *A travers l'Asie Mineure* (Athens and Paris: Diffusion de Boccard, 1980), 131 and for a comparative epigraphic evidence from Bithynia, L. Robert, *Études anatoliennes: recherches sur les inscriptions grecques de l'Asie Mineure* (Paris: E. de Boccard, 1937). Several ancient historians, including Strabon, Arrian of Nicomedia, and Stephen of Byzantium, Προύσα ετη αρχαιολογικα, 537 refer to a king Prousias, based on a late second-century AD coin bearing the name "Prousias, the founder of Prusa." Pliny the Elder, however, gives Hannibal as the founder of Prousa. Hannibal, after escaping from Carthage, ended up in Bithynia and worked as a naval commander for Prousias I from 188 to 183 BC. For a concise discussion of the foundation of Prousa and further bibliography, Bekker-Nielsen, T. Bekker-Nielsen, *Urban Life and Local Politics in Roman Bithynia the Small World of Dion Chrysostomos* (Aarhus: Aarhus University Press, 2008), 21–2.

6   V. Koukoules, *Βυζαντινών βίος και πολιτισμός*, 5 Vols. (Athens: Institut français d'Athène 1948–1957): 46–66. *The Oxford Dictionary of Byzantium* (New York: Oxford University Press, 1991), lists the following entries "Butcher," "Goat," "Meat," "Sheep," and "Swine," which highlights the role of Bithynia in the Byzantine agricultural production; M. F. Hendy, *Studies in Byzantine Monetary Economy 300-1450* (Cambridge, New York: Cambridge University Press, 1985), 562–6. Bithynia not only produced goods but also served as a transit point for goods from other regions. G. Dagron, "The Urban Economy-Seventh-Twelfth Centuries," in *The Economic History of Byzantium*, ed. A. E. Laiou (Washington DC: Dumbarton Oaks Research Library and Collection, 2002), 456–8.

7   The historical outline of events derives from the following sources: M. Balard, *La Romaine génoise (XIIe –début du XVI siècle)* (Rome: École française de Rome, 1978); C. Cahen, *Pre-Ottoman Turkey. A General Survey of the Material and Spiritual Culture and History c. 1071-1330* (London: Sidgwick & Jackson, 1968); C. Imber, *The Ottoman Empire 1300–1481* (Istanbul: Isis Press, 1990); H. İnalcık, *The Ottoman Empire. The Classical Age 1300-1600* (New York: Praeger 1973); E. Zachariadou, *Trade and Crusade Venetian Crete and the Emirates of Menteshe and Aydın (1300–1415)* (Venice: Istituto ellenico di studi bizantini e postbizantini di Venezia per tutti i paesi del mondo, 1983), 15–18.

8   Vryonis, *The Decline of Medieval Hellenism*, 268.

9   C. Cahen, *The Formation of Turkey. The Seljuk Sultanate of Rum: Eleventh to Fourteenth Centuries* (Harlow: Longman, 2001), 39–41 and 71.

10 Ibid.

11 Lindner, *Nomads and Ottomans*, 45–6.
12 Kafadar, *Between Two Worlds*, 141.
13 Foss, "Prusa," 3: 1750; İnalcık, "Bursa," 1: 1333–86; Giorgiali and Loumakis, "Prousa (Byzantium)."
14 For a discussion on the population estimates, see Lowry, *Ottoman Bursa*, 1–14, especially 6–7.
15 The Ottoman registers support the claim that Bithynia became dominantly Muslim only in the sixteenth century. See Lowry, *Ottoman Bursa*, which uses travelers' accounts and Ottoman cadastral registers, known as the *tahrir defters* (the earliest was compiled in 1487), studied by Ö. L. Barkan, and E. Meriçli, *Hüdavendigar Livası Tahrir Defterleri* (Tax Registers of the Hüdavendigar Province) (Ankara: Türk Tarih Kurumu Basımevi, 1988), 1–9, register no. 23, 1487: 1–32, to comment on the presence of non-Muslim local and foreign communities in the city as discussed by İnalcık, "The Question of the Emergence of the Ottoman State," 71–80.
16 Kafadar, *Between Two Worlds*, 122–5. The early Ottoman policy of keeping local laws and customs unchanged and incorporating the clerical and military inhabitants of the newly conquered lands into its administrative system has been discussed under the concept of *istimalet* by İnalcık, "Status of the Greek Orthodox Patriarchate," 409.
17 Lindner, *Explorations in Ottoman Prehistory*, 53.
18 See Bekker-Nielsen, *Urban Life*, for the many hats Dio wore in his lifetime, 119–45.
19 P. G. Walsh, *Pliny the Younger, Complete Letters* (Oxford: Oxford University Press, 2006), Book X: 23–6.
20 *Dio Chrysostom. Discourses*. Edited and translated by J. W. Cohoon and H. Lamar Crosby (Cambridge, MA: Harvard University Press, 1939–1951), 45. 13.
21 Ibid., 45. 12–15.
22 Ibid., 40. 11.
23 Ibid., 40. 11 and 47. 16–17; Seeing the colonnaded streets as a key element of the urban planning in the Eastern cities of the Roman Empire before the time of Hadrian is an important point, as discussed by R. Burns, *Origins of the Colonnaded Streets in the Cities of the Roman East* (Oxford: Oxford University Press, 2017), 181–4; G. Salmeri, "Dio, Rome, and the Civic Life in Asia Minor," in *Dio Chrysostom Politics, Letters, and Philosophy*, ed. S. Swain (Oxford: Oxford University Press, 2000), 67 dates the completion of the colonnade to 105–6; see Bekker-Nielsen, *Urban Life*, 119–45, for the reactions against Dio's urban interventions.
24 Walsh, *Pliny the Younger*, Book X: 23–6.

25 Bekker-Nielsen, *Urban Life*, 268–9; Walsh, *Pliny the Younger*, Book X.70–2. On the Greek and Roman history of the city, F. K. Dörner, "Prusa ad-Olympium," *Pauly Wissowa* 23 (1957): 1071–86; Kandes, *Προύσα ετη αρχαιολογικα*, 30.

26 Bekker-Nielsen, *Urban Life*, 268–9; Walsh, *Pliny the Younger*, Book X. 70–2. Judging from the emperor's answer, it is difficult to say whether this project was ever realized.

27 For an account on the monasteries on Mount Olympus, see B. Menthon, *Une terre de Légendes de Bithynie* (Paris: Bonne Presse, 1935), 8–9; Janin, *Les églises et les Monastéres*, 127–91. The former source needs to be used cautiously and supplemented with the latter one. For a general history and sources, see P. Charanis, "Monk as an Element of Byzantine Society," *Dumbarton Oaks Papers* 25 (1971): 61–84; R. Morris, *Monks and Laymen in Byzantium (843–1118)* (Cambridge: Cambridge University Press, 1995), 5–37. Edited by Klaus Belke, the *Tabula Imperii Byzantini 13: Bithynien und Hellespontos* (Vienna: Austrian Academy of Sciences, 2020).

28 Foss, "Prusa," 3: 1750; Mango and Ševčenko, "Some Churches on the South Shore," 207; Giorgiali and Loumakis, "Prousa (Byzantium)."

29 Janin, *Les églises et les Monastéres*, 191.

30 Nicephori Gregorae Gregoras, *Byzantina historia graece et latine*. Edited by I. Bekker (Bonn: E. Weber, 1829–1855), 44 as discussed further in Chapter 2, ft. 120.

31 See Chapter 1, note 5 in this book.

32 H. Lowry, *The Shaping of the Ottoman Balkans, 1350–1550: The Conquest, Settlement and Infrastructural Development of Northern Greece* (Istanbul: Bahçeşehir University Publications, 2007), 154–60; C. Bakirtzis, "The Urban Continuity and Size of Late Byzantine Thessaloniki," *DOP* 57 (2003): 45: 35–64.

33 For the Islamic City paradigm, my summary derives from E. Eldem, D. Goffmann and B. Masters, "Introduction," *The Ottoman City Between East and West–Aleppo, Izmir, and Istanbul* (Cambridge, New York: Cambridge University Press, 1999), 1–18. Earlier studies include I. Lapidus, "The Evolution of Muslim Urban Society," *Comparative Studies in Society and History* 15 (1978): 21–50; J. L. Abu-Lughod, "The Islamic City—Historic Myth, Islamic Essence, and Contemporary Relevance," *International Journal of Middle Eastern Studies* 19 (1989): 155–76; C. Cahen, "Mouvements populaires et autonomisme urbain dans l'Asie musulmane du moyen âge, I," *Arabica* 5:3 (1958): 225–50; C. Cahen, "Mouvements populaires et autonomisme urbain dans l'Asie musulmane du moyen âge, II," *Arabica* 6:1 (1959): 25–56.

34 J. Sauvaget, "L'enceinte primitive de la ville d'Alep," *Mélanges de l'Institut Français de Damas. Section Des Arabisants* 1 (1929): 131–59; J. Sauvaget, "Le plan antique de Damas," *Syria* 26.3–4 (1949): 314–58.

35 A. Raymond, "Islamic City, Arab City: Orientalist Myths and Recent Views," *British Journal of Middle Eastern Studies* 21.1 (1994): 7.

36 F. Acun, "A Portrait of the Ottoman Cities," *The Muslim World* 92:3–4 (2002): 255–85; G. Veinstein, "The Ottoman Town (Fifteenth-Eighteenth Centuries)," in *The City in the Islamic World*, eds. R. Holod, S. Jayussi, A. Petruccioli and A. Raymond (Leiden, Boston: Brill, 2008), 205–17; G. Boykov, "The T-Shaped Zaviye/İmarets of Edirne: A Key Mechanism for Ottoman Urban Morphological Transformation," *Journal of the Ottoman and Turkish Studies Association* 3.1 (2016): 29–30; H. İnalcık, "Istanbul: An Islamic City," *Journal of Islamic Studies* 1 (1990): 1–23; D. Kuban, *Istanbul, an Urban History: Byzantion, Constantinopolis, Istanbul* (Istanbul, 1996). For challenges to the idea that the spatial interventions were simply based on the Islamic city model, see Ç. Kafescioğlu, *Constantinopolis / Istanbul: Cultural Encounter, Imperial Vision, and the Construction of the Ottoman Capital* (University Park: Pennsylvania State University Press, 2009), chapters 1 and 2.

37 Lapidus, "Evolution of Muslim Urban Society," 21–50; Boykov, "The T-shaped Zaviye/İmarets of Edirne," 29–48.

38 For Arabo-Islamic and Turco-Balkan categories, see P. Pinon, "The Ottoman Cities of the Balkans," in *The City in the Islamic World*, In *The City in the Islamic World*, eds. R. Holod, S. Jayussi, A. Petruccioli and A. Raymond (Leiden, Boston: Brill, 2008), 146–7.

39 This is an oft-quoted statement in popular literature on Bursa. Keçecizade Fuad Paşa visited the baths in Bursa for theraupetic reasons in 1850. For its most recent reflection on Fuad Paşa's use of the term, N. İntepe, *Dibâce* (Istanbul: Kaynak Yayınları, 2009).

40 Lowry, *Nature of the Early Ottoman*, 56–7, 77, 195–6.

41 G. Necipoğlu, "From International Timurid to Ottoman: A Change of Taste in Sixteenth-Century Ceramic Tiles," *Muqarnas* 7 (1990): 136–70; P. Blessing, "Seljuk Past and Timurid Present," *Gesta* 56.2 (2017): 225–50.

42 For example, Nicaea and Constantinople; see Kafescioğlu, *Constantinopolis/Istanbul*, chapter 1.

43 For example, Komotini, Didymoteichon, and Thessaloniki. For a discussion of the Ottoman urban interventions in the Balkans, see S. Ćurčić, and E. Hadjitryphonos, *Secular Medieval Architecture in the Balkans 1300-1500 and Its Preservation* (Thessaloniki: Aimos, 1997), 19–39; Lowry, *The Shaping of the Ottoman Balkans*, 154–60.

44 According to the fourteenth-century *vita* of John Vatatzes, the majority of the thirteenth-century Laskarid urban interventions were in ruins around the time of the Ottoman conquest, Heisenberg, "Kaiser Johannes Batatzes," 197–201.
45 Kuran, "Three Ottoman Capitals," 118–22, especially 122; R. Ousterhout and C. Bakirtzis, *The Byzantine Monuments of Evros/Meriç River Valley* (Thessaloniki: European Center for Byzantine and Post-Byzantine Monuments, 2007), 169.
46 G. Necipoğlu, *Architecture, Ceremonial and Power: The Topkapı Palace in the Fifteenth and Sixteenth Centuries* (New York: Architectural History Foundation, 1991), 12–13, and as noted by Pancaroğlu, "Architecture, Landscape, and Patronage," 48; Kafescioğlu, *Constantinopolis/Istanbul*, 28–53.
47 Lowry, *Shaping of the Ottoman Balkans*, 154–60; Bakirtzis, "The Urban Continuity and Size of Late Byzantine Thessaloniki," 35–64.
48 S. Kostof, "Architectural History and the Student Architect: A Symposium," *Journal of the Society of Architectural Historians* 26.3 (1967): 189–91; 189–191. Kostof's "total context" can be summarized under four methods: "to study each building in its entirety because of the 'oneness' in architecture; to look at buildings in a broader physical sense later called 'setting'; to contend all buildings of the past are worthy of study because they form a community; and to scrutinize the nonphysical aspects that are essential to understanding the building."
49 This list only includes major fires in the city. For a complete list, see K. Baykal, *Tarihte Bursa Yaygınları* (Fires in the History of Bursa) (Bursa: Bursa Eski Eserleri Sevenler Kurumu Yayınları, 1948).
50 For a list of earthquakes where the epicenter was in Bursa, see N. Ambraseys and C. Finkel, *The Seismicity of Turkey and Adjacent Areas. A Historical Review, 1500-1800* (Istanbul: Eren Yayınları, 1985).
51 The modification has been described by St. Laurent, "Ottomanization and Modernization: The Architectural and Urban Development of Bursa and Genesis of Tradition," Ph.D. dissertation, Harvard University, 1989; St. B. Laurent, "Léon Parvillée, His Role as Restorer of Bursa's Monuments after the 1855 Earthquake and his Contribution to the Exposition Universelle of 1867," in *L'Empire ottoman; la République de Turquie et del la France*, eds. J.-L. Bacqué Grammont and H. Batu (Paris: Isis, 1986), 247–82; Z. Çelik, Z. *Displaying the Orient: Architecture of Islam at Nineteenth-Century World's Fairs* (Berkeley: University of California Press, 1992), 96–8; A. Ersoy, *Architecture and the Late Ottoman Historical Imaginary* (New York: Routledge, 2015), 79–102.
52 Ibid., Parallel major urban modifications include Mussolini's *il piccone risanatore* (healing pick) in 1932–42 and the modifications around Byzantine *Mese*,

Ottoman Divanyolu in Istanbul in the 1860s. Z. Çelik, *The Remaking of Istanbul: Portrait of an Ottoman City in the Nineteenth Century* (Seattle: University of Washington Press, 1993), chapters 4 and 5; M. Cerasi, "The Perception of Divan Yolu Through History," in *Afife Batur'a Armağan Mimarlık ve Sanat Tarihi Yazıları* (Essays on Architectural and Art History in Honor of Afife Batur), eds. A. Ağır, D. Mazlum and G. Cephanecigil (Istanbul: Literatür Yayınları, 2005), 111-24.

53 As noted by W. B. Denny, "Quotations In and Out of Context: Ottoman Turkish Art and European Orientalist Painting," *Muqarnas* 10 (1993): 219-30.

54 For an overview of the restorations especially on the latter, see İ. Yılmaz, "Bursa Sur Kapıları ve Taht-ı Kale Kapısı Rekonstrüksiyonu," *Uludağ Üniversitesi Fen-Edebiyat Fakültesi Sosyal Bilimler Dergisi* 26.1 (2014): 99-105.

55 For a description of the excavation results in Turkish and accompanying photos http://www.bursadakultur.org/tophanede_kilise.htm.

56 For studies on the mosaics, see R. Okçu, "Prusia ad Olympum Mozaikleri," (Mosaics from Prusia ad Olympum) *Journal of Mosaic Research* 3 (2009): 31-51; H. Çıtakoğlu, "Bursa/Hisar Bölgesi Mozaikleri ve Geometrik Desen Repertuarı," (Bursa/Hisar Region Mosaics and Geometric Pattern Repertoire) *International Journal of Social Inquiry* 9 (2016): 1-32. For a monograph on the salvage excavations conducted by the Bursa Archaeological Museum, see E. Özkan, and F. Ünal, *Hisarkeoloji*. (The Archaeology of the Castle) (Bursa: Osmangazi Belediyesi Yayınları, 2009). I thank the authors for their willingness to discuss the nature of their findings.

57 S. Çağaptay, "Archaeology Report: Results of the Tophane Area GPR Surveys, Bursa, Turkey," *Dumbarton Oaks Papers* 68 (2014): 387-404. I am grateful to the Turkish Ministry of Culture and Tourism (for the area of the tombs and parks) as well as the Ministry of Defense (for the Byzantine/Ottoman Palace), for granting me a permit to carry out the GPR survey with the collaboration of Larry Conyers (University of Denver) and April Kamp-Whittaker (Arizona State University).

58 Çağaptay, ibid., 394-9 and figures 3, 5, and 8.

59 Here, I visualize the entire scope of human intervention in Bursa. I greatly benefited from S. Kostof, "Architectural History and the Student Architect: A Symposium," *Journal of the Society of Architectural Historians* 26.3 (1967): 189-191 and D. Favro, "Ancient Rome through the Veil of Sight," in *Sites Unseen: Landscape and Vision*, eds. D. Harris and D. F. Ruggles (Pittsburgh, PA: University of Pittsburgh Press, 2007), 111-30.

Chapter 2

1. F. W. Hasluck, *Christianity and Islam under the Sultans* (Oxford, Clarendon Press, 1929), 1: 6–8.
2. The quotation is from I. Kopytoff, "The Cultural Biography of Things: Commoditization as Process," in *The Social Life of Things: Commodities in Cultural Perspective*, ed. A. Appadurai (Cambridge: Cambridge University Press, 1986), 67. For the symbolic and practical conversions in Islam: O. Grabar, *The Formation of Islamic Art* (New Haven: Yale University Press, 1987), 43–71.
3. For a discussion on the term, appropriation: R. Nelson and S. R. Shifff, *Critical Terms for Art History* (Chicago: University of Chicago Press, 1996), 117–29, especially 129. See O. Pancaroğlu, "Caves, Borderlands and Configurations of Sacred Topography in Medieval Anatolia," *Mésogeios* 25–26 (2005): 249–82; for the localization of the Tomb of Prophet Daniel, see O. Pancaroğlu, "Visible/Invisible: Sanctity," in *Eastern Mediterranean Port Cities: A Study of Mersin, Turkey– From Antiquity to Modernity*, eds. F. Yenişehirlioğlu, E. Özveren and T. Selvi Ünlü (Cham: Springer, 2009), 79–91; for the Shrine of Seyyid Gazi, Yürekli, *Architecture and Hagiography*, 93–7; Kiprovska, "Plunder and Appropriation," 60–5.
4. S. Humphreys, *Islamic History: A Framework for Inquiry* (Princeton, NJ: Princeton University Press, 1991), 273–9, discusses patterns of conversion in Islamic contexts. O. Grabar, The Formation of Islamic Art (New Haven: Yale University Press, 1987), 43–71; Pancaroğlu, "Architecture, Landscape and the Patronage," discusses the nature of the appropriation, 3, 9–10.
5. On the conversion of Saint Sophia into a Friday mosque and a monastery into a *madrasa*, see Aşıkpaşazade, *Osmanoğullarının Tarihi Tevârih-i Al'î Osman*, eds. K. Yavuz and Y. Saraç (Istanbul: Gökkubbe Yayınevi, 2007), 119; A. M. Schneider, *Die römischen und byzantinischen Denkmäler von Iznik-Nicaea* (Berlin: Archäologisches Institut des Deutschen Reiches, 1943); H. Yılmazyaşar, "İznik Ayasofya Kilisesi'nde Osmanlı Dönemi Yapısal Düzenlemeleri." (The Ottoman Interventions at the Nicaean Saint Sophia). *Ebru Parman'a Armağan: Sanat Tarihi ve Arkeoloji Yazıları*, ed. A. O. Alp (Ankara: Alter Yayınları, 2009), 361–84. Vryonis, *Decline of Medieval Hellenism*, 197–8 and fn. 361, also describes churches that were converted into mosques in Nikomedia/İzmit and Amastris/Amasra. The Orhan Mosque in Biga has patches of recessed brick technique in the foundation. Rebuilt after natural catastrophes on several occasions, the building today displays no other original (Byzantine) details.
6. The date of the Ottoman conquest of Trigleia, which remained predominantly Greek, is unclear. Based on their visit in the 1850s, M. Kleonymos, and Chr.

Papadopoulos, *Βιθυνίκα, Επίτομος Μονογραφία της Βιθυνίας και των πόλεων αυτής* (Constantinople: Typois I. A. Vretou, 1867), 43 and 137, mention fifty Muslim and five hundred Christian households (with no distinction among Christian denominations). The conversion of the Church of Saint Stephanos dates to 1560–61 (Hegirah 968); see Mango and Ševčenko, "Some Churches," 236–40 for further bibliography. Also M. S. Pekak, *Zeytinbağı (Trigleia) Bizans Dönemi Kiliseleri* (Byzantine Churches of Trigleia). Unpublished PhD Dissertation, Hacettepe University (Ankara, 1991); M. S. Pekak, "Zeytinbağı/ Trilye Bizans Dönemi Kiliseleri," (The Byzantine Churches of Trigleia) *XIII. Kazı ve Araştırma Sonuçları Toplantısı* (Ankara: Kültür ve Turizm Bakanlığı Yayınları, 1995), 307–38; Ousterhout, "Constantinople, Bithynia," 5–110; "Ethnic Identity," 48–62; S. Çağaptay, "The Church of the Panagia Pantobasilissa in Trigleia (ca. 1336) Revisited: Content, Context, and Community," *Annual Bulletin of the Istanbul Research Institute* 1 (2012): 56–8.

7   Ayverdi, *Osmanlı Mimarisinin*, 1–16, provides a catalog of buildings erected by Ertuğrul and Osman in Paphlagonia, Phrygia, and Bithynia.

8   For more on Byzantine construction postdating the conquest of Bursa and Bithynia, Çağaptay, "The Church of the Panagia Pantobasilissa in Trigleia," 45–59.

9   On the use of spoliation in the medieval Anatolian context, see G. Öney, "Anadolu Selçuklu Mimarisinde Antik Devir Malzemesi," (Ancient Period Spolia in Anatolian Seljuk Architecture) *Anadolu* 12 (1968): 17–38. S. Redford, "City Building in Seljuq Rum," in *Seljuqs: Politics, Society and Culture*, eds. C. Lange and S. Mecit (Edinburgh: Edinburgh University Press, 2011), 148–56, incorporates more visual evidence of the reuse of architectural sculpture and buildings in Sinop, Alanya, Aspendos and Konya. See also İ. Aktuğ-Kolay, "The Influence of Byzantine and Local Western Anatolian Architecture on the 14th Century Architecture of the Turkish Principalities," *Sanat Tarihi Defterleri / Özel Sayı -Okzident und Orient* 6 (2002): 199–213; S. E. Wolper, "Khidr, Elwan Çelebi and the Conversion of Sacred Sanctuaries in Anatolia," *The Muslim World* 90 (2000): 313, 316–17; B. Anderson, "The Complex of Elvan Çelebi: Problems in Fourteenth-Century Architecture," *Muqarnas* 31 (2014): 77–82; Yürekli-Görkay, "Osmanlı Mimarisinde Aleni Devşirme," 275; Yürekli, *Architecture and Hagiography*, 93–7; Kiprovska, "Plunder and Appropriation," 55–69.

10 S. Redford, "Alaeddin Mosque in Konya is Reconsidered," *Artibus Asiae* 51.1–2 (1991): 57–74; Öney, "Anadolu Selçuklu Mimarisinde," 17–38; Aktuğ-Kolay, "Influence of Byzantine and Local Western Anatolian Architecture," 199–213.

11 Here I follow Michael Camille's writings on the appropriation of the past, *The Gothic Idol: Ideology and Image-Making in Medieval Art* (Cambridge, New York: Cambridge University Press, 1989), 70–1.

12 Ibid., 71.
13 Kafadar, *Between Two Worlds*, 19–28. For a comparative Byzantine-Crusader coexistence, A. M. Weyl-Carr, "Correlative Spaces: Art, Identity and Appropriation in Lusignan Cyprus," *Modern Greek Studies Yearbook* 14–15 (1998–1999): 59–80.
14 Çağaptay, "Prousa/Bursa," 52, 53, 63, footnote 29. The building is named "Gümüşlü Kümbet" (literally, "silver-domed tomb"). Lead, not silver, was used in Byzantine monuments, but lead did not become the standard covering for Ottoman domes until much later. For the legendary interpretation of the tombs, see note 102 in this chapter. For the discussion of the reuser knowing about the original meaning and function of the object or building that is reused, see A. Cutler, "Reuse or Use? Theoretical and Practical Attitudes Toward Objects in the Early Middle Ages," *Settimane di Studio del Centro Italiano di Studi sull'Alto Medioevo* 46 (1999): 1055–83; F. B. Flood, "Pillars, Palimpsests, and Princely Practices: Translating the Past in Sultanate Delhi," *RES: Anthropology and Aesthethics* 43 (2003): 95–116.
15 Pancaroğlu, "Architecture, Landscape, and the Patronage," 43–5.
16 Aşıkpaşazade, *Osmanoğulları'nın Tarihi*, 339. The claiming was not always a speedy act. For example, Bursa's conquest, preceding the final capture in 1326, took a decade. The surrender of the city was eventually precipitated by worsening conditions within its walls, after the local Byzantine potentate known as Saroz (chief officer to the Byzantine ruler of the city) fled, embarking on a ship to Constantinople.
17 A copy of this cadastral map is stored in the Bursa Public Library.
18 Çağaptay, "Prousa/Bursa," 66, in Byzantine architecture, residential/palatial complexes enclosed within citadels are common, such as Eskihisar in Bithynia and the Blachernae in Constantinople. Bertrandon de la Broquière, *The Voyage d'outremer*, 136; R. Lubenau, *Beschreibung der Reisen des Reinhold Lubenau herasgegeben*. 3 Vols. (Königsberg: Pr. Beyer, 1914–1915), 3: 176; J. Hammer-Purgstall, *Umblick auf einer Reise von Constantinopel nach Brussa und von da zurück über Nicäa und Nicomedien* (Pesth: A. Hartleben, 1818), 42; Th. Smith, "An Account of the City of Prousa in Bithynia," *Philosophical Transactions* 1684 (14): 432. For the additions and changes to the palace complex over the years, J. Covel, *Dr. John Covel: Voyages en Turquie 1675–1677*, ed. J.-P. Grélois, Réalités Byzantinés Éditions 6. (Paris: P. Lethielleux, 1998) 150; J. Spon, and G. Wheler, *Voyage d'Italie, de Dalmatie, de Grece et du Levant: fait aux années 1675 et 1676* (La Haye: Alberts), 215. K. Baykal, Bursa'da Saray ve Köşk." (Palace and Kiosk in Bursa), in *Milli Saraylar Sempozyumu: Bildiriler* (Ankara: Kültür ve Turizm Bakanlığı Yayınları, 1984), 31–3 notes that the building began to be used as the military headquarters beginning in 1846 and went through major remodeling during the reign of Abdülhamid II (r. 1876–1909).
19 Bekker-Nielsen, *Urban Life*, 53.

20 *Dr. John Covel*, figures 14, 18, 19, 21, and 23; G. Kiourtzian, "L'Époque Protobyzantine À Travers les Monuments Épigraphiques," in *La Bithynie au Moyen Âge*, ed. B. Geyer and J. Lefort, (Paris: E. Lethielleux, 2003), 43–64; Bekker-Nielsen, *Urban Life*, 53.

21 Sieges and threats were common in the Hellenistic period; see Bekker-Nielsen, *Urban Life*, 26–8.

22 C. Foss, "The Defenses of Asia Minor against the Turks," *The Greek Orthodox Theological Review* 27.2 (1982): 159–61; J. Lefort, "Tableau de la Bithynie au XIIIe siècle," in *The Ottoman Empire (1300-1389)*, ed. E. Zachariadou. (Rethymnon: Crete University Press, 1993), 110–13, plate A.

23 Ottomans attempted to conquer the city in 1302, 1304, and 1305, all during the time of Osman. For the nature of damage, Ruy González de Clavijo, *Embassy to Tamerlane 1403-1406*. Edited and translated by G. Le Strange (New York: Harper, 1928), 269.

24 D. Kastritsis, *The The Sons of Bayezid: Empire Building and Representation in the Ottoman Civil War 1402-1413* (Leiden: Brill, 2007), 45–8, 78–80, 96–111.

25 Redford, "City Building in Seljuq Rum," 256–7; P. Blessing, Urban Space Beyond Walls: Siting Islamic Funerary Complexes in Konya," in *Tomb–Memory–Space, Concepts of Representation in Pre-Modern Christian and Islamic Art*, ed. F. Giese, A. Pawlak and M. Thome (Berlin, Boston: De Gruyter, 2018) 25–43 discusses how in the thirteenth century the Rum Seljuk court officials with connections to the Mongol-Ilkhanid rulership began building complexes outside the city walls of Konya, which created new neighborhoods.

26 For later-Ottoman renovations, Gabriel, *Une capitale turque*, 23–7. Ayverdi, *Osmanlı Mimarisinin*, 116, discusses the difficulty of separating what is datable to the pre-Karamanid siege versus post-Karamanid remodeling.

27 Ottoman- and Turkish-period names are in italics; modern names are in parentheses.

28 C. Foss, and D. Winfield, *Byzantine Fortifications: An Introduction* (Pretoria: University of South Africa, 1986), 138–9. Foss and Winfield make conflicting claims about the fortifications of Bursa: one reference to the *Saltanat kapı* treats it as if it still stands, while another says that it no longer exists.

29 Ayverdi, *Osmanlı Mimarisinin*, 116 argues that the outer line must have been built in the early Ottoman period.

30 Ibid., citing Gabriel as the source for old photographs, cites plate numbers from 23 to 30, but Ayverdi is mistaken, as Gabriel's plate number is 10.

31 *Dr. John Covel*, 164–8, figures b 19, 20, 21, and 22 and 373–4. For the inscribed pieces inserted in the walls, and for the tower, figure b 23. For the inscriptions discussed above, see Kiourtzian, "L'Époque Protobyzantine," 59–60.

32 For the survival of the *decumanus maximus*, Bekker-Nielsen, *Urban Life*, 52–3, fig.12; Burns, *Origins of the Colonnaded Streets*, 183 fig. 8.08. The fifteenth-century rebuildings aimed to restore the walls after the Karamanid siege, the seventeenth-century remodelings focused on the south side, and the nineteenth-century restorations aimed to revive the walls after the 1855 earthquake, Gabriel, *Une capitale turque*, 23–7.

33 Gabriel, ibid.; Ayverdi, *Osmanlı Mimarisinin*, 116.

34 Hammer-Purgstall, *Umblick auf einer Reise*, 42; Smith, "An Account of the City of Prousa," 432, also talks about the fact that the palace had walls around it: "the Seraglio which is walled round." Also, *Dr. John Covel*, 150; Baykal, "Bursa'da Saray ve Köşk," 31–3.

35 Ayverdi, *Osmanlı Mimarisinin*, 117. Later, in the late 1930s when the construction for a hospital started in the upper city, a series of arcaded underground structures made of brick and mortar were revealed as has been noted by M. Ataş, *Bursa Klavuzu* (Bursa Guide) (Istanbul: Baha Matbaası, 1944), 24. For the results of the GPR survey, Çağaptay, "Tophane Area GPR Surveys," 401–2, figures, 14–16.

36 Salvage excavations were conducted in the late 1990s and early 2000s by the Bursa Archaeological Museum several hundred meters to the west of the tombs and the inner citadel. Özkan and Ünal, *Hisarkeoloji*, passim.

37 Battuta, traveling in Bithynia, managed to meet Orhan not in Bursa but in İznik. See Gibb, *The Travels of Ibn Battuta*, 2: 451–2. See also, for example, the documents relating to Gregory Palamas' captivity in 1354–5: G. Arnakis, "Gregory Palamas among the Turks and Documents of His Captivity as Historical Sources," *Speculum* 26 (1951): 104–18. On that occasion, Orhan was in a village in the mountains around Bursa in the company of his Byzantine physician, where a debate was arranged between Palamas and some enigmatic wise men in Orhan's court (the Chionai). Bertrandon de la Broquière, *Le voyage d'outremer*, 170–2, 176–7. For further information on Palamas' conversations with Orhan, see Chapter 3, notes 22–3 in this book.

38 As was the case in the contemporaneous Ayasoluk Palace of the Aydinids, Büyükkolancı, Ayasuluk'ta Yeni Bulunan Kale Köşkü ve Hamamı." (The Recently Discovered Citadel Palace and the Bathhouse in Ayasoluk), in *XIII. Ortaçağ ve Türk Dönemi Kazıları ve Sanat Tarihi Araştırmaları Sempozyumu Bildirileri* (Denizli: Pamukkale Üniversitesi Fen-Edebiyat Fakültesi Yayınları, 2009), 145.

39 I develop the idea of a pitched tent or movable dwelling from my reading of Ibn Battuta as discussed in Gibb, *The Travels of Ibn Battuta*, 2: 440. Battuta was invited by the Aydinid ruler Mehmed Bey (1308–34) to visit his *kharqa* (a portable structure with a timber skeleton covered with layers of felt and topped

with a cupola) located in the mountains. For comparative movable dwelling examples from the Rum Seljuk world, S. Redford, "Thirteenth-Century Rum Seljuk Palaces and Palace Imagery," *Ars Orientalis* 23 (1993): 219-20; A. C. S. Peacock, "Court and Nomadic Life in Saljuq Anatolia," in *Turko-Mongol Rulers, Cities and City Life*, ed. D. Durand-Guédy (Leiden, Boston: Brill, 2013), 191-221; 193-6; the Turco-Mongol realm, C. Melville, "The Itineraries of Shāhrukh b. Timur (1405-47)," in *Turko-Mongol Rulers, Cities and City Life*, ed. D. Durand-Guédy (Leiden, Boston: Brill, 2013), 285-315; and the late Byzantine itinerant models of monarchy, S. Çağaptay, "How Western Is It? The Palace at Nymphaion and Its Architectural Setting," in *First International Sevgi Gönül Memorial Symposium on Byzantine Studies* (Istanbul: Koç Üniversitesi Yayınları, 2010), 360-1. The palace at Yenişehir possibly predated that of Bursa, Neşri, *Kitâb-ı Cihannümâ*, 1: 112-13.

40 See C. Yüksel Muslu, *The Ottomans and the Mamluks Imperial Diplomacy and Warfare in the Islamic World* (London: I.B. Tauris, 2014), 69-71, for a discussion on the marriage and its impact on the diplomatic relations and the Mamluk sources talking about the event.

41 My interpretation is inspired by Nebahat Avcıoğlu's influential piece titled "Istanbul: The Palimpsest City in Search of Its Architext," *RES: Anthropology and Aesthetics* 53-54 (2008): 190-210, especially 191-2, which discusses how and if "imperial cities often claimed to be born out of palaces."

42 Katib Çelebi, *Cihannümâ* (Konstantiniyye: Dâr al-Ṭabāʿah al-Âmire, 1145=1732), 681. The word "kurb" in Ottoman Turkish implies a sense of proximity. I agree with Ayverdi, *Osmanlı Mimarisinin*, 293 footnote 2 that a remodeling prior to a major wedding ceremony event is highly likely. Alternatively, it would indicate a new building complex built near Bursa for which we do not have any other reference following the wedding.

43 For the circumcision, Aşıkpaşazade, *Osmanoğullarının Tarihi*, 48-9; for the enthronement, ibid., 81-2; for the wedding, ibid., 94.

44 Ibid.

45 For the visual siting of the Edirne Palace, P. Kontolaimos, "A Landscape for the Sultan, An Architecture for the Eye: Edirne and Its Fifteenth-Century Royal Tower," *Landscape History* 37.2 (2016): 19-33, for the results of the excavations, M. Özer, *Edirne Sarayı (Saray-ı Cedid-i Amire) Kısa Bir Değerlendirme* (The Palace at Edirne: A Short Analysis) (Istanbul: Bahçeşehir Üniversitesi Yayınları, 2014) *passim*.

46 For the details of this wedding and the paintings describing the bride riding an elephant discussed by S. Redford, "Byzantium and the Islamic World, 1261-1557," in *Byzantium: Faith and Power 1261-1557*, ed. H. Evans (New York:

MET, 2004), 394–5. For the reading of Sitt Hatun within the context of Edirne, A. Singer, "Enter, Riding on an Elephant: How to Approach Early Ottoman Edirne," *Journal of the Ottoman and Turkish Studies Association* 3.1 (2016): 89–109.

47 Singer, "Enter, Riding on an Elephant," 99.
48 Çağaptay, "Prousa/Bursa," 66; Lubenau, *Beschreibung der Reisen*, 3: 176; Broquière, *The Voyage d'outremer*, 136; Hammer-Purgstall, *Umblick auf einer Reise*, 42; Smith, "An Account of the City of Prousa," 432. For the additions and changes to the palace complex, *Dr. John Covel*, 150; Spon and Wheler, *Voyage d'Italie de Dalmatie*, 215; and Baykal, "Bursa'da Saray ve Köşk," 31–3.
49 *Bursa Kadı Sicilleri* (Bursa Court Registers), 330, 5.
50 As will be discussed below in the Old Bath and Kükürtlü Bath complexes.
51 C. F. Texier, and R. P. Pullan, *Byzantine Architecture: Illustrated by Examples of Edifices Erected in the East during the Earliest Age of Christianity* (London: Day & Son, 1864), 159; L. Robert, "Sur un type monétaire de Prousa de l'Olympe et sur des épigrammes," *Hellenica* 2 (1946): 98–9. For Byzantine authors mentioning the Byzantine emperors and the members of the imperial family, Cedrenus, *Georgius Cedrenus [et] Ioannis Scylitzae ope*, ed. I. Bekker (Bonn: E. Weber, 1839), II: 27; for Irene and Constantine VI: *Theophanes Continuatus, Ioannes Cameniata, Symeon Magister, Georgius Monachus*, ed. I. Bekker (Bonn: E. Weber, 1838), 4: 49 and also Theophanes, *Theophanis Chronographia*, ed. C. de Boor (Leipzig: B.G. Teubner, 1883 and 1885), 471; for Leo VI: Porphyrogenitus, *Constantine VII Porphyrogenitus, Emperor of the East, 905-959. De Administrando Imperio*, ed. G. Moravcsik and trans. R. Jenkins (Washington DC: Dumbarton Oaks Research Library and Collection, 1967), 246–8.
52 Bekker–Nielsen, *Urban Life*, 119, footnote 9.
53 For the history and plan of the Old Bath: C. F. Texier, *Description de l'Asie Mineure* (Paris: Firmin Didot, 1839), 116–17; Gabriel, *Une capitale turque*, 166, figure 128 and plate 96; Baykal, *Bursa Anıtları*, 30. Both Ayverdi, *Osmanlı Mimarisinin*, 276–83 and S. Çetintaş, *Türk Mimari Anıtları: Osmanlı Devri, Bursa'da Murad I ve Bayezid I Binaları* (Turkish Works of Architecture: The Ottoman Period, The Buildings of Murad I and Bayezid I) (Istanbul: Milli Eğitim Basımevi, 1952), 12–20 reject the idea of earlier foundations. The latter author, however, mentions that the octagonal hot plunge room (caldarium) once had a figural mosaic decorating its pond. I thank Heath Lowry for this reference.
54 L. Robert, *Études anatoliennes: recherches sur les inscriptions grecques de l'Asie Mineure* (Paris: E. de Boccard, 1937), 231; L. Robert, "Sur un type monétaire de Prousa de l'Olympe et sur des épigrammes," *Hellenica* 2 (1946): 96.

55 Robert, "Sur un type monétaire de Prousa de l'Olympe," 97 and pl.1.
56 The coin bears the name Iulia Mamae as discussed in ibid.; M. (Usman) Anabolu, "Olympos Dağı Eteklerindeki Prusa (Bursa) Sikkesindeki Therme ile İlişkili Olarak," *Belleten* 59.226 (1995): 583; Bekker-Nielsen, *Urban Life*, 25.
57 For Kükürtlü: Gabriel, *Une capitale turque*, 170; Ayverdi, *Osmanlı Mimarisinde Fatih Devri*, fig. 226; Baykal, *Bursa Anıtları*, 32.
58 Gibb, *The Travels of Ibn Battuta*, 2: 450.
59 K. Afroditi, "Prusa (Antiquity)," *The Encyclopaedia of the Hellenic World*, Asia Minor, (published online, (August 29, 2008) and accessed online October 15, 2018); Athenaeus, (*Athénée de Naucratis) Les Deipnosophistes, livres I et II*, ed. and trans. A. M. Desrousseaux (Paris: Société d'édition "Les Belles Lettres," 1956), 2: 43 a; Leontios Scholasticus. *Anthologia Graeca*, IX = Anthologia Palatina. Bibliothèque nationale de France (Par. Suppl. gr. 384), IX: 630. Bekker-Nielsen, *Urban Life*, 25 for further bibliography.
60 Procopius, *Buildings*, trans. H. B. Dewing with G. Downey, Loeb 343 (Cambridge, MA: Harvard University Press, 1940), 5.3.16-20.
61 Ibid. For a recent analysis, see Pickett, "Water and Empire," 115-17 and Tables 1 and 4.
62 Ibid.; also, A. M. Mansel, *Yalova ve Civarı. Yalova und Umgebung* (Istanbul: Istanbul Müzeleri Neşriyatı, 1936), 56-7.
63 For "θερμά," *Stephani Byzantinii Ethnica*, ed. M. Billerbeck and A. Neumann-Hartmann. [Corpus fontium historiae Byzantinae. Series Berolinensis; Volume 43.4] (Boston, MA: De Gruyter, 2016), 234-5.
64 *Anthologia Graeca,* IX: 676.
65 Robert, "Sur un type monétaire de Prousa de l'Olympe," 101-2; Mansel, *Yalova ve Civarı /Yalova und Umgebung,* 48-57.
66 There are exceptions to this rule. For instance, the Kükürtlü Bath, a still functioning bath in Bursa, whose main section was redesigned by Murad I, was not added to the *waqf*, and he requested that no payment be required of those who bathed in the spas.
67 For the restoration history of the complex, Ayverdi, *Osmanlı Mimarisinin*, 276-83 and Çetintaş, *Türk Mimari Anıtları*, 12-20.
68 Ibid.
69 Gabriel, *Une capitale turque*, 170.
70 A. Ubicini, *La Turquie actuelle* (Paris: Hachette, 1855), 30. Patrikios' martyrdom was represented on an eleventh-century hexaptych now located in the Monastery of Saint Catherine at Mount Sinai, as discussed by G. Galavaris, *An*

Eleventh Century Hexaptych of the Saint Catherine's Monastery at Mount Sinai (Athens: Mount Sinai Foundation, 2009), 105.

71 For a comparison, see Kafescioğlu, *Constantinopolis/Istanbul*, 103–9.

72 S. Ćurčić, "Architecture in the Age of Insecurity: An Introduction to Secular Architecture in the Balkans, 1300–1500," in *Secular Medieval Architecture in the Balkans 1300-1500 and Its Preservation*, eds. S. Ćurčić and E. Hadjitryphonos (Thessaloniki: AIMOS, 1997), 47. Kafescioğlu, ibid., 104–5 draws parallels between the Umayyad and Ottoman bathing establishments and their take on the idea of monumentality as well as each culture's interaction with the late antique material culture.

73 Marlia Mundell-Mango, "Thermae, Balnea/ Loutra, Hamams: The Baths of Constantinople," in *Istanbul and Water*, Ancient Near Eastern Studies Supplement 47, eds. P. Magdalino and N. Ergin Ancient Near Eastern Studies Supplement 47 (Leuven: Peeters, 2015), 145, 151, and 153.

74 Janin, *Les églises et les monastéres*, 174–5.

75 S. Eyice, "Bursa'da Osman ve Orhan Gazi Türbeleri," (The Mausolea of Osman and Orhan in Bursa) *Vakıflar Dergisi* 5 (1963): 131–47; Pancaroğlu, "Architecture, Landscape, and the Patronage," 43; Çağaptay, "Visualizing the Cultural Transition," Chapter 2; idem, "Prousa/Bursa," 52–3; V. M. Tekinalp, "Remodelling the Monastery of Hagios Ioannes Prodromos in Prusa ad Olympum (Modern Bursa, Turkey)," in *the Architecture of Byzantium and Kievan Rus from the 9th to the 12th Centuries* (St. Petersburg: Transactions of the State Hermitage Museum, 2010), 164.

76 Baykal, *Bursa Anıtları*, 15; Gabriel, *Une capitale turque*, 30, 43–4; Ayverdi, *Osmanlı Mimarisinin*, 59–61; Kuran, "Three Ottoman Capitals," 115–16.

77 Some support the idea that the inscription originally belonged to Şehadet, such as F. Taeschner, "Beiträge zur frühosmanischen Epigraphik und Archäologie," *Der Islam* 20 (1932): 109–86, especially 127–37 and idem, "Beiträge zur frühosmanischen Epigraphik und Archäologie," *Der Islam* 22 (1935): 69–73, especially 69–70. Others, such as R. Hartmann, *Im neuen Anatolien, Reiseeindrücke* (Leipzig: Hinrichs, 1928), 19; M. T. Koyunluoğlu, *İznik ve Bursa Tarihi.* (The History of İznik and Bursa) (Bursa: Vilayet Matbaası, 1935), 163; Baykal, *Bursa Anıtları*, 16, argue that the piece must have come from somewhere else. Gabriel, *Une capitale turque*, 45, claims that the inscription is expatriated from its original location, the first Ottoman mosque in the upper citadel. Kuran, "Three Ottoman Capitals," 115 ft. 8 argues that the inscription was immured in the east entrance of Şehadet to make the memory of Orhan's mosque visible. Ayverdi, *Osmanlı Mimarisinin*, 59 and A. Kuran, *The Mosque*

in Early Ottoman Architecture (Chicago: University of Chicago Press, 1968), 161–4.

78 Eyice, "Bursa'da Osman ve Orhan Türbeleri," 147.

79 Gibb, *The Travels of Ibn Battuta*, 2: 322; Gabriel, *Une capitale turque*, 43–4 refers to the Ottoman practice of conversion as discussed by travelers, such as Menthon and claims that besides the mausolea that were converted from buildings in a monastery, another church was converted to a mosque. Eyice, "Bursa'da Osman ve Orhan Türbeleri," 131–47, summarizes the diverging statements in travelers' accounts on the city.

80 O. Pancaroğlu, "Devotion, Hospitality and Architecture in Medieval Anatolia," *Studia Islamica* 108.1 (2013): 48, ft. 2, notes that due to the inconsistencies in Ibn Battuta's narratives, it is difficult to say whether he traveled in Anatolia from 1331–2 or from 1332–4.

81 *Mühimme Defteri* (Ankara: T. C. Başbakanlık Devlet Arşivi Genel Müdürlüğü), 28 (984/1576): 165. I agree with Ayverdi, *Osmanlı Mimarisinin*, 66 who claims that the building mentioned here as the Orhan *Cami* must be Orhan's Friday mosque in the old city, rather than his convent-*masjid* in the lower city, as the latter was big enough to accommodate a large congregation, and its plan was not flexible enough to remodel, as well as the fact that the *Ulu Cami* was located just next to it.

82 Evliya Çelebi, *Seyahatnâme*, 2: 10. He claims that each wall of the structure measures around 110 *ayak* (corresponding to around 38 centimeters does not make any sense at all.)

83 For Covel's manuscript, *Dr John Covel*, 146–8, figure b 4 as discussed in Çağaptay, "Prousa/ Bursa," 57–61, fig. 6; Tekinalp, "Remodelling the Monastery of Hagios Ioannes Prodromos," 165, fig. 3. For Smith's quotation, "An Account of the City of Prousa," 431.

84 I thank Lars Karlsson for bringing this valuable image to my attention. Johann Bernard Fischer von Erlach, a practicing architect and historian produced *Entwurff Einer Historischen Architektur* (Leipzig: Selbstverl, 1725), 78, plate 2, titled "The Grand Mosque of the Turkish ruler Orhan II (albeit misidentified as Orhan II) built in the old town of Bursa."

85 D. Sestini, *Voyage dans La Grèce asiatique, à la péninsule de Cyzique à Brusse et à Nicée* (London and Paris: Chez Leroy, 1789), 101–5; R. Pococke, *A Description of the East and Some Other Countries*, 2 Vols. (London, 1743–1745), 299–300.

86 M. Crinson, *Empire Building Orientalism and Victorian Architecture* (New York and London: Routledge, 1996), 19.

87 C. A. Bernard, *Les bains de Brousse en Bithynie* (Constantinople: Mille frères, 1842), 69–70.

88 Broquiere, *The Voyage d'outremer*, 32–4. Ayverdi, *Osmanlı Mimarisinin*, 58–9; Gabriel, *Une capitale turque*, 45–6; R. Mantran, "Les inscriptions arabes de Brousse," *Bulletin d'Ètudes Orientales de L'Institut Français de Damas* 14 (1952–1954): 88–114..
89 This is discussed further in Chapter 3.
90 Çağaptay, "Prousa/Bursa," 65–6.
91 "Orhan tâbeserâhın medresesine vakıf olan hamamın tamiri . . ." *Bursa Court Registers*, year 1484, Vol. 4: 30.
92 For its remodeling history from the sixteenth century onward until its destruction in the 1855 earthquake, Ayverdi, *Osmanlı Mimarisinin*, 94.
93 Ayverdi, *Osmanlı Mimarisinin*, 93 citing from *Bursa Court Registers*, Vol. 4, 51.
94 As discussed by Ayverdi, *Osmanlı Mimarisinin*, 94, *Bursa Court Registers*, year 1260 (1844): 310. The register uses the word *ittisâl*, meaning adjacent or conjoined.
95 It reads: "Manastırı Bursa'da bu medrese itdi." Neşri, *Kitâb-ı Cihannümâ*, 1: 186.
96 For the history of the building, Ayverdi, *Osmanlı Mimarisinin*, 91–3; see footnote 152 in this chapter for a discussion on the possible location of the *madrasa* given the results of a GPR survey.
97 Yılmaz, *Caliphate Redefined. The Mystical Turn in Ottoman Political Thought* (Princeton: Princeton University Press, 2018), 98–100 for further discussion and bibliography. Comparative evidence is found in the Aydınid context, when Cairo-trained Hacı Paşa was appointed as the first *madrasa* teacher and wrote treatises and introductions, as discussed by S. N. Yıldız, "From Cairo to Ayasoluk: Hacı Paşa and the Transmission of Islamic Learning to Western Anatolia in the Late Fourteenth Century," *Journal of Islamic Studies* 25 (2014): 263–97.
98 Çağaptay, "Visualizing the Cultural Transition," Chapter 2. The buildings were destroyed in the earthquake of 1855 and replaced by less evocative buildings that survive today. A still-standing example of a Byzantine church/chapel turned into a mausoleum is the Tomb of Lala Şahin Paşa in Kirmasti/Mustafakemalpaşa; see Çağaptay, "Frontierscape," 176–7. See also Melikoff, *La Destan d'Umur Pasha*, 47; Neşri, *Kitâb-ı Cihannümâ*, 1: 81 and 145; Hoca Sadeddin, *Tacü't-tevarih* 1: 73; Aşıkpaşazade, *Osmanoğulları'nın Tarihi*, 101, 112, and 368. Sources also refer to a monastery turned into a *madrasa*.
99 Çağaptay, "Prousa/Bursa," 64–5. The same "minimal" approach is valid for the conversions of churches into mosques. Ousterhout, "The East, The West," 170. A much-cited case of a Byzantine building subjected to Ottoman conversion is St. Sophia, in which much of the original interior decoration was left intact, even though Christian visual connotations were regarded as non-Islamic by

later generations. See G. Necipoğlu, "The Life of an Imperial Monument: Hagia Sophia after Byzantium," in *Hagia Sophia from the Ages of Justinian to the Present*, eds. R. Mark and A. Çakmak (Cambridge and New York: Cambridge University Press, 1992), 206–7.

100 Çağaptay, ibid., 65, footnote 76. The Ottomans had acquired these items as provincial governors of the dilapidated Rum Seljuk state. They included a drum, worry beads, a diploma, robes, flags, and a sword, as noted by Neşri, *Kitâb-ı Cihannümâ* 1: 111 and 175; Sestini, *Voyage dans la Gréce*, 101–5; Hammer-Purgstall, *Umblick auf einer Reise*, 47–9; Dr. John Covel, 146–7; Redford, "Byzantium and the Islamic World," 392.

101 In a forthcoming piece entitled "A Complicating Narrative," Aslı Akışık notes that according to the fifteenth-century account of Chalkokondyles, Osman died in Bursa. I thank Aslı Akışık for sharing a copy of her work with me prior to its publication.

102 Çağaptay, "Prousa/Bursa," 52, 53, 63 and footnote 29. The legacy of the silver-domed tomb remained in the popular imagination of Ottoman Turks for centuries.

103 These two names were used interchangeably during the Ottoman period. Âşıkpaşazade, *Osmanoğulları'nın Tarihi*, 112 and Neşri, *Kitâb-ı Cihannümâ*, 1:115.

104 Texier and Pullan, *Byzantine Architecture*, 157; Ayverdi, *Osmanlı Mimarisinin*, 105–6; Gabriel, *Une capitale turque*, 25–32; K. Ådahl, ed., *C. G. Löwenhielm Artist and Diplomat in Istanbul 1824-1827* (Uppsala: Uppsala University Press, 1993), 27; A. Pralong, and J. P. Grélois, "Les monuments byzantins de la ville haute de Brousse," in *La Bithynie au Moyen Âge*, ed. B. Geyer and J. Lefort (Paris: P. Lethielleux, 2003), 134–49; Çağaptay, "Prousa/Bursa," 53, fig. 2. The circular structures of Profitis Elias were examined by Th. Papazotos, "The Identification of the Church of 'Profitis Elias' in Thessaloniki," *Dumbarton Oaks Papers* 45 (1991): 121–7.

105 Pralong and Grélois, ibid., and Tekinalp, "Remodelling the Monastery of Hagios Ioannes Prodromos," 164–79 recapitulate similar identifications by travelers and attempt to find comparable buildings, but these two works do not aim to interpret the reuse of the buildings and what that reuse meant to the Ottomans. For the meaning of reuse and conversion, Çağaptay, "Prousa/Bursa," 62–7; Texier, *Description de l'Asie Mineure*, 61–2 and 130; Hammer-Purgstall, *Umblick auf einer Reise*, 47–9; Janin, *Les églises et les monastéres*, 174. The most creative identification was done by V. Schultze, *Altchristliche Städte und Landschaften*,

2 Vols. (Gütersloh: C. Bertelsmann, 1922), 1: 39, who misleadingly identified the tomb of Osman as the remains of the palace at Pythia (modern-day Yalova on the coast of the Sea of Marmara) as discussed in this Chapter, notes 59–63.

106 Texier and Pullan, *Byzantine Architecture*, 169 and 171, plate 56.

107 Çağaptay, "Prousa/Bursa," 53. Pralong and Grélois, "Les monuments byzantins," 144 however, identified the building as a baptistery by looking at the drawing done by Texier.

108 Eyice, "Bursa'da Osman ve Orhan Türbeleri," 131–47; and S. Eyice, "Two Mosaic Pavements from Bithynia," *Dumbarton Oaks Papers* 17 (1963): 373–83.

109 For Löwenhielm: Çağaptay, "Prousa/Bursa," 48–50, 53–60 and 66–7, figures 3, 4, 7 and 8; Ådahl ed. *C. G. Löwenhielm Artist*, 27 and 29; Yenal, *Bir Zamanlar Türkiye – Turkey As It Was. Carl Gustaf Löwenhielm Bir İsveç Elçisinin 1820'lerdeki Türkiye Albümü – A Swedish Diplomat's Turkish Portfolio in the 1820s* (Istanbul: Yapı Kredi Yayınları, 2003). For Catenacci: Pralong and Grélois, "Les monuments byzantins," 134–49. For Cassas: Pralong and Grélois, "Tombeau d'Orcan," 139. For Texier, Çağaptay, ibid., 47–49 and 53–54, fig. 2; Tekinalp, "Remodelling the Monastery of Hagios Ioannes Prodromos," 164–79.

110 Texier and Pullan, *Byzantine Architecture*, 150, were the first to offer this comparison.

111 B. Ward-Perkins, *Roman Imperial Architecture*, 3rd edn (New Haven: Yale University Press, 1994), 433–5 and fig. 294 and 295.

112 E. H. Swift, *Roman Sources of Christian Art* (New York: Columbia University Press, 1951), Plate XIX; R. Krautheimer, *Rome: Profile of a City, 312-1308* (Princeton: Princeton University Press, 2000), 150. For a different set of comparisons, see Tekinalp, "Remodelling the Monastery of Hagios Ioannes Prodromos," 173–5.

113 Çağaptay, "Prousa/Bursa," 53; M. W. Jones, "Principles of Design in Roman Architecture. The Setting Out of Centralized Buildings," *Papers of the British School at Rome* 57 (1989): 106–51.

114 Ayverdi, *Osmanlı Mimarisinin*, 105–6.

115 Çağaptay, "Prousa/Bursa," 53; Pralong and Grélois, "Tombeau d'Orcan à Brousse," 138–9.

116 Ådahl et al., *C. G. Löwenhielm Artist*, 27 and 29; E. Yenal, *Bir Zamanlar Türkiye – Turkey As It Was*.

117 Çağaptay, "Prousa/Bursa," 53, fig. 4; Pralong and Grélois, "Les monuments byzantins," 134–49.

118 R. Krautheimer, *Early Christian and Byzantine Architecture*. Fourth edition with S. Ćurčić (New Haven: Yale University Press, 1984), 382–3; R. Ousterhout, *Master Builders of Byzantium* (Princeton: Princeton University Press, 1999), 26–7 for the former; Krautheimer, ibid., 430–4; Ousterhout, ibid., 243–4 for the latter.

119 Çağaptay, "Prousa/Bursa," 56–60. For Covel's manuscript, *Dr John Covel*, 146–8; F. W. Hasluck, "Bithynica," *The Annual of the British School at Athens* 13 (1906–1907): 287–308 also studied this manuscript and made comments on the sketches done by Covel. Evliya Çelebi, *Seyahatnâme*, 2: 10–11; Eyice, "Two Mosaic Pavements," 376; Y. Demiriz, *Örgülü Bizans Döşeme Mozaikleri*. (Interlaced Byzantine Mosaic Pavements). (Istanbul: Yorum, 2002), 15. The ambiguity over whether the dome was supported by columns or piers may result from an inconsistency in architectural terminology among the travelers: Spon and Wheler, *Voyage d'Italie de Dalmatie*, 216 and Covel, ibid., 148 use the word "pillars"; Texier and Pullan, *Byzantine Architecture*, 157 use the word "columns"; and L. de Laborde, *Voyage de l'Asie Mineure* (Paris: Firmin Didot, 1838), 23 and Miss Pardoe, *The City of the Sultan and Domestic Manners of the Turks in 1836*, 2 Vols. (London: Henry Colburn, 1837), 193 use the term "six gigantic columns of masonry."

120 H. Buchwald, "Lascarid Architecture," *Jahrbuch Österreichischen Byzantinistik* 28 (1979): 278–9.

121 Ibid., 292–3.

122 For the former, Pralong and Grélois, "Les monuments byzantins," 139 and for the latter, Krautheimer, *Early Christian*, 358–9; Ousterhout, *Master Builders*, 108–9. For a different set of further comparisons, Çağaptay, "Prousa/Bursa," 53–7; Tekinalp, "Remodelling the Monastery of Hagios Ioannes Prodromos," 166–9 and 173–5.

123 For a slightly different dating attempt, Çağaptay, ibid., 57–9. C. Pinatsi, "New Observations on the Pavement of the Church of Haghia Sophia in Nicaea," *Byzantinische Zeitschrift* 99.1 (2006): 119–26. Eyice, "Bursa'da Osman ve Orhan Türbeleri," 374–9 and idem, "Two Mosaic Pavements," 373; Y. Demiriz, *Örgülü Bizans Döşeme Mozaikleri* (Interlaced Byzantine Mosaic Pavements) (Istanbul, 2002), 15; Evliya Çelebi, *Seyahatnâme*, 2: 10–11.

124 As attested by the current state of the coffins in the building.

125 H. Maguire, "The Medieval Floors of the Great Palace," in *Byzantine Constantinople: Monuments, Topography and Everyday Life*, ed. N. Necipoğlu (Leiden: Brill, 2001), 153–74.

126 Çağaptay, "Prousa/Bursa," 61. For marble revetments and the *opus* sectile floor in Prousa: the fourteenth-century chronicler Ephraim of Ainos describes the variety of stones used in the church as marble revetments (verse no: 7926, Ephraim) (Ainos), *Historia chronica*, O. Lampsides (Athens: Academy of Athens, 1984–1985), 280; *Dr. John Covel*, 142 "marble in green"; Hammer-Purgstall, *Umblick auf einer Reise*, 48; Bernard, *Les bains de Brousse en Bithynie*, 70 "en marbre noir, sur une colonne supportant la vôute," and "verde antico"; Laborde, *Voyage de l'Asie Mineure*, 23–4: "sur un pilier, en marbres de plusieurs couleurs"; Sestini, *Voyage dans La Grèce*, 101–2; J. Dallaway, *Constantinople Ancient and Modern: With Excursions to the Shores and Islands of the Archipelago and to the Troad* (London: Cadell, 1797), 280; T. Renouard de Bussierre, *Lettres sur l'Orient: écrites pendant les années 1827 et 1828* (Paris: Levrault, 1829), 154: "plusieurs croix."

127 Demiriz, *Örgülü Bizans Döşeme*, 98 prefers to associate the execution of the floor as a part of the restoration program that took place in the mid-eleventh century.

128 G. Millet, *Monuments byzantins de Mistra: matériaux pour l'étude de l'architecture et de la peinture en Grèce aux XIVe et XVe siècles* (Paris: E. Leroux, 1910), Plate 42.2.

129 Çağaptay, "Prousa/Bursa," 57–9; Pinatsi, "New Observations," 126.

130 Vryonis, *Decline of Medieval Hellenism*, 197–8 and footnote 361.

131 Hasluck, *Christianity and Islam*, 1: 6–19.

132 Wolper, "Khidr, Elwan Çelebi," 313, 316–17; Pancaroğlu, "Devotion, Hospitality," 73–4.

133 See F. W. Hasluck, "Ambiguous Sanctuaries and Bektashi Propaganda," *Annual of the British School of Athens* 20 (1913–14): 102; idem, *Christianity and Islam*, 1: 48–9; S. Eyice, "Çorum Mecitözü'nde Aşık Paşa-Oğlu Elvan Çelebi Zaviyesi," (Aşık Paşa-Oğlu Elvan Çelebi Zaviyesi at Mecitözü in Çorum) *Türkiyat Mecmuası* 15 (1969): 234–9; Wolper, "Khidr, Elwan Çelebi," 313, 316–17; Anderson, "Complex of Elvan Çelebi," 73–97 for an analysis of the scholarship on the building from the sixteenth century onward.

134 Wolper, "Khidr, Elwan Çelebi," 313, 316–17.

135 A. Y. Ocak, "Elvan Çelebi," *Türk Diyanet Vakfı İslam Ansiklopedisi* (1995) 11: 63–4; G. Kut and A. Y. Ocak, "Aşık Paşa," *Türkiye Diyanet Vakfı İslam Ansiklopedisi* 4 (1991): 4: 1–3.

136 Anderson, "Complex of Elvan Çelebi," 91–4.

137 Çetintaş, *Türk Mimari Anıtları*; Ayverdi, *Osmanlı Mimarisinin*; Gabriel, *Une capitale turque*.

138 Eyice, "Bursa'da Osman ve Orhan Türbeleri," 114–47 offers a set of proposed construction. He also proposes a tenth-century date for the Mausoleum of Orhan, idem, "Monuments byzantins anatoliens inédits ou peu-connus," *Corsi di Cultura sull'arte Ravennate e Bizantina* 18 (1971): 313.

139 Gabriel, *Une capitale turque*; Eyice, ibid.; Pralong and Grélois, "Les monuments byzantins," 139–49; Tekinalp, "Remodelling the Monastery of Hagios Ioannes Prodromos," 164–79.

140 St. Laurent, "Ottomanization and Modernization"; for a review of the reactions by the travelers who were in and around the city at the time of the earthquake and in its aftermath, see Lowry, *Ottoman Bursa*, 81–4.

141 A critical reading of this genre and an exemplary set of these accounts in the context of Prousa is in Lowry, *Ottoman Bursa*, preface.

142 Çağaptay, "Prousa/Bursa," 60; A. Pralong, "Matériel Archéologique Errant," in *La Bithynie au Moyen Âge. Geographie et habitat*, eds. B. Geyer and J. Lefort (Paris: E. Lethielleux, 2003), 225–86. For comparative capital examples: Mansel, *Yalova ve Civarı /Yalova und Umgebung*, 57, Plate, 10; J. Kramer, "Kämpferkapitelle mit den Monogrammen Kaiser Justinus II. und seiner Gemahlin, der Kaiserin Sophia in Yalova Kaplıcaları (Termal)," in *Festschrift für Klaus Wessel zum 70. Geburstag*, ed. M. Restle (Münich: Editio Maris, 1988), 178–84 and figures 1, 3, 9, and 11; S. Y. Ötüken, *Forschungen im nordwestlichen Kleinasien, Antike und byzantinische Denkmäler in der Provinz Bursa* (Tübingen: Ernst Wasmuth Verlag, 1996), 17.

143 Çağaptay, "The Church of the Panagia Pantobasilissa in Trigleia," 45–59. Based on the fieldwork done in 1968, 1971, 1972, and 1973, Mango and Ševčenko's article remains a crucial source in understanding the architectural productivity and decorative program in Bithynia from the middle to the late Byzantine period. See Mango and Ševčenko, "Some Churches on the South Shore," 235–98, especially 279–98; Pekak, "Zeytinbağı (Trigleia) Bizans Dönemi Kiliseleri."

144 Çağaptay, "Prousa/Bursa," 60–1; Dr. John Covel, 146–8; A. Cutler and M. Johnson, "Synthronon," *Oxford Dictionary of Byzantium* (New York and Oxford: Oxford University Press, 1991), 3; Smith, "An Account of the City of Prousa," 431–3; Spon and Wheler, *Voyage d'Italie de Dalmatie*, 432; Bouras, "Templon," *Oxford Dictionary of Byzantium* (New York and Oxford: Oxford University Press, 1991), 3: 2023–4.

145 Çağaptay, ibid., 61; Pralong and Grélois, "Les Monuments byzantins," 139–41; Tekinalp, "Remodelling the Monastery of Hagios Ioannes Prodromos," 168.

146 This transformation has been discussed by Ousterhout, *Master Builders*, 86–92 contextualizing several churches following a similar transformation such as the churches at Amorium (in Phyrgia), Kydna (in Pamphylia), Selçikler (in

Lydia), all first built in the form of basilicas with and without baptisteries and transformed into cross-domed churches (Figures: 55, 56, and 57). The excavations of the church in Choma in Lycia unearthed similar architectural results; see Çağaptay, "The Church at Choma: A Revisiting of the Development of a Regional Style," *Byzantine Studies Conference Abstracts* 28 (2002): 62–3, which summarizes the author's MA thesis titled "The Church at Choma (Elmalı, Antalya) and Its Materials" (Bilkent University, 2001).

147 Çağaptay, "Prousa/Bursa," 61; Smith, "An Account of the City of Prousa," 431–3. The emperor Constantine V (r. 741–75) has been described as the most odious iconoclastic emperor of the Iconoclastic era. As Smith does not cite a source with this information, his attribution may well be without merit, solely based on seventeenth-century understanding of attributing churches with a big mosaic cross depicted in the main apse to the Iconoclastic period, especially to the reign of Constantine V, following well-established examples, such as the Church of Saint Irene in Constantinople.

148 Çağaptay, ibid.; Nicephori Gregorae, *Byzantina historia graece et latine*, ed. I. Bekker (Bonn: E. Weber, 1829–1855), 44: "The queen built the church naos inside the metropolis of the inhabitants of Prousa lying near Mount Olympus in the name of Saint John of Prodromos"; Pachymeres, *Relations historiques III*: 46–7, 78–9 and 100–1; Ephraim of Ainos, *Historia chronica*, 1990: verses 7916, 7925–9 (verse 7925, "She (Irene) founded a very beautiful church (*domus*) of Prodromos in Prusa whose beauty is described by words with a great variety of marbles. It was founded as a *symeneion* (place for the monks) for the worshippers of God."

149 Çağaptay, "Tophane GPR Survey," 396–400, figures 8–12.
150 Ibid., 394–7, figures 3–7.
151 Ibid., 395, figure 3.
152 Ibid., 394–6, figures 3 and 5. See notes 92–96 in this chapter on locating Orhan's *madrasa* within the old city.
153 Ibid., 401, figure 14.
154 Ibid., 401, figures 15–18.
155 As mentioned in Chapter 1, note 55 in this book. For a report and scholarly interpretations of the excavations in Turkish, see www.bursadakultur.org/tophanede_kilise.htm
156 Schultze, *Altchristliche Städte und Landschaften*, 1: 337; Eyice, "Bursa'da Osman ve Orhan Türbeleri," 101, footnote 49.
157 Eyice, "Bursa'da Osman ve Orhan Türbeleri," 101. Also see Procopius, *Buildings*, 5.3.16–20.

Chapter 3

1 For an overview of the discussions on the terminology, see Zeynep Oğuz, "Multifunctional Buildings of the T-Type in Ottoman Context: A Network of Identity and Territorialization," Unpublished MA thesis, METU, 2006, 1–2 examining the terminology, as well as the context in which this form and function came into being in those buildings. I have discussed elsewhere Çağaptay, "Visualizing the Cultural Transition," Chapter 4; idem, "The Road from Bithynia to Thrakia," 433–5; idem, "Frontierscape," 158, footnotes, 29–36, the problems in the modern scholarship regarding the terminology surrounding the function of these complexes, as well as the scholarly emphasis on their religious identity at the cost of ignoring the "multifunctionality" that these buildings might have. More recently, Salgırlı, "Architectural Anatomy," 318, footnote 27, argues that "multipurpose" would be a better term, indicating a deliberate choice behind the introduction of the side rooms (convent rooms) to the plan.

2 G. Necipoğlu, *The Age of Sinan: Architectural Culture in the Ottoman Empire* (London: Reaktion, 2005), 49–50.

3 Pancaroğlu, "Architecture, Landscape and the Patronage," 42–5; Kuran, "Three Ottoman Capitals," 114–18. For a comparison coming from the mid-thirteenth century, see the Rum Seljuk realm in Konya, which displays examples of new funerary complexes built outside the city walls by the non-royal members of the court, P. Blessing, "Urban Space Beyond Walls: Siting Islamic Funerary Complexes in Konya," in *Tomb–Memory–Space, Concepts of Representation in Pre-Modern Christian and Islamic Art*, ed. F. Giese, A. Pawlak, and M. Thome (Berlin, Boston: De Gruyter, 2018), 25–7.

4 Repeating verbatim, H. Lowry, and A. Bryer, "Introduction," in *Continuity and Change in Late Byzantine and Early Ottoman Society*, eds. H. W. Lowry and Anthony Bryer (Birmingham and Washington DC: Dumbarton Oaks Research Library and Collection, 1986), 2–4, to discuss the methodological techniques for dealing with the Byzantine charters and Ottoman *defters*: "First, on a familial level, the former can give information on the size and shape of a family, whereas the latter can only provide information on the average size of a family. Second, on an institutional level, the former provide the reader with imperial and private acts of donation, purchase, sale, exchange, and mortgage of property, clerical and monastic economy, whereas the latter are not tailored to function as the registers of religious holdings, nor as registers of population and land, but rather as a compilation of revenues obtained from land and people."

5   A pioneering study supplementing these two kinds of materials with archaeological and other types of literary evidence is by Lowry and Bryer, ibid.
6   Kandes, *Προύσα ετη αρχαιολογικα*, 13–16 and 23–5, described the pre-Ottoman neighborhoods of the city, which were confined to the upper city and the immediate surroundings. Lowry, *Ottoman Bursa*, 15–38 uses travelers' accounts and Ottoman cadastral registers, known as the *tahrir defters* (the earliest was compiled in 1487), studied by Barkan and Meriçli, *Hüdavendigâr Livası*, 1–9, register no. 23, 1487: 1–32, to comment on the presence of non-Muslim local and foreign communities in the city. Ö. *XVI. Yüzyılın Sonlarında Bursa. Yerleşimi, Yönetimi, Ekonomik ve Sosyal Durumu Üzerine bir Araştırma*. (Bursa at the End of the Sixteenth Century. A Research on Its Settlement, Administration, Economic and Social Aspects) (Ankara: Türk Tarih Kurumu Yayınları, 2006), 115–16: H. İnalcık, "The Question of the Emergence of the Ottoman State," *International Journal of Turkish Studies* 2.2 (1981–82): 71–80.
7   Ergenç, *XVI. Yüzyılın Sonlarında Bursa*, 115. The notion of ethnic and religious homogeneity in the creation of a neighborhood has been challenged in several other studies on Ottoman cities throughout the ages, for example, Istanbul, Kafescioğlu, *Constantinopolis/Istanbul*, 178–81.
8   T. Papademetriou, *Render unto the Sultan: Power, Authority, and the Greek Orthodox Church in the Early Ottoman Centuries* (Oxford: Oxford University Press, 2015), 189, footnotes 28–30. For a discussion of on the sporadic presence and latent representation of the metropolitans from Prousa at the Holy Synod in Constantinople in the fourteenth century, G. Terezakis, "The Diocese of Prousa," *The Encyclopaedia of the Hellenic World, Asia Minor* (published online September 20, 2018 and accessed online October 1, 2018) indicating a period of insecurity and crisis.
9   The Armenian bishopric in Bursa is documented in 1307. Cahen, *The Formation of Turkey*, 202–15.
10 W. Weiker, *Ottomans, Turks and the Jewish Polity: The History of the Jews of Turkey* (Lanham: University Press of America, 1992), 29. Lowry, *Ottoman Bursa*, 15–38. There were seven inscriptions dating to AD 820 referring to Jews living in Prousa and there is also a colophon mentioning the name Shlomo ha-Nasi as a member of the Jewish congregation in Bursa; he was the son of Rabbi Jesse ha-Nasi of Tırnovo, Bulgaria, as noted by A. Galanté, *Histoire des Juifs d'Anatolie*, 2 Vols. (Istanbul: Imp. M. Babok, 1937–39), 94; idem, *Appendice à l'Histoire des Juifs*, 18–21; Bornstein-Makovetsky, "Bursa (Prousa)," (Consulted Online October 1, 2018).

11 İlyas Efendi, "Türk Hakimiyetinde Museviler," *Dergâh Mecmuası* 1338.2 (1919): 21; O. Çetin, *Sicillere Göre Bursa'da İhtida Hareketleri ve Sosyal Sonuçları* (Changing Religions According to the Ottoman Registries and Its Social Impacts), 2nd edn (Ankara: Türk Tarih Kurumu Basımevi, 1999), 29; Bornstein-Makovetsky, "Bursa (Prousa)"; Baykal, *Bursa Anıtları*, 13, claims that the synagogue was built in the Byzantine period. M. Franco, *Essai sur l'histoire des Israélites de l'Empire Ottoman depuis les origines jusqu'à nos jours* (Paris: A. Durlacher, 1897), 27–8. For an overview of the Jewish presence in the city, see H. Tuna, "Social, Cultural and Economic Situation of the Jews in Bursa in the Tanzimat Period." Unpublished MSci Thesis. Middle East Technical University, Ankara, 2013, 8–19.

12 A. Erbahar, "Etz Ahayim Synagogue, Bursa," *The Encyclopedia of Jews in the Islamic World* (Consulted Online October 1, 2018). The Etz Ahayim was destroyed by a fire in the 1940s. Two other synagogues were built in the same neighborhood, known as Gerush and Mayor; the former is still in use. For a general history of the synagogues in Bursa and Turkey, see N. Güleryüz, *The Synagogues in Turkey* (Istanbul: Gözlem Yayınları, 2008).

13 For the Church of the Holy Apostles, see Kandes, Προύσα ετη αρχαιολογικα, 143. For the Church of Taxiarches and a discussion on its inscription, see Kandes, Προύσα ετη αρχαιολογικα, 144.

14 Ö. L. Barkan and E. Meriçli, *Hüdavendigar Livası Tahrir Defterleri* (Tax Registers of the Hüdavendigar Province) (Ankara: Türk Tarih Kurumu Basımevi, 1988), 7–8; Lowry, *Ottoman Bursa*, 28–32; Köseoğlu, *Tarihte Bursa Mahalleleri*, 11, 16, and 38; G. F. Patrinelis, "Ειδήσεις για την Ελληνική κοινότητα της Προύσας (15ος-17ος αι.)," (News for the Greek Community in Bursa) Δελτίο Κέντρου Μικρασιατικών Σπουδών (Bulletin of the Center for Asia Minor Studies) 7 (1988): 11–13, 16–17, and 21.

15 Kandes, Προύσα ετη αρχαιολογικα, 142–3.

16 Lowry, *Ottoman Bursa*, 15–38.

17 The Armenian Catholic church began to be used as a silk spinning factory and is now located in the Namazgah district. The Armenian Gregorian was demolished in the 1980s. R. Kaplanoğlu, "Bursa Kiliseleri," (Churches of Bursa) *Bursa Araştırmaları Dergisi* 30.8 (2010): 19–20.

18 Ergenç, *Bursa*, 325–8; H. İnalcık, "Bursa XV. Asır Sanayi ve Ticaret Tarihine Dair Vesikalar," *Belleten* 24 (1960): 45–102.

19 See İ. Selçuk, "State Meets Society: A Study of *Bozakhāne* Affairs in Bursa," in *Feeding People, Feeding Power: Imarets in the Ottoman Empire*, eds. N. Ergin, C. K. Neumann, and A. Singer (Istanbul: Eren, 2007), 24–5 for further analysis.

20 Lowry, *Ottoman Bursa*, 3 citing from A. Özkılınç, ed. *166 Numaralı Muhasebe-i Vilayet-i Anadolu Defteri (937/1530)* (Number 166 Registry of the Anatolian Province Accounts) (Ankara: Başbakanlık Devlet Arşivleri Genel Müdürlüğü, 1995), 6.

21 Schlemmer, *Johannes Schiltberger: Als Sklave,* 118; "The city contains 200,000 houses . . . and eight hospices where people are received whether they be Christians, Muslims, or Jews," Bertrandon de la Broquière, *The Voyage d'outremer,* 83 lists bread and wine being served in the *imarets* of Bursa in 1432 and caviar and olive oil consumed only by the Greeks, 84. Wheler, *A Journey into Greece*, 216 refers to the needy in the city, explaining that, regardless of faith, they can go and have food in the *imarets*. For a detailed analysis, see Lowry, *Ottoman Bursa*, 30–8.

22 G. G. Arnakis, "Gregory Palamas among the Turks and Documents of His Captivity as Historical Sources," *Speculum* 26 (1951): 104–18; Kitapçı Bayrı, *Warriors, Martyrs, and Dervishes*, 119–20.

23 The identity of the Chionai is a matter of debate. Arnakis and Wittek argued, respectively, that the word "Chion" or "Chionas" was a Greek corruption of the word *ahi* or *hoca*. Arnakis, "Gregory of Palamas," 113–14; G. Arnakis, "Gregory Palamas, the Chiones and the Fall of Gallipoli," *Byzantion* 22 (1952): 305–12; P. Wittek, "Chiones," *Byzantion* 21 (1951): 421–3. Later scholars, including M. Balivet, "Byzantins Judaisants et juifs islamises des *Kuhhan* (Kahin) aux *Xionai* (Χιόνιος)," *Byzantion* 52 (1982): 24–59; Zachariadou, E. "Religious Dialogue between Byzantines and Turks during the Ottoman Expansion," in *Religionsgesprache Im Mittelalter*, eds. B. Lewis and F. Niewöhner (Wiesbaden: Harassowitz, 1992), 289–304; J. Meyendorff, "Grecs, Turcs, et Juifs en Asie Mineure au XIVe Siècle," *Byzantinische Forschungen* 1 (1966): 212–13; D. Sahas, "Gregory of Palamas on Islam," *The Muslim World* 73.1 (1983): 9; and G. M. Prohorov, "Prenie Grigorija Palamys Chiony: Turki'i Problema Zidovskaja Mudrostvujuscih," *Trudy Otdela Drevnerusskoj Literatury* 27 (1972): 329–69, argue that if the Chionai were Jewish, they were most likely recent converts but nevertheless occupied an important position in the Ottoman court. More recently, R. A. Miller, "Religious v. Ethnic Identity," 27–9, claims that determining whether the Chionai were *ahis, hocas*, Jews, or Jewish converts does not sufficiently answer the question of their origins. Miller argues that Palamas might have observed them as the rhetorical descendants of Marcellinus' Chionitae, a native Greek speaker writing in Latin in the fourth and fifth centuries and hence they might be originating from the Mongol-Ilkhanids Iran, 40–1. In a forthcoming piece, Kastritsis, "Ottoman Urbanism before 1453," challenges this view on the basis of

shallow understanding of the text itself and the Byzantine literary context. I thank Dimitri Kastritsis for sharing his insight on the matter.

24 Lowry, *Ottoman Bursa,* 19 and 35–6 citing from M. Kritovoulos, *History of Mehmed the Conqueror by Kritovoulos,* ed. C. Riggs (Princeton: Princeton University Press, 1954), 93; Ö. L. Barkan, and E. H. Ayverdi, *Istanbul Vakıfları Tahrir Defteri: 1546 Tarihli* (1546 Cadastral Register from Istanbul) (Istanbul: Baha Matbaası, 1970), 16.

25 For an earlier discussion, see Chapter 1, footnote 28; Lowry, *Ottoman Bursa,* 6–7 and 37–8. According to Evliya Çelebi, *Seyahatnâme,* 2: 10–11, the old city consisted of 2,000 houses, 7 mosques, 1 bath, and 20 shops in the seventeenth century.

26 Neşri, *Kitab-ı Cihan-Nüma,* 1: 187; Necipoğlu, *The Age of Sinan,* 71–6, the quotation comes from ibid., page 71, "The concept of improvement by cultivating, building, inhabiting, populating and civilizing."

27 Hüseyin Hüsameddin, "Orhan Bey'in Vakfiyesi," (Orhan's Endowment Deed) *Türk Tarih Encümeni Mecmuası* 17.7 (1926–1927): 289–90. Only the *convent-masjid* survives today.

28 The inscription on the door gave the date of construction as 1339 (Hegirah 740) as well as the rebuilding in 1417, after the Karamanid raid of 1413. Ousterhout, "Constantinople and Bithynia," 85, identifies the construction date as 1334. For analyses of the inscription and the date, see Ayverdi, *Osmanlı Mimarisinin,* 61–89; E. H. Ayverdi, " Bursa'da Orhan Gazi Camii ve Osmanlı Mimarisinin Menşei Meselesi" (The Origins of Ottoman Architecture and the Case of the Mosque of Orhan) *Vakıflar Dergisi* 6 (1965): 75; G. Goodwin, *A History of Ottoman Architecture* (London: Thames and Hudson, 1971), 34–5; Kuran, *The Mosque in Early Ottoman Architecture,* 98–101. The dedicatory inscription has been studied by Mantran, "Les inscriptions arabes de Brousse," 90.

29 For a detailed discussion of the complex, Ayverdi, *Osmanlı Mimarisinin,* 18–216 and Gabriel, *Une capitale turque,* 46–9; Çağaptay, "Frontierscape," 166–9. Scholars disagree on the extent of the damage and how much of the present-day structure was rebuilt in 1417–18 and after the 1855 earthquake. For example, see Wilde, *Brussa,* 11–12; Ayverdi, ibid., 62; and Çetintaş, *Türk Mimari Anıtları,* 18–19. For a recent view into the function and timeline and extent of repairs, see S. Emir, *Erken Osmanlı Mimarlığında Çok-İşlevli Yapılar: Kentsel Kolonizasyon Yapıları Olarak Zaviyeler* (Multi-Functional Buildings in Early Ottoman Architecture: Zaviyes as Urban Colonizing Edifices), 2 Vols. (İzmir: Akademi Kitabevi, 1994), 35–44, for example, claims on the basis of textual evidence and structural analysis that the edifice was built to function as a

convent and regained the status of a mosque in the second half of the sixteenth century when a minaret was added.

30 Ibid.
31 As noted by Ayverdi, ibid., 64; "olan mesakin ve metabin ve metabih ve örtülü" (comprising of residential, therapeutic, and cooking facilities and roofed); Hüsameddin, "Orhan Bey'in Vakfiyesi," 286, also 289–90; M. Hızlı, "Bursa'da Selâtîn İmaretleri," (Bursa's Sultanic Imarets), *Uludağ Üniversitesi İlahiyat Dergisi* 10.1 (2001): 35; H. B. Öcalan, S. Sevim and D. Yavaş, ed. *Bursa Vakfiyeleri* (Bursa Waqfs) (Bursa: Bursa Kültür Sanat ve Turizm Vakfı Yayınları, 2013), 66–7.
32 See Çağaptay, "Frontierscape," 166, figures 4–6.
33 Çağaptay, ibid., 167; Tunay claimed that the key to distinguishing fourteenth-century Byzantine buildings from their Ottoman counterparts is to analyze the form of the windows and openings, which were round in the former and had pointed arches in the latter: M. I. Tunay, "Masonry of Late Byzantine and Early Ottoman Periods," *Zograf* 12 (1981): 76–9. Tunay's argument is challenged by R. G. Ousterhout, "The Byzantine Heart," *Zograf* 17 (1986): 36–44 and more recently, idem, *Master Builders*, chapter 6 and especially p. 200.
34 To name a few examples: the Mosque of Alaeddin, the convent-*masjids* of Orhan and Murad I in Bursa; the Hacı Özbek Mosque and the Nilüfer Hatun *Imaret* in İznik; the Mehmed Dede *Zaviye* in Yenişehir; the Mosque of Orhan in Bilecik.
35 Çağaptay, ibid., 167; Ćurčić, *Secular Medieval Architecture*, 49. Although at first glance the use of the Byzantine round arch at the convent-*masjid* of Orhan seems to be overshadowed by the slightly pointed arch, in some of the wall planes of the same period, the use of the Byzantine round arch form overpowers that of other types of arches.
36 Ćurčić, ibid., 49.
37 Çağaptay, "Frontierscape," 169. In the late Romanesque and early Gothic periods, both types of arches existed side by side, such as in Notre Dame la Grande at Poitiers and St. Denis. These may reflect eclectic uses of architectural forms from different cultures as discussed by M. Trachtenberg, "Gothic and Italian Gothic: Toward a Redefinition," *Journal of the Society of Architectural Historians* 50 (1991): 22–37.
38 Çağaptay, ibid., 169. The juxtaposition of different types of arches was also common in other centers of production such as Greece and Serbia. C. Bouras, "The Impact of Frankish Architecture on Thirteenth-Century Byzantine Architecture," in *The Crusades from the Perspective of Byzantium and the Muslim World,* eds. A. E. Laiou and Roy P. Mottahedeh (Washington DC:

Dumbarton Oaks Research Collection and Library, 2001), 247–62 has suggested Byzantine and Islamic pedigrees for the juxtaposed arches. The development of side-by-side arches was evident in the fifteenth- and sixteenth-century military architecture of the Ottoman Balkans, such as the so-called Jezava Gate (1430–39) in Serbia and the westernmost tower of the Heptapyrgion in Thessaloniki, Ćurčić, *Secular Medieval Architecture in the Balkans*, 48–50. For its appearance in Islamic architecture, see K. A. C. Creswell, *A Short Account of Early Muslim Architecture*. Revised edition by J. W. Allen (Aldershot: Scolar Press, 1989), 55, 58–86, 101–4, 116, 131, 143, 157, and 195.

39 M. B. Tanman, "Ekrem Hakkı Ayverdi'nin Erken Devir Osmanlı Mimarisine Dair Tespitleri," in *Ekrem Hakkı Ayverdi'nin Hâtırasına Osmanlı Mimarlık Kültürü*, ed. H. Aynur and A. H. Uğurlu (Istanbul: Kubbealtı Neşriyatı, 2016), 235–36.

40 Çağaptay, "Frontierscape," 169–70, fig. 7; M. Meinecke, *Patterns of Stylistic Changes in Islamic Architecture: Local Traditions versus Migrating Artists*. H. Kevorkian Lecture Series (New York: New York University Press, 1996), 102; Tanman, "Erken Dönem Osmanlı Mimarisinde Memlük Etkileri," 82–90, especially 85; idem, "Mamluk Influences in the Architecture of the Anatolian Emirates," in *The Arts of the Mamluks in Egypt and Syria: Evolution and Impact*, ed. D. Behrens Abouseif (Goettingen: Bonn University Press, 2012), 283–300, 290; Çağaptay, "Frontierscape," 169–70, fig. 7.

41 Ayverdi, *Osmanlı Mimarisinin*, 419–40; Necipoğlu, *The Age of Sinan*, 79. Çağaptay, ibid., 180–1; According to Z. Yürekli, "Architectural Patronage and the Rise of the Ottomans," in *A Companion to Islamic Art and Architecture*, eds. F. Barry Flood and Gülru Necipoğlu (Hoboken, NJ: Wiley Blackwell, 2017), 739–41, the reign of Bayezid I coincides with the Ottoman interest in hiring builders who had worked for the other principalities in Anatolia.

42 Çağaptay, ibid., 170–1; Gabriel, *Une capitale turque*, 51–63; Ayverdi, *Osmanlı Mimarisinin*, 231–64. The building does not have an inscription, but the endowment deed provides the date of completion. E. Tak, "Diplomatik Bilimi Bakımından XVI.-XVII. Yüzyıl Kadı Sicilleri ve Bu Sicillerin İhtiva Ettiği Belge Türlerinin Form Özellikleri Ve Tanımlanması" (16th and 17th Century Court Registers and Their Examinations and Contents in Accordance with Diplomacy), Unpublished PhD Dissertation, Marmara University: Istanbul, 2009, Chapter 3, Gökbilgin, "Murad I. Tesisleri," 221. The endowment deed is dated 1385–86.

43 Ćurčić, "Architecture in the Byzantine Sphere," 66, notes similarities such as the banded wall construction technique, banded voussoirs, occasional use of brick patterning, and the large decorative tympana which recall several Palaiologan churches.

44 Çağaptay, "Frontierscape," 171, fig. 11. For a discussion on the Ohrid's Saint Sophia and Arta's Panagia Paregoritissa, see Krautheimer, *Early Christian and Byzantine Architecture*, 417–28; O. Aslanapa, *Osmanlı Devri Mimarisi* (The Architecture of the Ottoman Period) (Istanbul: İnkilap Kitabevi, 2005), 18, discusses the decorative similarities between Ohrid's Saint Sophia and Murad I's convent-*masjid*.

45 Çağaptay, ibid., 171 and 174; B. Pantelić, *The Architecture of Decani and the Role of Archbishop Danilo II* (Wiesbaden: Reichert, 2002), 4 and 26–9.

46 Çağaptay, ibid., 171; R. Ivancević, "Two Thirteenth-Century Portals in Istria: Models of Traditional and Innovative Uses of Classical Art," *Hortus Artium Medievalium* 1996 (2): 57–64.

47 Çağaptay, ibid., 176–77, figures 15–17. Another structure is the Tomb of Lala Şahin Paşa in Kirmasti/Mustafakemalpaşa bearing a similar corbel frieze. For the spectrum of this feature, see Ousterhout, "Constantinople, Bithynia," 75–110.

48 İnalcık, "Murad I," 31: 159–62.

49 Çağaptay, ibid., 176; Ousterhout, "Ethnic Identity," 55; *Master Builders*, 140–5; "The East, The West," 121.

50 Çağaptay, ibid. The use of pseudo-spolia was common in Anatolian Seljuk architecture, with the Alaeddin Mosque in Konya a good example of this phenomenon. Pseudo-spolia in the context of Crusader Jerusalem has been examined by R. Ousterhout, "Architecture as Relic and the Construction of Sanctity: The Stones of the Holy Sepulchre," *Journal of the Society of Architectural Historians* 62.1 (2003): 21–3.

51 For comments on misuse of the terms "survival" and "continuity," see P. Horden, and N. Purcell, *The Corrupting Sea: A Study of Mediterranean History* (Oxford; Malden, MA: Blackwell Publishers, 2000), 27 and 308–11; Wolper, "Khidr, Elwan Çelebi," 309–22.

52 Şaman Doğan, "Bursa Murad Hüdavendigar Camii ve Niğde Ak Medrese," 211–20. It must be noted that the building in Niğde is constructed completely of stone masonry and functioned only as a *medrese* and not as a mosque. In addition, although the building is double-storied, the first floor lacks openings and the second floor has twin pointed openings carried on single colonnettes.

53 Çağaptay, "Frontierscape," 175. For the first quotation: *Usul*, 10; H. Wilde, *Brussa: eine entwickelungsstäte türkischer architektur in Kleinasien unter den ersten Osmanen* (Berlin: E. Wasmuth, 1909), 12–13. For the second one, S. Gerlach, *Tage-Buch, der von zween glorwürdigsten Römischen Käysern* (Frankfurt: J.D. Zunners, 1674), 258.

54 A. Gabriel, "Bursa'da Murad I Camii and Osmanlı Mimarisinin Menşei Meselesi." (The Mosque of Murad I in Bursa and the Question of the Origins of Ottoman Architecture) *Vakıflar Dergisi* 2 (1942): 3, 36.
55 Ayverdi, *Osmanlı Mimarisinin*, 235.
56 Çağaptay, "Frontierscape," 175; Tanman, "Erken Dönem Osmanlı Mimarisinde Memlük Etkileri," 85–8; S. Çetintaş, *Türk Mimari Anıtları: Osmanlı Devri, Bursa'da Murad I ve Bayezid I Binaları*. (Turkish Works of Architecture: The Ottoman Period, The Buildings of Murad I and Bayezid I) (Istanbul: Milli Eğitim Basımevi, 1952), 28 which attributes the structure to Turkish builders.
57 R. Ousterhout, "In Pursuit of the Exotic Orient," *Journal of Aesthetic Education* 35.4 (2001): 113–18, Book Review of *Venice and the East: The Impact of the Islamic World on Venetian Architecture 1100–1500*, ed. Deborah Howard (New Haven: Yale University Press, 2000), 113–18.
58 Çağaptay, "Frontierscape," 175. A strong Genoese presence also existed in Pera, as well as in the Foça-Chios region. G. Necipoğlu, "Visual Cosmopolitanism and Creative Translation: Artistic Conversations with Renaissance Italy in Mehmed II's Constantinople," *Muqarnas* 29 (2012): 3, footnotes 13 and 119. For Murad I's campaigns in the Balkans, and his alliance with the Genoese against the Venetians, see İnalcık, "Murad I," 31: 159–62.
59 Çağaptay, ibid., E. Hoffman, "Pathways of Portability: Islamic and Christian Interchange from the Tenth to the Twelfth Century," *Art History* 24 (2001): 17–50; J. Elsner, "Significant Details: Systems, Certainties and the Art Historian as Detective," *Antiquity* 64 (1990): 950–2; D. Kotoula, "Maniera Cypria and Thirteenth Century Icon Production on the Island of Cyprus: A Critical Approach," *Byzantine and Modern Greek Studies* 28 (2004): 89–100.
60 Çağaptay, ibid., 176. I borrow heavily from J. R. Sackett, "Style and Ethnicity in Archaeology: The Case of Isochretism," in *The Uses of Style in Archaeology*, eds. M. W. Conkey and C. A Hastorf (Cambridge: Cambridge University Press, 1989), 32–43.
61 Bayezid built two other T-type buildings in Bursa, one named after the Kazeruni skeikh of Persian origins and another one in Yıldırım, a subdistrict of Bursa. He also commissioned the construction of other inverted-T-type buildings in Balıkesir, Alaşehir and Edirne.
62 Yürekli, "Architectural Patronage and the Rise of Ottomans," 750 reminds us of how this style of arch is also noted in the Jalayirid and Timurid manuscripts executed in Herat, Baghdad, and Tabriz.
63 A. Kuran, *The Mosque in Early Ottoman Architecture*, 77–8.

64 Ayverdi, *Osmanlı Mimarisinin*, 419–40; Necipoğlu, "Anatolia and the Ottoman Legacy," 150–3; Necipoğlu, *The Age of Sinan*, 77–80; Yürekli, "Architectural Patronage and the Rise of Ottomans," 739–41; Blessing, "Seljuk Past and Timurid Present," 225–8.
65 Necipoğlu, *The Age of Sinan*, 50.
66 Ibid., 60. Edirne offers interesting cases of architectural statements commemorating the fight against the infidels. For example, the Old Mosque, commissioned by Süleyman and Musa, Bayezid's rival sons and completed in 1414 by Mehmed I, his third son, stands as a testimony to the victory of the latter over the other two brothers. Following in his father's footsteps, in the city center of Edirne, Murad II built his own Friday mosque known as the New Mosque, also known as the Üç Şerefeli (Triple-Galleried) (1438–47), he had vowed to finish the construction of the mosque if he returned triumphant from the battleground in Hungary. Goodwin, *History of Ottoman Architecture*, 55–7 and 77–8. For a detailed discussion on the succession strife in the Ottoman court in this period, Kastritsis, *The Sons of Bayezid*, 41–194.
67 Necipoğlu, ibid., 50.
68 Baykal, *Bursa Anıtları*, 15; Gabriel, *Une capitale turque*, 30, 43–44; Kuran, "Three Ottoman Capitals," 115.
69 Wittek, *Rise of the Ottoman Empire*, 14. Chapter 2, note 77.
70 I follow the translation by Ayverdi, *Osmanlı Mimarisinin*, 59; herein a full transcription is provided as well. Lowry, *Nature of the Early Ottoman*, 33–41, especially 37; plate 1 reviews the readings by Ayverdi idem, and Wittek, *Rise of the Ottoman Empire*, 14. Recently, Yılmaz, *Caliphate Redefined*, 104, footnote 24 offers a slightly different reading.
71 The term has been used interchangeably: *gazi* meant the holy warrior and *gaza* stood for the holy war. For a discussion on the epigraphic content and style, as well as the use of the word *gazi* in the other principalities, see Lowry, *Nature of the Early Ottoman*, 33–44.
72 Kafadar, *Between Two Worlds*, 1–5.
73 For a review of the earlier scholarship and its review, see Kafadar, ibid., 47–59.
74 Kafadar, ibid., 80; Lowry, *Nature of the Early Ottoman*, 19–20, 25.
75 Kafadar, ibid.
76 See Yılmaz, *Caliphate Redefined*, 105–6 for a discussion and further bibliography on how the contemporaneous principality rulers, such as the Menteshid, used similar titles and their associated meanings around the time of the dissolution of the Mongol–Ilkhanid power. For the early Ottoman coins, see Artuk, "Early Ottoman Coins," 457–63.

77 Eyice, "Bursa'da Osman ve Orhan Türbeleri," 147, see also Chapter 2, notes 83–87 and 146–48 in this book.
78 Ibid., Evliya Çelebi, *Seyahatnâme*, 2: 10. For further discussion, Chapter 2, notes 78–87 in this book.
79 A. D. Mordtmann, *Anatolien, Skizzen und Reisebriefe aus Kleinasien 1850–1859* (Hannover: H. Lafaire, 1925), 351.
80 The patron of the mosque was for some time a matter of debate; Gabriel, *Une capitale turque*, 45, claims that it was built by Orhan, noting the inscription above the east door as well as the misorientation of the mosque—the orientation to Mecca is 34° south-southwest—that follows the ones built in the reign of Orhan. However, later published *waqf* registration made clear that the mosque was endowed by Murad I; see Ayverdi, *Osmanlı Mimarisinin*, 267. For the endowment deed, see Gökbilgin, "Murad I. Tesisleri," 217–34.
81 Gabriel, *Une capitale turque*, 45–6.
82 Ayverdi, *Osmanlı Mimarisinin*, 274.
83 Baykal, *Bursa ve Anıtları*, 55.
84 R. Anhegger, "Beiträge zur Frühosmanischen Baugeschichte," in *Zeki Velidi Togan Armağanı/Symbolae in honorem Zeki Velidi Togan* (Istanbul: Maarif Basımevi, 1950), 301–30; S. H. Eldem, "Bursa'da Şehadet Camii Konusunda bir Araştırma." (A Research on Şehadet Camii) *Türk Sanatı Tarihi Araştırma ve İncelemeleri* I (1963): 313–26.; Gabriel, *Une capitale turque*, 45–6; see Ayverdi, *Osmanlı Mimarisinin*, 267–74 for a lengthy discussion on the plan and restitution attempts.
85 Eyice, "Bursa'da Osman ve Orhan Gazi Türbeleri," 145 and footnote 71.
86 Pralong and Grélois, "Tombeau d'Orcan à Brousse," 138–9.
87 Ibid., 139 and figure 74.
88 This drawing is in the maps and prints collection of the National Museum of Fine Art. Another view drawn from Pınarbaşı, in the collections of the same museum, includes the view of the mosque from a different angle and shows the same construction details, but shows only one dome. The second dome is overshadowed by cypress trees. The photos are by Abdullah Frères.
89 Ayverdi, *Osmanlı Mimarisinin* 1: 294; Aşıkpaşazade, *Osmanoğullarının Tarihi*, 61. Neşri, *Kitab-ı Cihan-Nüma* 1: 203 and 1: 309; Hoca Sadeddin Efendi, *Tacü't-tevarih*. Edited by İ. Parmaksızoğlu (Ankara: Kültür Bakanlığı Yayınları, 1974–9), 1: 81; *Oruç Beğ Tarihi*, 44.
90 For an introduction to this period, see Kastritsis, *The Sons of Bayezid*, 1–12, Besides chasing the image of Alexander, Bayezid I also sought to earn the caliphal title by demanding that the Abbasids confer the title to him. P. Wittek, "Le Sultan de Rûm," *Annuaire de l'Institute Philologie et d'Histoire Orientales*

et Slaves 6 (1938): 381–2. For further references on Alexander the Great, see Necipoğlu, "Visual Cosmopolitanism and Creative Translation," 3–8.

91 For the examples in the context of Edirne, see the earlier discussion. For the military campaigns under Bayezid I and his victory over the Crusader armies, see K. Kreiser, "Zur Kulturgeschichte der Osmanischen Moschee," in *Türkische Kunst und Kultur aus osmanischer Zeit*, ed. H.-C. von Bothmer, B. Kellner-Heinkele and D. Rohwedder, 2 Vols. (Recklinghausen: Aurel Bongers, 1985), 75–86.

92 Ayverdi, *Osmanlı Mimarisinin*, 419–40; Necipoğlu, "Anatolia and the Ottoman Legacy," 150–3; Necipoğlu, *The Age of Sinan*, 77–80; Yürekli, "Architectural Patronage and the Rise of Ottomans," 739–41.

93 Ayverdi, ibid., 410–11; Aslanapa, *Yüzyıllar Boyunca Türk Sanatı (14. Yüzyıl)* (Turkish Art Through the Ages, 14th Century) (Ankara: Milli Eğitim Bakanlığı, 1977), 68; Meinecke, *Die Mamlukische Architektur*, I: 140–1. The name of the artist is Abd al-Aziz ibn al-Daqqi al-Ayntabi.

94 Tanman, "Erken Osmanlı Mimarisinde Memlük Etkileri," 82–9.

95 M. S. Graves, "The Lamp of Paradox," *Word & Image* 34.3 (2018): 237–50, especially 244–6.

96 For a discussion of earlier examples, see J. Bloom, "On the Transmission of Designs in Islamic Architecture." *Muqarnas* 10 (1993): 21–8. For contextualizing the Ayasoluk Mosque within the realm of the prototypes of the Grand Mosque of Damascus, see O. Aslanapa, *Turkish Art and Architecture* (New York: Praeger, 1971), 102–3; Tanman, "Mamluk Influences," 292–3. Two further builders bearing the same family name and originating from Damascus worked on the Ottoman building projects: the *Madrasa* of Mehmed I in Merzifon and the Mosque of Bayezid Paşa in Amasya, as discussed by idem, 288.

97 Redford, "Alaeddin Mosque in Konya and the Antique," 57–74, especially 59 and 70. Several examples dating to the Rum Seljuk period are attributed to Syrian builders, such as the Alanya, Antalya, and Sinop castles, the Sultan Han near Aksaray, as well as the Alaeddin Mosque in Konya. Tanman, "Mamluk Influences," 290. Circulation of Mamluk artisans in Ottoman territory was especially evident before 1453. Even much later, the Süleymaniye *defters* show collaboration among multiethnic builders, Necipoğlu, *The Age of Sinan*, 564.

98 Meinecke, *Die Mamlukische Architektur*, I: 138.

99 Tanman, "Mamluk Influences," 284.

100 Ayverdi, *Osmanlı Mimarisinin*, 419–40; Necipoğlu, "Anatolia and the Ottoman Legacy," 153; Necipoğlu, *The Age of Sinan*, 79; Tanman, "Erken Osmanlı Mimarisinde Memlük Etkileri," 82–9; Tanman, "Mamluk Influences," 292–9. More recently, on Bayezid I's aspirations as a builder, Yürekli, "Architectural Patronage and the Rise of Ottomans," 739–41.

101 Trigleia was unfortified, open to both sea and land attacks, and other Bithynian towns and cities fell—Prousa in 1326, Nicaea in 1331. It is therefore likely that the city did not remain under Byzantine control for long. Nonetheless, records suggest that the Christian community remained vital—note the conversion of the Saint Stephanos (present-day Fatih Cami) into a mosque in the year 1560-1 (Hegirah 968). For a discussion of the demographic evidence, and the Christian architectural and artistic efforts that thrived after the Ottoman conquest of Trigleia, see Çağaptay, "The Church of the Panagia Pantobasilissa," 56-7.

102 For the proliferation of monasteries on holy mountains in the ninth century, see K. Belke, "Heilige Berge Bithyniens," in *Heilige Berge und Wüsten: Byzanz und sein Umfeld. Referate auf dem 21. Internationalen Kongress für Byzantinistik*, London, 21-26. August 2006, ed. P. Soustal (Vienna: Verlag der Österreichischen Akademie der Wissenschaften), 1-14. In my "The Church of the Panagia Pantobasilissa," 48-9, I have proposed that the lengthening of the nave may have been intended to provide more space for tombs and burials, rejecting the earlier arguments by previous scholars.

103 For discussions of courtly chivalric ethos, cultural overlays, and conversions in Anatolia, see Kafadar, *Between Two Worlds*; Redford, "Byzantium and the Islamic World," 389-96, especially 390. For a discussion of intermarriages, see Bryer, "Greek Historians on the Turks," 471-93.

104 Kafadar, ibid., 19-28 discusses how the local Christians coped with the changes in the regime. For a succint reading of reuse and appropriation, see Grabar, *The Formation of Islamic Art*, 43-71; Flood, "Pillars, Palimpsests, and Princely Practices," 95-116; B. F. Flood, "The Medieval Trophy as an Art Historical Trope: Coptic and Byzantine 'Altars' in Islamic Contexts," *Muqarnas* 18 (2001): 41-72, especially 41. Flood also notes that the study of reused architectural material in Islamic contexts has been done systematically. For a detailed analysis of spolia in the Islamic context, see S. Redford, "The Seljuks of Rum and the Antique," *Muqarnas* 10 (1993): 148-56, and G. Goodwin, "The Reuse of Marble in the Eastern Mediterranean in Medieval Times," *Journal of the Royal Asiatic Society* (1977): 17-30.

105 Ousterhout, "Ethnic Identity," 57; Goodwin, *History of Ottoman Architecture*, 16-19, also notes that the second phase was built later than the convent-*masjid* of Orhan in Bursa, though the plan is older. For the rebuilding attempts by Abdülaziz, Ersoy, "Architecture and the Search for Ottoman Origins," 210.

106 For a detailed analysis of this period, see Kastritsis, *The Sons of Bayezid*, 41-63.

107 Necipoğlu, "From International Timurid to Ottoman," 136-70; Blessing, "Seljuk Past and Timurid Present," 225-8. As mentioned by Necipoğlu, *The Age*

of Sinan, 77–80, this is the case not only in Ottoman architecture but also in the architecture of other emirates, such as that of the Aydinid İsa Bey Mosque near Ayasoluk; the architect was of Damascene origin. Yürekli, "Architectural Patronage and the Rise of Ottomans," 739–51.
108 H. Bhabha, *The Location of Culture* (London, New York: Routledge), 55.

Chapter 4

1 As discussed in Chapter 3, note 1 in this book.
2 A. I. Doğan, *Osmanlı Mimarisinde Tarikat Yapıları, Tekkeler, Zaviyeler ve Benzer Nitelikteki Fütuvvet Yapıları* (Tarikat Structures, Dervish Lodges, Zaviyes and Similar Futuwwa Buildings in Ottoman Architecture) (Istanbul: Istanbul Teknik Üniversitesi Yayınevi, 1977), 55–80; these terms have been used to imply the idea of a convent. These labels are sometimes used in the same context in the Ottoman chronicles, such as Aşıkpaşazade referring to buildings commissioned by Orhan, see Aşıkpaşazade, *Osmanoğullarının Tarihi Tevârih-i Al'i Osman*, ed. K. Yavuz and Y. Saraç (Istanbul: Gökkubbe Yayınevi, 2007), chapter 1.
3 Eyice, "İlk Osmanlı Devrinin Dini – İçtimai," 23–4; Pancaroğlu, "Devotion, Hospitality," 60–72.
4 Doğan, *Osmanlı Mimarisinde Tarikat*, 179–282. For the *mahfil* or *majlis* discussion, see Pancaroğlu, ibid., 69.
5 A. Y. Ocak, "Zaviyeler, Dini, Sosyal ve Kültürel Tarih Açısından Bir Deneme (Zaviyes: Religious, Social, Cultural and Historical Review)," *Vakıflar Dergisi* 12 (1978): 247–69, for further discussion on Kazeruni, 260.
6 G. G. Arnakis, "The Futuwwa Traditions in the Ottoman Empire Akhis, Dervishes and Craftsmen," *The Journal of Near Eastern Studies* 12.4 (1953): 24. For a recent view into the dynamics of the social and male stratifications and a lens into the world of *ahis*, see R. Goshgarian, "Beyond the Social and the Spiritual: Redefining the Urban Confraternities of Late Medieval Anatolia" (Unpublished PhD dissertation, Harvard University, 2008). R. Goshgarian, "Opening and Closing: Coexistence and Competition in Associations Based on Futuwwa in Late Medieval Anatolian Cities," *British Journal of Middle Eastern Studies* 40.1 (2013): 36–52; R. Goshgarian, "Social Graces and Urban Spaces: Brotherhood and the Ambiguities of Masculinity and Religious Practice in Late Medieval Anatolia," in *Architecture and Landscape in Medieval Anatolia, 1100–1500*, eds. P. Blessing, and R. Goshgarian (Edinburgh: Edinburgh University Press, 2017), 114–31, discussing the *ahis* and their social and commercial makeup; Selçuk, "State and Society in the Marketplace," and İ. Selçuk,

"Suggestions on the Social Meaning and Functions of the *Akhi* Communities and Their Hospices in Medieval Anatolia," in *Architecture and Landscape in Medieval Anatolia, 1100–1500*, eds. P. Blessing, and R. Goshgarian (Edinburgh: Edinburgh University Press, 2017), 955–113, on state-sponsored economic life and *ahis*; and Kitapçı Bayrı, *Warriors, Martyrs, and Dervishes*, 28–36, on Turkish-Muslim frontier narratives, identity, and geography.

7   Ibid.
8   Goshgarian, "Beyond the Social," 22 and idem, "Opening and Closing," 38.
9   Arnakis, "Futuwwa Traditions," 234; Selçuk, "Suggestions on the Social Meaning," 107–8.
10 Ocak, "Ahi (akhī)," in *EI3*: Consulted online on October 12, 2018. First published online: 2013; Selçuk, "Suggestions on the Social Meaning," 95–8.
11 As cited in R. E. Dunn, *The Adventures of Ibn Battuta: A Muslim Traveler of the 14th Century* (Berkeley: University of California Press, 1986), 145–6.
12 Ibid.
13 Wolper, *Cities and Saints*, 20–3; Yürekli, *Architecture and Hagiography*, 107–8.
14 Ibid., 44–55; for a broader reading along the theme of shared physical space used by the *ahis* and sufis, see Pancaroğlu, "Devotion, Hospitality," 54 and 62. For a recent overview of the *ahis* as active agents of commercial life, see Selçuk, "Suggestions on the Social Meaning," 95–113. For a similar setup among the late medieval Armenian confraternities, see Goshgarian, "Social Graces and Urban Places," 114–31.
15 Selçuk, "Suggestions on the Social Meaning," 97–100 and 108.
16 As discussed by Z. Oğuz, "Multifunctional Buildings of the T-Type," 3. Eyice, "Osmanlı Mimarisinin İlk Devrinin Bir Camii Tipi Hakkında," 88; Kuran, *The Mosque in Early Ottoman Architecture*, 25 argues that the development of this building type should be examined by focusing only on its central hall with the *mihrab* niche within the transformation of the Ottoman mosque.
17 Doğan, *Osmanlı Mimarisinde Tarikat*, 179–282.
18 Chapter 3, footnote 1 Çetintaş, *Türk Mimari Anıtları*, 6, 10–11, 15–16, 19–27, and 52–4; S. Çetintaş, *Yeşil Cami ve Benzerleri Cami Değildir* (The Green Mosque and the Like are not Mosques) (Istanbul: Maarif Basımevi, 1958), 1–26.
19 Ayverdi, Osmanlı Mimarisinin, 83 critiques for not fully understanding the "milli zihniyet ve vekâar" (trans. national pride and ideology) in lieu of Çetintaş, *Yeşil Cami ve Benzerleri*, 1–4.
20 For a review of scholarship on the matter, see Oğuz, "Multifunctional Buildings of the T-Type," 1–3 and *passim*., Çağaptay, "Visualizing the Cultural Transition," Chapter 4; idem, "From Bithynia to Thrakia," 433–5; idem, "Frontierscape," 158, footnotes 29–36.

21 Ayverdi, *Osmanlı Mimarisinin*, 76 discusses a seventeenth-century date; Çetintaş, *Türk Mimari Anıtları*, 19 claims an eighteenth-century date; Gabriel, *Une capitale turque*, 47, argues for a nineteenth-century date, for minaret addition. Emir, *Erken Osmanlı Mimarlığında*, 35–44, for example, claims on the basis of textual evidence and structural analysis that the edifice was built to function as a convent and regained the status of a mosque in the second half of the sixteenth century when a minaret was added. For an overview on the issue, see A. O. Uysal, "Zaviyeli Camilerde Minare Problemi" (The Problem of a Minaret in Zawiya Mosques), *Türk Etnografya Dergisi* 20 (1997): 48. For the problem of misaligned mihrabs in early Ottoman mosques, see F. E. Barmore, "Turkish Mosque Orientation and the Secular Variation of the Magnetic Declination," *Journal of Near Eastern Studies* 44.2 (1985): 81, 98.

22 Gabriel, *Une capitale turque*, 56; Uysal, "Zaviyeli Camilerde Minare Problemi," 49; S. Salgırlı, "Soap Bars and Silk Cocoons: Microecologies of Connectivity in Late Medieval Mediterranean Architecture," *Journal of Early Modern History* 23 (2019), 138, footnote 36 for a discussion on how the minaret would be an afterthought to the design.

23 Ayverdi, *Osmanlı Mimarisinin*, 252; Çetintaş, *Türk Mimari Anıtları*, 6.

24 Necipoğlu, *The Age of Sinan*, 49–50.

25 S. Eyice, "Osmanlı Türk Mimarisinin İlk Devrinin Bir Cami Tipi Hakkında." (On an Early Ottoman-Turkish Mosque Type). Paper Presented at *Milletlerarası I. Türk Sanatları Kongresi Tebliğleri, 19-24 Ekim 1959* (Ankara: Kültür Bakanlığı Yayınevi, 1962), 187–8, 188; S. Eyice, "İlk Osmanlı Devrinin Dini – İçtimai Bir Müessesesi: Zaviyeler ve Zaviyeli Camiler." (A Social and Religious Organization of the Early Ottoman Era: Zaviyes and Zaviye Mosques), *Istanbul Üniversitesi İktisat Fakültesi Mecmuası* 23.1–2 (1963): 1–80, Kuran, *The Mosque in Early Ottoman Architecture*, 84, 88–9.

26 Eyice, "İlk Osmanlı Devrinin Dini – İçtimai," 1–80; Kuran, *The Mosque in Early Ottoman Architecture*, 104–7. H. Saladin, *Manuel d'art musulman, l'architecture I* (Paris: Librairie Alphonse Picard, 1907), 486, identified the Mamluk buildings in Egypt as originating from the Central Asian house scheme. E. Diez, *Die Kunst der islamischen Völker* (Berlin: Neubabelsberg, 1915), 129, on the other hand, gave the credit to the domestic architecture in Byzantine architecture.

27 See Kuran, *The Mosque in Early Ottoman Architecture*, 104–7 for further discussion on the transformation of the plan and for a revised dating discussion. For a recent revision on the datings of these buildings and their cultural contexts, see P. Blessing, *Rebuilding Anatolia after the Mongol Conquest: Islamic Architecture in the Lands of Rum 1240–1330* (Farnham, Surrey, UK and

Burlington, VT, USA: Ashgate, 2014), for the former, 140–2 and 104–15 for the latter.

28 M. Van Berchem, "Origine de la madrasah," *Mèmoires de la Mission archéologiques française de Caire* 19.2 (1894): 254–69.

29 Ibid., 254–69; R. Hillenbrand, "Madrasa, III. Architecture," *The Encyclopaedia of Islam* TWO, 5 (1990): 1136.

30 R. Bulliett, *The Patricians of Nishapur: A Study of Medieval Islamic Social History* (Cambridge, MA: Harvard University Press, 1972), 72–5.

31 Emir, *Erken Osmanlı Mimarlığında*, 3–5 and 13; P. R. Lindner, "How Mongol were the Early Ottomans?" in *The Mongol Empire and Its Legacy*, ed. R. Amitai-Preiss and D. O. Morgan (Leiden, Boston: Brill, 1999), 282–9. Using numismatic evidence from Söğüt, Lidner argues that the early Ottomans were subordinate to the Mongol–Ilkhanids and that scholars of the early twentieth century working on the origins of the Ottomans, such as Fuad Köprülü, suffered from horror Tartarorum. This scholarly impasse has been torn down by Sedat Emir who ascribes a sole Mongol-Ilkhanid origins for the plan of an inverted-T. For a review of Emir's findings, Wolper, Cities and Saints, 104–6.

32 Ousterhout, "Constantinople, Bithynia," 787; Lindner, *Nomads and Ottomans*, 6–7; Lindner, "How Mongol were the Early Ottomans," 282–9.

33 T. Allsen, *Commodity and Exchange in the Mongol Empire: A Cultural History of Islamic Textiles* (New York: Cambridge University Press, 1997), 30–45 and 95–6; idem, *Culture and Conquest in Mongol Eurasia* (Cambridge, New York: Cambridge University Press, 2001), 59–211; J. C. Y. Watt, "A Note on Artistic Exchanges in the Mongol Empire," in *The Legacy of Genghis Khan: Courtly Art and Culture in Western Asia 1256–1353*, eds. L. Komaroff and S. Carboni (New York, New Haven: MET and Yale University Press, 2002), 62–73; L. Komaroff, "The Transmission and Dissemination of a New Visual Language," in *The Legacy of Genghis Khan: Courtly Art and Culture in Western Asia 1256-1353*, eds. L. Komaroff and S. Carboni (New York, New Haven: MET and Yale University Press, 2002), 168–95.

34 Wolper, *Cities and Saints*, 4, identifies these buildings as "dervish lodges" which provided spaces for communal activities, including prayer, study, teaching, conversation with visitors, accommodation of travelers, and distributing food to the poor. For the Rum Seljuk elite surviving under the Mongol rule, ibid., 1–16; Blessing, *Rebuilding Anatolia, passim*. For a more recent reading, see Pancaroğlu, "Devotion, Hospitality," 65–70.

35 Note 31 in this chapter; Lindner, *Nomads and Ottomans*, 6–7.

36 Chapter 3, footnote 1 in this book. Pancaroğlu, "Devotion, Hospitality," 48–81; T. DaCosta Kaufmann, *Towards a Geography of Art* (Chicago and London:

The University of Chicago Press, 2004), emphasizes a focus on cross-regional networks in order to define a broader reading of cultural overlaps and move beyond narrowly defined geographical categories.

37 For a discussion on the construction practices, see Chapter 3. For an analysis of this technique and its revival in the eighteenth century, see Z. Ahunbay, "Decorative Coatings on Some Eighteenth-Century Buildings in Istanbul," in *Afife Batur'a Armağan Mimarlık ve Sanat Tarihi Yazıları*. (Essays on Architectural and Art History in Honor of Afife Batur), ed. A. Ağır, D. Mazlum and G. Cephanecigil (Istanbul: Literatür Yayınları, 2005), 205–11.

38 Çağaptay, "Visualizing the Cultural Transition," Chapters 3 and 4; Ousterhout, "Constantinople, Bithynia," 75–110; and "Ethnic Identity," 48–62; G. Necipoğlu, "Creation of a National Genius: Sinan and the Historiography of Classical Ottoman Architecture," *Muqarnas* 14 (2007): 145, idem, "Anatolia and the Ottoman Legacy," 150.

39 I base my discussion heavily on D. F. Ruggles, "The Dual Heritage of Sicilian Monuments," in *The Cambridge History of Arabic Literature: The Literature of Al-Andalus*, ed. R. Menocal, R. Scheindlin and M. Sells (Cambridge: Cambridge University Press, 2000), 373–4.

40 Ousterhout, "Ethnic Identity," 58–62; Tunay, "Masonry of the Late Byzantine and Early Ottoman Periods," 79, and others.

41 Ousterhout, *Master Builders*, 200.

42 Ibid.

43 Çağaptay, "Frontierscape," 164–6, footnotes 86–92. In Hacı Bektaş Veli's *Vilayetname* (Book of Sanctity), a semi-legendary autobiography written in the late fifteenth century, focuses on a certain Nikomedianus working for Orhan and Murad I. E. Gross, *Das Vilâjet-nâme des Haǧǧi Bektasch: Ein türkisches Derwischevangelium* (Leipzig: Türkische Bibliothek, 1927), 151–2; Ersoy, "Architecture and Late Ottoman Historical Imaginary," 144, refute this assumption that Christodoulos was the name of the builder of Murad I's convent-*masjid*, as this would likely have been fabricated later as a response to the Byzantine look of the building.

44 Necipoğlu, "Anatolia and the Ottoman Legacy," 150. These buildings bear "distinctive ground plans with clearly delineated square and rectangular units [and] are unlike the curvilinear, blending spaces of Byzantine churches."

45 "The disintegration of the prototype into its single elements, the selective transfer of these parts, and their reshuffling in the copy." R. Krautheimer, "Introduction to an Iconography of Medieval Architecture," *Journal of the Warburg and Courtauld Institutes* 5 (1942): 14.

46 T. Mathews, and A.-C. Daskalakis Mathews, "Islamic Style Mansions in Byzantine Cappadocia and the Development of the Inverted-T-Plan," *Journal of the Society of Architectural Historians* 56.3 (1997): 305–6, and figure 19. Another comparable complex is the Kasr al-Jiss (Gypsum Palace) of the mid-ninth century near Samarra.

47 Fustat's T-types were examined by G. T. Scanlon, "Preliminary Report: Excavations at Fustat," *Journal of the American Research Center in Egypt* 4 (1965): 7–30; G. T. Scanlon and W. B. Kubiak, "Fusṭāṭ Expedition Preliminary Report 1971, Part I," *Journal of the American Research Center in Egypt* 16 (1979): 110; Mathews and Daskalakis-Mathews, ibid., 306–8, fig. 21.

48 Mathews and Daskalakis-Mathews, "Islamic-Style Mansions in Byzantine Cappadocia," 304–9. Ali Bahgat Bey and A. Gabriel, *Les fouilles d'al-Foustat et les origins de la maison arabe en Égypte* (Paris: E. de Boccard, 1921), introduction.

49 For the contextualization of the plan, G. Necipoğlu, "An Outline of Shifting Paradigms in the Palatial Architecture of the Pre-Modern Islamic World," *Ars Orientalis* 23 (1993): 5 and 10, footnote 34; Shahid, "Lakhmids," *The Encyclopaedia of Islam,* TWO, 4: 634–40.

50 The translation is from Mathews and Daskalakis-Mathews, "Islamic-Style Mansions in Byzantine Cappadocia," 307.

51 Ibid. For further discussion, *Tabbaa, Constructions of Power and Piety,* 86–8.

52 Mathews and Daskalakis-Mathews, "Islamic-Style Mansions in Byzantine Cappadocia," 306–7, fig. 20.

53 The most common hall layout include the Fatimid shrines in Cairo, such as that of al-Juyushi (1085) and Sayyida Ruqayya (1133), which both modify the *majlis* plan. For an overview, N. Rabbat, "Mamluk Throne Halls: *Qubba* or *Iwān*?" *Ars Orientalis* 23 (1993): 204–6.

54 Examples are the Ayyubid Palace in the Aleppo Castle, residential quarters at Shawbak and Karak. Tabbaa, "Defending Ayyubid Aleppo," 176–82.

55 For earlier reiterations, see S. Hazeem, "The Development of the Cairene *qāʿa*: Some Considerations," *Annales Islamologiques* 23 (1987): 31–53; A. I. Laila, "Residential Architecture in Mamluk Cairo," *Muqarnas* 2 (1984): 47–59, for later Mamluk examples, N. Rabbat, "Mamluk Throne Halls," 204–6; idem, *Mamluk History Through Architecture: Monuments, Culture and Politics in Medieval Egypt and Syria* (London: I. B. Tauris, 2010), 131.

56 Rabbat, "Mamluk Throne Halls," 204–6; idem, *Mamluk History Through Architecture,* 131.

57 A. Lézine, "Les salles nobles des palais mamelouks," *Annales islamologiques* 10 (1972): 63–148; Rabbat, *Mamluk Architecture,* 131; Pancaroğlu, "Devotion, Hospitality," 69.

58 Mathews and Daskalakis-Mathews, "Islamic-Style Mansions," 304–9. R. Ousterhout, *A Byzantine Settlement at Çanlı Kilise* (Washington D.C.: Dumbarton Oaks Research Library and Collection, 2006), 147–9, suggests that architectural borrowing came out of the shared Roman past among the elite.

59 Mathews and Daskalakis-Mathews, ibid., 304–9; Ousterhout, "Secular Architecture," *passim*; idem, *A Byzantine Settlement*, 147–9 and 193–200; idem, *A Byzantine Settlement*, 147–9; V. Kalas, "Cappadocia's Rock-Cut Courtyard Complexes: A Case Study for Domestic Architecture in Byzantium," in *Housing in Late Antiquity: From Palaces to Shops*, eds. L. Lavan, L. Özgenel, and A. C. Sarantis (Leiden, Boston: Brill, 2007), 393–414. In earlier scholarship, the inverted-T's in early Ottoman architecture are claimed to be rooted in Byzantine architecture, Wilde, *Brussa*, 10; C. Gurlitt, "Die Bauten Adrianopels," *Orientalisches Archiv* 1 (1909–1910): 51–2; E. Mamboury, *Istanbul touristique* (Istanbul: Çituri Biraderler Matbaası, 1951), 115; G. Martiny, "Zur Entwicklungsgeschichte der Osmanischen Moschee," *Ars Orientalis* 4 (1961): 107–12, 108.

60 Ousterhout, *A Byzantine Settlement*, 148, citing the late-Roman villa at Piazza Armerina.

61 D. Katz, "A Changing Mosaic: Multicultural Exchanges in the Norman Palaces of Twelfth-Century Sicily," Unpublished PhD dissertation, University of Toronto, 2016, 189–90 and 245–7.

62 Emir, *Erken Osmanlı Mimarlığında*, 12–14 discusses the now-lost small water font at the convent-*masjid* of Orhan.

63 G. Kubler, *The Shape of Time: Remarks on the History of Things* (New Haven: Yale University Press, 1982), 63; A. Lermer, and A. Shalem, *After One Hundred Years: The 1910 Exhibition "Meisterwerke Muhammedanischer Kunst Reconsidered"* (Leiden, Boston: Brill, 2010), 7.

64 My summation of Kubler is based on, P. M. Lee, "'Ultramoderne': Or, How George Kubler Stole the Time in Sixties Art," *Grey Room* 2 (2001): 46–50; P. M. Lee, *Chronophobia: On Time in the Arts of the 1960s* (Cambridge: MIT Press, 2004), especially 253–6.

Chapter 5

1 My model of economic development on the basis of the value of the land where the value of the goods produced there diminish according to the distance from the center conforms to the model suggested by J. H. von Thünen, *Der isolierte Staat in Beziehung auf Landwirtschaft und Nationalökonomie*. (Hamburg:

F. Perthes, 1826), as also applied to the Hispano-Umayyad Spain, Ruggles, *Gardens, Landscape and Vision*, 11.

2 S. Çağaptay, "Bilecik," in *The Encyclopaedia of Islam*, THREE, ed. Kate Fleet, Gudrun Krämer, Denis Matringe, John Nawas and Everett Rowson. Consulted online July 2, 2019. First published online: 2019, 8–9.

3 Aşıkpaşazade, *Osmanoğulları'nın Tarihi*, 56–67.

4 This term was coined by Spiro Kostof in his unpublished 1976 lectures at Columbia University, "Seat of Peter: The Medievalizing of Rome." The term describes a gradual definition of urban fabric through a variety of socioeconomic, political, and other factors, including city planning or regulation. For remarks on this lecture, see the introduction, Z. Çelik, D. Favro and R. Ingersoll, ed. *Streets: Critical Perspectives on Public Space* (Berkeley: University of California Press, 1994), 1–5.

5 As discussed by Lowry, *Ottoman Bursa*, 47–8; Lubenau, *Beschreibung der Reisen*, III: 77–97.

6 Barkan and Meriçli, *Hüdavendigar Livası Tahrir Defterleri*, 252 discuss that yellow lentils were produced in Bithynia during the fifteenth century.

7 Laiou, "The Agrarian Economy Thirteenth-Fifteenth Centuries," in *The Economic History of Byzantium*, ed. A. E. Laiou (Washington D.C.: Dumbarton Oaks Research Collection and Library, 2002), 311–75, especially 321 and Pachymeres, *Relations historiques*, 293; C. Morrisson and J. C. Cheynet, "Prices and Wages in the Byzantine World," in *The Economic History of Byzantium*, ed. A. E. Laiou (Washington D.C.: Dumbarton Oaks Research Collection and Library, 2002), 815–78. On page 836, the authors discuss that the pricing of Bithynian (produced in Trigleia) wine was even higher than the rest of the wine types, costing 6 to 7/10 hyperpyra for 10 measures. The price inflation for wine was greater even than for wheat. For garden and landscape-related vocabulary in the Ottoman archival documents, N. Trepanier, "Harvesting Garden Semantics in late Medieval Anatolia," in *Architecture and Landscape in Medieval Anatolia, 1100–1500*, eds. P. Blessing and R. Goshgarian (Edinburgh: Edinburgh University Press, 2017), 187–99.

8 J. Koder, *Gemüse in Byzanz: Die Frischgemüseversorgung Konstantinopels im Licht der Geoponika* (Vienna: Fassbaender, 1993), *passim* and idem, "Fresh Vegetables for the Capital," in *Constantinople and Its Hinterland*, ed. C. Mango, G. Dagron and G. Greatrex (Aldershot: Ashgate, 1995), 49–56. Despite the small urban garden plots emerging in Constantinople, the lettuce from the Mount was praised and sought by the capital, J. Darrouzès, *Epistoliers byzantins du Xe siècle* (Paris, 1960), 324, 328 and 329; Lefort, "Les communications entre Constantinople et a Bithynie," in *Constantinople and Its Hinterland*, ed.

C. Mango and G. Dagron (Aldershot: Ashgate, 1995), 207–18; Dagron, "The Urban Economy," 393–461.

9 P. Tafur, *Pero Tafur Travels and Adventures, 1435–1439*, trans. M. Letts (Piscataway, NJ: Gorgias Press, 2007), 149; corroborating evidence also comes from Schlemmer, *Johannes Schiltberger: Als Sklave*, 34 and 40 and Broquière, *The Voyage d'outremer*, 131–5, as discussed in detail by Lowry, *Ottoman Bursa*, 9, 16, and 40–2.

10 Evliya Çelebi, *Seyahatnâme*, 2: 3–5.

11 Wheler, *A Journey into Greece*, 214. Other valuable sources on the trees, especially mulberry, is Sestini, *Voyage dans la Grèce asiatique*: 169, 183–6. For an analysis of the travelers' accounts and Evliya Çelebi's interpretations, Lowry, *Ottoman Bursa*, 39–70.

12 For an inspirational model, see Cordoba functioning as an urban center in the Andalusian landscape, see Ruggles, *Gardens, Landscape and Vision*, 10–11.

13 For a similar tension, see Kafescioğlu, *Constantinopolis/Istanbul*, 2.

14 Lubenau, *Beschreibung der Reisen*, III: 77–8.

15 Ubicini, *La Turquie actuelle*, 43–63.

16 İsmail Beliğ (Bursevi), *Güldeste-i riyâz-ı irfan ve vefayât-ı dânişverân-ı nâdiredan* (Bursa: Hüdavendigâr Vilâyeti Matbaası, 1302=1884–1885), 212–13.

17 Ayverdi, *Osmanlı Mimarisinin*, 102. For a discussion on its surroundings and its features, Evliya Çelebi, *Seyahatnâme*, 2: 48–50.

18 Hasluck, *Christianity and Islam*, I: 230.

19 For a survey of the travelers' accounts on the description of Abdal Murad and his complex and its transformation, see Lowry, *Ottoman Bursa*, 85–98.

20 As discussed in Chapter 3.

21 Crane, "Ottoman Sultan's Mosques," in the *Ottoman City and Its Parts*, ed. I. Bierman et al. (New Rochelle, NY: A. D. Caratzas, 1991), 173–243.

22 Wolper, *Cities and Saints*, 42–72; Blessing, "Urban Space Beyond Walls," 25–43.

23 Boykov, "The T-shaped Zaviye/İmarets of Edirne," 33–4.

24 Ibid.

25 Necipoğlu, *The Age of Sinan*, 77.

26 Kafescioğlu, *Constantinopolis/Istanbul*, 79, Çağaptay, "Prousa/Bursa," 68, footnote, 91.

27 Necipoğlu, *The Age of Sinan*, 77. The *külliye* established by Orhan in the lower city is exceptional in this case, as the body of Orhan was interred in the upper city.

28 Barkan, "İstila Devirlerinin Kolonizatör Türk Dervişleri ve Zaviyeler," (Turkish Dervishes and Lodges in the Age of Raids), *Vakıflar Dergisi* 2 (1942): 279–365.

29 Aflaki, *Manaqib al-'Arifin: Les saints des derviches tourneurs*. Edited and Translated by C. Huart. 2 Vols. (Paris: E. Leroux, 1918–1920), 208.

30 Lowry, *Nature of the Early Ottoman*, 82. For earlier scholarship on the matter, see Tak, "Diplomatik Bilimi," 185, ft. 740.
31 See H. Lowry, "Random Musings on the Origins of Ottoman Charity: From Mekece to Bursa, Iznik and Beyond," in *Feeding People, Feeding Power: Imarets in the Ottoman Empire*, ed. N. Ergin, C. K. Neumann, and A. Singer (Istanbul: Eren, 2007), 71–2, for the Covel citation, 77.
32 Schlemmer, *Johannes Schiltberger: Als Sklave*, 118.
33 On the aspect of alliances, see Kafadar, *Between Two Worlds*, 122–38.
34 A more complex ideological route has been established between the imperial mausolea and mosques in Ottoman Istanbul, Necipoğlu, "Dynastic Imprint on the Cityscape: The Collective Message of Imperial Funerary Mosque Complexes in Istanbul," 23–36 and idem, *The Age of Sinan*, 79–82.
35 Tak, "Diplomatik Bilimi," 181 and 185. There are four endowment deed documents associated with the reign of Orhan: the first one is the original one dated to 1324 and is written in Persian, there are two other copies written in Arabic and dated to 1359-60, and the last one is undated. The one dated to 1359-60 is published by Hüseyin Hüsameddin, "Orhan Bey'in Vakfiyesi," 284–301, especially 286–90; Hızlı, "Bursa'da Selâtîn İmaretleri," 33–62. For a discussion on the 1324 endowment deed, see I. H. Uzunçarşılı, "Gazi Orhan Bey Vakfiyesi," (The Endowment Deed of Orhan) *Belleten* 19, no. 5 (1941): 277–88; Gökbilgin, *Osmanlı Müesseseleri Teşkilatı ve Medeniyeti Tarihine Genel Bakış* (A General View into the History of the Organization of the Ottoman Institutions and Civilization) (Istanbul: Edebiyat Fakültesi Yayınları, 1977), 13; I. Beldiceanu-Steinherr, *Recherches sur les actes des règnes des sultans Osman, Orkhan et Murad I* (Monaco: Societas academicǎ romȃnǎ, 1967), 127–30; Hızlı, "Bursa'da Selâtîn İmaretleri," 35–7. For a more recent analysis, see Öcalan et al., *Bursa Vakfiyeleri*, 66–7 and Vedat Turğut, "Orhan Gazi Dönemi Vakıfları," *Orhan Gazi ve Kocaeli Tarihi Araştırmaları* 10 (2019): 1–84, especially 5–6.
36 Ayverdi, *Osmanlı Mimarisinin*, 61–89; Gabriel, *Une capitale turque*, 46–9.
37 Hüsameddin, "Orhan Bey'in Vakfiyesi," 289–90.
38 Pancaroğlu, "Devotion, Hospitality," 75–6. Note that Ayverdi, *Osmanlı Mimarisinin*, 95 discusses the imaret and the zaviye as individual buildings as part of the complex.
39 Ayverdi, *Osmanlı Mimarisinin*, 96;
40 K. Kepecioğlu, *Bursa Hamamları* (Bursa: Halkevi Yayınları, 1935), 9; Ayverdi, *Osmanlı Mimarisinin*, 111.
41 Çetintaş, *Türk Mimari Anıtları*, 25–8.
42 These two buildings partially survived until the mid-1930s. Ayverdi, *Osmanlı Mimarisinin*, 94.

43 Ayverdi, *Osmanlı Mimarisinin*, 117; the reference to the lower citadel or *aşağı hisar* was made in the inscription of the Mosque of Umur Bey, dated to the fifteenth century, as cited by Ayverdi, footnote 1.
44 Tak, "Diplomatik Bilimi," chapter 3, the endowment deed is dated to 1385–6; Hızlı, "Bursa'da Selâtîn İmaretleri," 42–6; Gökbilgin, "Murad I. Tesisleri," 217–22; Beldiceanu-Steinherr, *Recherches sur les actes des règnes des sultans*, 213–18.
45 See Z. Oğuz Kursar, "Sultans as Saintly Figures in Early Ottoman Mausolea," in *Sacred Spaces and Urban Networks*, ed. S. Yalman and H. A. Uğurlu (Istanbul: Koç Üniversitesi Yayınları, 2019), 85–6 especially footnotes, 65–8 for further bibliography and discussion on Murad I as a martyr and a holy figure. For Murad I as a holy warrior, see Yürekli, *Architecture and Hagiography*, 67–8.
46 Chapter 4, note 22 in this book for a discussion of the minaret as an afterthought in the design process. My interpretation is based on Pancaroğlu, "Devotion, Hospitality," 77, footnote 76; Gökbilgin, "Murad I. Tesisleri," 217–22; Beldicenau-Steinherr, *Recherches sur les actes des règnes des sultans*, 213–18.
47 Pancaroğlu, "Devotion, Hospitality," 77.
48 For the changes and remodelings that each underwent after the early Ottoman period, see Ayverdi, *Osmanlı Mimarisinin*, 276–87.
49 Tanman, "Erken Dönem Osmanlı Mimarisinde Memlük Etkileri," 87–8 and idem, "Mamluk Influences," 286.
50 Pancaroğlu, "Architecture, Landscape, and the Patronage," 43–5; S. Sevim, "I. Murad'ın Vakıfları ve Temlikleri," in *Sultan 1. Murad Hüdavendigar ve Dönemi* (Murad I Hüdavendigar and His Period), ed. İ. Selimoğlu (Bursa: Osmangazi Belediyesi Yayınları, 2012), 377 discusses the extent of the land as part of the endowment. I thank Dr. Eser Çalıkuşu for sharing the copy of the article with me.
51 Ocak, "Zaviyeler," 261; Oğuz Kursar, "Sultans as Saintly Figures in Early Ottoman Mausolea," 85–6; Yürekli, *Architecture and Hagiography*, 67–8 on Murad I's multiple identities in Sufi chronicles.
52 Yılmaz, *Caliphate Redefined*, 122–4.
53 The phrasing is as follows: "zaviyetü'ş-şerife ve'l-'imaretü'l latife," E. H. Ayverdi, "Yıldırım Bayezid'in Bursa Vakfiyesi ve Bir İstibdalnamesi," (Bursa Waqf Charter and A Document on Exchange of Properties) *Vakıflar Dergisi* 8 (1969): 37–46.
54 Ayverdi, *Osmanlı Mimarisinin*, 420–2; idem, "Yıldırım Bâyezid'in Bursa Vakfiyesi," 37–46; Hızlı, "Bursa'da Selâtîn İmaretleri," 46–8. The date given as 1399–1400 indicated not only the construction in the complex but also the other Bayezid-endowed buildings in the city as noted by Tak, "Diplomatik Bilimi," 185.
55 Necipoğlu, *The Age of Sinan*, 50.

56 Goodwin, *History of Ottoman Architecture*, 46–51; Aslanapa, *Osmanlı Devri Mimarisi*, 22–5.
57 P. Magdalino, "The Byzantine Aristocratic Oikos," in *The Byzantine Aristocracy, IX to XIII Centuries*, ed. M. Angold. British Archaeological Reports, International Series 22 (Oxford: British Archaeological Reports, 1984), 92–111; Kandes, Προύσα ετη αρχαιολογικα, 13–16 and 23–5.
58 For Küşteri or Şüşteri, Ayverdi, "Yıldırım Bayezid'in Bursa Vakfiyesi," 44–5. For the commemorative role of the *külliyes*, Pancaroğlu, "Architecture, Landscape, and the Patronage," 46. Overall, within the Ottoman context, the *waqf* system gave a direction to the establishment of the *külliye* and provided financial means for the development of the *külliye* and the continuity of its services. The *waqf* system was important to the development and growth of urban life. It acted as a reassurance to the Ottoman state on prospective urbanization matters.
59 Here, I subscribe to M. Trachtenberg, *Dominion of the Eye: Urbanism, Art and Power in Early Modern Florence* (Cambridge and New York: Cambridge University Press, 1997), ix–xviii.
60 Crane, "Ottoman Sultan's Mosques," 173–243; Kuran, "Three Ottoman Capitals," 114–17; Pancaroğlu, "Architecture, Landscape, and the Patronage," 43–6; Kafescioğlu, *Constantinopolis/Istanbul*, 70–2.
61 Trachtenberg, *Dominion of the Eye*; 63–71; S. Kostof, *City Shaped: Urban Patterns and Meanings Through History* (London: Thames and Hudson, 1991), 43-93.
62 Ibid.
63 D. Favro, "Meaning and Experience: Urban History from Antiquity to the Early Modern Period," *Journal of the Society of Architectural Historians* 58 (1999): 368.
64 Here I use the Lefebvrian conceptualization of the term, wherein it emphasizes multiple meanings that a building embodies, H. Lefebvre, *Production of Space*, trans. D. Nicholson-Smith (Oxford, UK, Cambridge, MA: Blackwell), 220–8.
65 J. Agnew, "Representing Space: Space, Scale and Culture in Social Science," in *Place/ Culture/ and Representation*, eds. J. Duncan and D. Ley (London: Routledge, 1993), 251–71; E. Casey, *Getting Back into Place: Toward a Renewed Understanding of the Place World* (Bloomington: Indiana University Press, 1993); Lefebvre, *Production of Space*; G. Pollock, "Beholding Art History: Vision, Place, and Power," in *Vision and Textuality*, ed. S. Melville and B. Readings (Macmillan: Imprint Palgrave, 1995), 38–66; P. Rabinow, *The Foucault*

Reader (New York, Pantheon, 1984), 239–56; J. Tagg, "Introduction/Opening," in *Grounds of Dispute: Art History, Cultural Politics and the Discursive Field*, ed. J. Tagg (Minneapolis: University of Minnesota Press, 1992), 1–39. Similar theoretical approaches applied to Islamic landscapes and urban constructs include Ruggles, *Gardens, Landscape, and Vision*, 9–11; L. Thys-Şenocak, "Yeni Valide Mosque Complex in Eminönü, Istanbul (1597–1665)," in *Women, Patronage, and Self-Representation in Islamic Societies*, ed. D. F. Ruggles (Albany: State University of New York Press, 2001), 69–89; and Kafescioğlu, *Constantinopolis/Istanbul*, 1–11.

66 Pancaroğlu, "Devotion, Hospitality," 80–1. The architect of this complex was İvaz Paşa whose design and engineering skills were praised in the inscription of the Mosque of Mehmed 1 in Dimetoka (*c.* 1420) as discussed by E. H. Ayverdi, "Dimetoka'da Sultan Çelebi Mehmet Câmii," *Vakıflar Dergisi* 3 (1957): 15.

67 For the Old Mosque in Edirne, Chapter 3, note 66 in this book. For the *Yeşil* Complex: E. H. Ayverdi, *Osmanlı Mimarisinde Çelebi ve Sultan Murad Devri. (Ottoman Architecture during the reigns of Çelebi and Sultan Murad)*, Vol. 2. (Istanbul: Istanbul Fetih Cemiyeti, 1972), 195–6. Examining the reasons behind the restoration of the Mehmed I's mosque by Abdülaziz as a means to legitimize the Ottoman dynastic myth in the nineteenth century, Chapter 3, footnote 105 in this book, as discussed more broadly by "Kafadar, *Between Two Worlds*, 95; Kastritsis, *The Sons of Bayezid*, 198; Ersoy, "Architecture and the Search for Ottoman Origins," 209–10.

68 Ayverdi, *Osmanlı Mimarisinin*, 419–40; Necipoğlu, "Anatolia and the Ottoman Legacy," 150–3; idem, "From International Timurid to Ottoman," 136–70; idem, *The Age of Sinan*, 77–80; Blessing, "Seljuk Past and Timurid Present," 225–8; Yürekli, "Architectural Patronage and the Rise of Ottomans," 739–52.

69 Ayverdi, *Osmanlı Mimarisinde Çelebi ve Sultan Murad Devri*, 298–327; Gabriel, *Une capitale turque,* 105–129. An important yet unpublished study by Richard Turnbull, "The Muradiye Complex in Bursa and the Development of the Ottoman Funerary Tradition," Unpublished PhD dissertation, New York University, 2008 was inaccessible to me.

70 I follow Kastritsis' terminology, "Ottoman Urbanism before 1453 and the Question of Early Ottoman Capital Cities," forthcoming.

71 A. Akışık, "A Complicating Narrative: Laonikos Chalkokondyles on Ottoman Fratricide," forthcoming; Kafadar, *Between Two Worlds*, 105–9 discusses the change in the political environment and the fact that the Ottoman chronicles

referring to the beginning of fratricide under Bayezid I would coincide with the end of the frontier ethos during his reign.

72 H. İnalcık, "Kanunname," *Türkiye Diyanet Vakfı İslam Ansiklopedisi* 24 (2001): 333–7. For further reading on Chalkokondyles, comparisons with his contemporaries, and the question of his audience, see Akışık, "A Complicating Narrative," forthcoming.

73 The following people were buried in the complex: in Murad II's mausoleum: Alaeddin, Orhan, Ahmet, and Şehzade Sultan (Murad II); between the convent-*masjid* and the mausoleum of Murad II: Ahmed, Şehinşah, Mehmet and Korkut, Kamer Sultan, and Fatma Sultan (sons and daughters of Bayezid II); beyond the convent-masjid: the tomb of Cem Sultan (son of Mehmed I) and the tomb of Mustafa (son of Süleyman), which included the tombs of his mother, Mahidevran, and co-prince brother Bayezid's sons, Ahmet and Orhan. Other tombs belong to imperial wives and consorts, such as Hüma Hatun of Murad II, Gülşah of Mehmed II, and Şirin of Bayezid II. The complex also had the tomb of Mehmed II's midwife.

74 This is the term used in the endowment deeds of both Bayezid I and Mehmed I's complexes in Bursa, as discussed in Kastritsis, "Ottoman Urbanism before 1453," forthcoming.

75 As discussed Chapter 1, note 5 in this book.

76 For a discussion on the identification of Edirne as the "abode of *gazis*" based on the fifteenth-century hagiographic text of *Saltukname*, S. Yerasimos, *La fondation de Constantinople et de Sainte-Sophie dans le traditions turques* (Paris: IFEA and Jean Maisonneuve, 1990), 207–10; Kafadar, Between Two Worlds, 148–9; Kastritsis, "Ottoman Urbanism before 1453," forthcoming.

77 Singer, "Enter, Riding on an Elephant," 97.

78 As discussed by Singer, ibid., 96.

79 As mentioned in the *Vilayetname*, 146 "a *tekye* (lit.*tekke*, a dervish convent) without a *bağ* (garden) and a *bağ* without water are impossible," underscoring the importance of gardens or agricultural lands surrounding buildings of religious nature. For further discussion, Trepanier, "Harvesting Garden Semantics," 187–90. For how the gardens earned sanctity via the additions of tombs in the Islamic context, see D. F. Ruggles, *Islamic Gardens and Landscapes* (University of Pennsylvania Press, 2008), 103.

80 Aşıkpaşazade, *Osmanoğullarının Tarihi*, 5; Kafadar, *Between Two Worlds*, 45–6.

81 Kafadar, ibid.; Akdağ, "Osmanlı İmparatorluğunun Kuruluş ve İnkişafı Devrinde Türkiye'nin İktisadi Vaziyeti," (Turkey's Economic Condition During the Establishment and Growth Eras of the Ottoman Empire), *Belleten* 13 (1949): 497–571. For a review of Akdağ's work by İnalcık, "Osmanlı İmparatorluğunun

Kuruluş ve İnkişafı Devrinde Türkiye'nin İktisadi Vaziyeti Üzerine bir Tetkik Münasebetiyle," (In Lieue of an Analysis of The Economic State of Turkey the Ottomans during the Formative Period), *Belleten* 15 (1951): 629-84. Akdağ, later developed the same view in the following publication, *Türkiye'nin İktisadi ve İçtimaî Tarihi (The Economic and Social History of Turkey)* (Istanbul: Cem Yayınları, 1959). For a post-İnalcık review of Akdağ's theory, Kafadar, *Between Two Worlds*, 45.

82   Repeating Laiou verbatim: "Agrarian Economy," 321: "In the fourteenth century, there was still export of wine from Bithynia, but the level of agricultural production must have fallen off very dramatically. There is evidence at the same time for relative prosperity in Turkish-occupied Anatolia, as an indication of the importance of the peace." Laiou hints at the fact that agricultural production must have fallen off considerably as well. For the development of peaceful relationships and its impact on commerce, see E. Zachariadou, "Notes sur la population de l'Asie Mineure turque au XIVe siècle," *Byzantinische Forschungen* 12 (1987): 228.

83   For caravanserais and *hans* functioning as vehicles to claim land and political legitimacy, Pancaroğlu, "Devotion, Hospitality," 52-5. İnalcık, *Ottoman Empire. Classical Age*, 146-50, on the role of *hans* and *caravanserais* in Ottoman commerce, also see Lowry, *Ottoman Bursa*, 39-70; H. Gerber, *Economy and Society in an Ottoman City, 1600-1700* (Jerusalem: Hebrew University of Jerusalem, 1988), 10-11.

84   Maritime communication followed a route from Constantinople to Kyzikos and Lopadion (via the Ryndakos River) and reached Kios, located on the south shore of the Sea of Marmara. The most important Bithynian port must be Pylai (east of Yalova) as discussed by Avramea, "Land and Sea Communications, Fourth-Fifteenth Centuries," in *The Economic History of Byzantium: From the Seventh through the Fifteenth Century*, ed. A. E. Laiou, Vol. 1 (Washington DC: Dumbarton Oaks Research Collection and Library, 2002), 57-90.

85   Çağaptay, "Visualizing the Cultural Transition," Chapter 4; R. Kaplanoğlu, *1455 Tarihli Kirmasti Defterine Göre Osmanlı Kuruluş Devri Vakıfları*. (Early Ottoman Period According to the 1455 Kirmasti Defter). (Bursa: Avrasya Etnografya Vakfı Yayınları, 2014), 31-71; Salgırlı, "Soap Bars and Silk Cocoons," 121-51.

86   Fleet, *European and Islamic Trade*, 140-1; Elisséeff, "Khan," *The Encyclopaedia of Islam* TWO, 4 (1990): 1010-11; E. Sims, "Markets and Caravanserais," in *Architecture in the Islamic World*, eds. E. Grube and G. Michell (London: Thames and Hudson, 1984), 97-111; Mandel, *I caravanserragli Turchi*; For

an overview of Rum Seljuk *hans* and caravanserais, see A. T. Yavuz, "Anadolu Selçuklu Dönemi Kervansarayları Tipolojisi," (Typology of the Anatolian Seljuk Caravanserais) *IV. Milli Selçuklu Kültür ve Medeniyeti Semineri Bildirileri, Konya* (Konya: Selçuklu Araştırma Merkezi Yayınları, 1995), 183–98; A. T. Yavuz, "Kervansaraylar," *Anadolu Selçukluları ve Beylikler Dönemi Uygarlığı Kitabı*, Vol. 2. (Ankara: Kültür ve Turizm Bakanlığı Yayınları, 2006), 435–45; Pancaroğlu, "Devotion, Hospitality," 52–6.

87   S. Faroqhi, "In Search of Ottoman History," in *New Approaches to State and Peasant in Ottoman History*, ed. H. Berktay and S. Faroqhi (London: Frank Cass, 1992), 211–41, discussing the lack of sources as it follows on pages 227–8: "scholars squeezed the last drop of information out of a few inscriptions, chronicles and occasional references in early Ottoman or Venetian documents." Travelers such as Ruy Gonzàlez de Clavijo, Bertrandon de la Broquière, and Benedetto Dei give some insight into commercial life, whereas Byzantine sources, for example Pachymeres, Kantakouzenos, Gregoras, Doukas, and Chalkokondyles, contribute little to our understanding of the economic matters of the period. Apart from those, there are also Ibn Battuta and al-'Umari, as well as the Ottoman sources, for example Ahmedi, Aşıkpaşazade, Oruç, anonymous chronicles, and Şükrullah.

88   İnalcık, *Economic and Social History*, 222.

89   Fleet, *European and Islamic Trade*, 68 and 140.

90   Vryonis, *Decline of Medieval Hellenism*, 30–42, especially 33 and footnote 164. Constantine Porphyrogenitos (*De Ceremoniis* I: 270) mentions such institutions in the region of the Sangarius, at Nicomedia, and at Pylai in Bithynia.

91   The community consisting of Genoese, Florentine, and Venetian merchants have several mentions in travelers' accounts. Kline, *The Voyage d' Outremer*, 83, for example, gives details about the living quarters of a Genoese and a Florentine acquaintance. Spanish traveler, Pero Tafur visited the city not long after in 1437 and stayed at his Genoese friend's house, *Pero Tafur Travels and Adventures*, 149.

92   B. Dei, *La cronica dall'anno 1400 all'anno 1500*. Edited by R. Barducci (Florence: F. Papafava, 1985), 133.

93   İnalcık, "Bursa: XV. Asır," 45–102 has studied and published those court records for the years 1478–80. These merchants included the Genoese Sangiacomi, Florentine Alessio, and Venetian Mariotti. The Pera-based Italian merchant, Giovanni di Francesco Maringhi, also negotiated matters between local Bursan merchants and those of Florence in 1501–02. Lowry, *Ottoman Bursa*, 24–5 provides a list of Catholic, Jewish, and Greek Orthodox tradesmen residing in Bursa, 44–5 and 64.

94 H. İnalcık, Osmanlı İdare, Sosyal ve Ekonomik Tarihiyle İlgili Belgeler: Bursa Kadı Sicillerinden Seçmeler," (Ottoman Records on Administrative, Social and Economic History: A Group of Court Records from Bursa), *Belgeler* 1988 (13): 1–91; H. İnalcık, "Osmanlı İdare, Sosyal ve Ekonomik Tarihiyle İlgili Belgeler: Bursa Kadı Sicillerinden Seçmeler." (Documents on Ottoman Administrative, Social and Economic History: Selections from Court Records in Bursa), *Belgeler* 10 (1980–1): 1–41, uses the *şeriye sicils* (religious court records) for information on the involvement of the non-Muslims in the socio-commercial life of the city. These include an Italian renting a house with a garden, several Genoese merchants involved in the slave trade, and commercial contracts signed between the members of the Latin community and the local non-Muslim community.

95 Evliya Çelebi, *Seyahatnâme*, 2: 3–5, 13–14, 17–18.

96 Ibid., 2: 13–16.

97 Ibid., Lowry, *Ottoman Bursa*, 39–70.

98 Chapter 3, note 47 in this book.

99 A print by Texier was published in the Turkish Ministry of Culture's publications on Anatolia as *Türkiye in Gravürs: Anatolia I-II*. Trémaux's photo taken in 1854, gives a better idea of the construction technique, E. Özendes, *The First Capital Bursa* (Istanbul: YEM Yayınları, 1999).

100 Özendes, *First Capital Bursa*.

101 Selçuk, "Suggestions on the Social Meaning," 102, ft. 31.

102 Kuran, *The Mosque in Early Ottoman Architecture*, 23. Ćurčić and Hadjitryphonos, *Secular Medieval Architecture*, notes a similar design principle in post-Byzantine monuments in the Aegean, such as the monastery of Saint Zoni on Samos, illustrating monastic quarters surrounding a courtyard with a church in the middle.

103 For a detailed study on the origin of the word and its usage in the Mediterranean world, see O. R. Constable, *Housing the Stranger in the Mediterranean World: Lodging, Trade, and Travel in Late Antiquity and the Middle Ages* (Cambridge, New York: Cambridge University Press, 2003). For the Bursan context of keeping a record of annual production and taxation, Kaplanoğlu, *1455 Tarihli Kirmasti Defterine Göre*, 73.

104 For the origin and use of this lodging type, see Constable, ibid., as well as chapters 7 and 8.

105 Gerber, *Economy and Society in an Ottoman City*, 48–51. For a fascinating biography of the Kapan Han built by Murad I and its commercial networks, Salgırlı, "Soap Bars and Silk Cocoons," 121–51.

106 Pancaroğlu, "Architecture, Landscape and the Patronage," 46–8. This is in contrast to what has been suggested in the context of Andalusian Spain; see Ruggles, *Gardens, Landscape and Vision*, 9.

Chapter 6

1. Gabriel, *Une capitale turque*, 209-10: "Lorsqu'on analyse les monuments de Brousse, loin d'y constater une rupture avec la tradition seldjoukide, on y recueille, au contraire, de multiples attestations de sa persistance. (C'est là que) naquit et se développa cet art dénommé ottoman qui régna sur les diverses régions de l'Anatolie occidentale et s'étendit jusqu'en Thrace."
2. Crane, "Ottoman Sultan's Mosques," 173–4.
3. Salgırlı, "Soap Bars and Silk Cocoons," 125.
4. E. Meyer, "Turquerie and Eighteenth-Century Music," *Eighteenth-Century Studies* 7.4 (1974): 474–88.
5. http://lvivgallery.org.ua/museums.
6. As eloquently discussed by Necipoğlu, "Visual Cosmopolitanism and Creative Translation," 3–4 and further bibliography.
7. Tanpınar, "Bursa'nın Daveti," in *Yaşadığım Gibi*, ed. B. Emil (Istanbul: Dergâh Yayınları, 1996), 215–16. Translation of the Tanpınar's text is by İffet Orbay, *Bursa*, as it appears on the inside of the front cover of her book.
8. As it appears on the inside of the back cover of Orbay, *Bursa*.
9. As discussed earlier, Çıtakoğlu, "Bursa/Hisar Bölgesi Mozaikleri," 1–32, Okçu, "Prusia ad Olympum Mozaikleri," figures 27–33.
10. Chapter 1, note 55 and Chapter 2, notes 155–6 in this book.
11. Selçuk, "State Meets Society," 24–5.
12. Tuna, "Social, Cultural and Economic Situation of the Jews in Bursa," 49, for a discussion on the Jewish cemetery, 46–9; with figures 146–9.
13. W. MacDonald, *The Architecture of the Roman Empire. An Introductory Study*. 2 Vols. (New Haven and London: Yale University Press), 2: 9.
14. St. Laurent, "Ottomanization and Modernization," and idem, "Léon Parvillée," 247–82.
15. Ahmed Vefik also hired Leon Parvillée, who not only restored the mausolea, as well as the Green Complex of Mehmed I, as discussed in the first chapter, but was also instrumental in bringing together the drawings, elevations of the buildings for presenting the Ottoman architectural heritage to the learned European circles through the publication of his *Architecture et décoration turques au XVe siècle*

(Paris: Ve A. Morel, 1874). Parvillée's role in the preparation of *Usul-u Mi'mari-i Osmani* or *L'architecture ottomane* commissioned by the Ottoman government on the occasion of the 1873 Vienna Exposition is also noteworthy. For a detailed discussion, Çelik, *Displaying the Orient*, 155–6 and A. Ersoy, *Architecture and the Late Ottoman Historical Imaginary*, Chapter 3.

16 For Luigi Piccinato's other urban planning and architectural design projects, focusing on the medieval city of Florence, the railway station in Naples, the stadium in Pescara, as well as road planning in Rome as discussed by F. Malusardi, *Luigi Piccinato e l'urbanistica moderna* (Rome: Officina, 1993), 110–14.

17 Piccinato, "L'esperienza del piano di Bursa," *Urbanistica* 36–7 (1962): 110–36 with a summary in English, 30–1. For the impact of Piccinato's historic preservation attempts in Bursa, Çağaptay, "Prousa to Bursa: The Reinvention of an Ottoman Capital," in *Remembering and Forgetting the Ancient City*, ed. S. Ottewill-Soulsby and J. Martínez Jiménez (Cambridge: Cambridge University Press, 2021), forthcoming.

18 St. Laurent, "Ottomanization and Modernization"; idem, "Léon Parvillée," 247–82; Çelik, *Displaying the Orient*, 96–8; Ersoy, "Architecture and the Search for Ottoman Origins," 79–102.

19 Malusardi, *Luigi Piccinato*, 110–14.

20 Piccinato, "L'esperienza," 136.

21 https://adventuresinankara.com/2015/01/13/bursa-the-neatest-city-in-turkey-youve-probably-not-thought-about-guest-post/

22 Here, I rely on D. Cosgrove, "Landscape and Landschaft," *German Historical Institution* 35 (2004): 57–71.

23 Ibid., 59.

24 Ibid., 60. As a parallel, in seventeenth-century England individual counties were described in a way that acknowledged their distinctive features while allowing them to be incorporated into a national image. K. Olwig, *Landscape, Nature and the Body Politic: From Britain's Renaissance to America's New World* (Madison: University of Wisconsin Press, 2002), 16–19.

25 A more complex ideological route has been established between the imperial mausolea and mosques in Ottoman Istanbul, Necipoğlu, "Dynastic Imprint on the Cityscape," 23–36 also Kafescioğlu, *Constantinopolis/Istanbul*, 66–74.

26 Pancaroğlu, "Architecture, Landscape and the Patronage," 46–8. Cosgrove, "Landscape and Landschaft," 62. Cosgrove's emphasis on the term "distanciated gaze" is rooted in feminist perspectives on vision, as discussed by G. Rose, *Feminism and Geography* (Minneapolis: University of Minnesota Press, 1993), 87–112. For a further discussion on Ross, D. Harris and D. F. Ruggles,

"Introduction," in *Sites Unseen: Landscape and Vision* (Pittsburgh, PA: University of Pittsburgh Press, 2007), 20–1. Based on Rose's theory, they discuss that "the geographer's gaze is male, he sees the landscape as female, and therefore mysterious and elusive."

27 P. Nora, ed., *Realms of Memory: Rethinking the French Past* (New York: Columbia University Press, 1999), 3: ix–xii.

28 Sackett, "Style and Ethnicity in Archaeology," 32–43. For a comparative case in hybrid architecture of Medieval Greece, see H. Grossman, "Syncretism Made Concrete: The Case for a Hybrid Moreote Architecture in Post-Fourth Crusade Greece," in *Archaeology in Architecture: Papers in Honor of Cecil L. Striker*, eds. D. Deliyannis and J. Emerick (Mainz: Von Zabern, 2005), 73.

29 A similar symbolic framing by the Ottomans was Mehmed II's attitude toward the Byzantine city of Constantinople. He built his palace near the ruins of a Byzantine palace, but his *külliye* (begun in 1463) was built away from the Byzantine areas. Necipoğlu, *Architecture, Ceremonial and Power*, 4–22 and Kafescioğlu, *Constantinopolis/Istanbul*, 55–60.

30 For an inspirational discussion of characters, see Salgırlı, "Soap Bars and Silk Cocoons," 138, citing from R. Kaplanoğlu, *1455 Tarihli Kırmastı Defterine*, 34 and 53.

31 Here I draw on R. C. Holub, *Crossing Borders: Reception Theory, Poststructuralism, Deconstruction* (Madison: University of Wisconsin Press, 1992), 1–10.

32 N. Bryson, "The Gaze in the Expanded Field," in *Vision and Visuality*, ed. H. Foster (Seattle: Bay Press, 1988), 87–108, especially 91–2.

33 M. Baxandall, *Painting and Experience in Fifteenth-Century Italy* (Oxford: Oxford University Press, 1986), 29–39.

34 For a selection of these photos, see Özendes, *The First Capital Bursa*.

35 Here, I use the term in an inclusive sense to refer to combination of architecture and landscape, as well as urban spaces and any environmental feature altered by human intervention. The term "cultural landscape" was coined by C. Sauer, "The Morphology of Landscape," *University of California Publications in Geography* 2 (1925): 19–54. For an analysis of Sauer's methodology and his impact on the development of the term, see D. Harris, "Postmodernization of Landscape," *Journal of Society of Architectural Historians* 58.3 (1999–2000): 434.

Bibliography

Primary Sources

Ahmedî. *İskendernâme*. Edited by Y. Akdoğan. Ankara: Türk Tarih Kurumu Basımevi, 1988.

Akropolites, George. *Chronicon Constantinopolitanum George Akropolites: The History, Introduction, Translation and Commentary*. Edited by R. Macrides. Oxford and New York: Oxford University Press, 2007.

Aşıkpaşazade. *Osmanoğullarının Tarihi Tevârih-i Al'î Osman*. Edited by K. Yavuz and Y. Saraç. Istanbul: Gökkubbe Yayınevi, 2007.

Athenaeus. *(Athénée de Naucratis) Les Deipnosophistes, livres I et II*. Edited and translated by A. M. Desrousseaux. Paris: Société d'édition "Les Belles Lettres," 1956.

Bursa Kadı Sicilleri (Bursa Court Registers).

Cedrenus. *Georgius Cedrenus [et] Ioannis Scylitzae ope*. Edited by I. Bekker. Bonn: E. Weber, 1839.

Çelebi, Evliya. *Seyahatnâme*. Volume 2. Istanbul: İkdam Matbaası, 1314=1896–1897.

Çelebi, Katib. *Cihannümâ*. Konstantiniyye: Dâr al-Ṭabâ'ah al-Âmire, 1145=1732.

Choniates, N. *Nicetae Choniatae Historia*. Edited by J. A. Van Dieten. Berlin, New York: De Gruyter, 1975.

Dio Chrysostom. *Dio Chrysostom. Discourses*. Edited and translated by J. W. Cohoon and H. Lamar Crosby. Cambridge, MA: Harvard University Press, 1939–1951.

Ephraim (Ainos). *Historia chronica*. Edited by O. Lampsides. Athens: Academy of Athens, 1984–1985.

Gregoras, Nicephori Gregorae. *Byzantina historia graece et latine*. Edited by I. Bekker. Bonn: E. Weber, 1829–1855.

Hoca Sadeddin Efendi. *Tacü't-tevarih*. Edited by İ. Parmaksızoğlu. Ankara: Kültür Bakanlığı Yayınları, 1974–1979.

İsmail, Beliğ (Bursevi). *Güldeste-i riyâz-ı irfan ve vefayât-ı dânişverân-ı nâdiredan*. Bursa: Hüdavendigâr Vilâyeti Matbaası, 1302=1884–1885.

Kritovoulos, M. *History of Mehmed the Conqueror by Kritovoulos*. Edited by C. Riggs. Princeton: Princeton University Press, 1954.

Leontios Scholasticus. *Anthologia Graeca*, IX = Anthologia Palatina. Bibliothèque nationale de France, (Par. Suppl. gr. 384), IX.

Mühimme Defteri, 28 (984/1576). Ankara: T. C. Başbakanlık Devlet Arşivi Genel Müdürlüğü.

Neşri. *Kitâb-ı Cihannümâ. Neşri Tarihi*. Edited by F. R. Unat and M. A. Köymen. Ankara: Türk Tarih Kurumu Basımevi, 1949–1957.

Oruç Bey. *Oruç Beğ Tarihi*. Edited by N. Atsız. Istanbul: Tercüman Yayınları, 1972.

Pachymeres, G. *Relations historiques*. Edited by A. Faillier and V. Laurent. 2 Vols. [Corpus fontium historiae Byzantinae Series Parisiensis 24.1–2] Paris: Les Belles Lettres, 1984.

Pliny the Younger. *Pliny's Letters*. Edited by A. Church and W. J. Brodribb. Philadelphia: Lippincott. 1879–1880.

Porphyrogenitos. *Constantine VII Porphyrogenitus, Emperor of the East, 905-959. De ceremoniis*. Paris: Les Belles Lettres, 1935.

Porphyrogenitus. *Constantine VII Porphyrogenitus, Emperor of the East, 905-959. De Administrando Imperio*. Edited by G. Moravcsik and translated by R. Jenkins. Washington, D.C.: Dumbarton Oaks Research Library and Collection, 1967.

Procopius. *Buildings*. Translated by H. B. Dewing with G. Downey, Loeb 343. Cambridge, MA: Harvard University Press, 1940.

Ruy González de Clavijo. *Embassy to Tamerlane 1403-1406*. Edited and translated by G. Le Strange. New York: Harper, 1928.

Solakzade. *Tarih-i Âl-i Osman*. Istanbul: Mahmut Bey Matbaası, 1298 = 1880–1881.

Stephen of Byzantium. *Stephani Byzantinii Ethnica*. Edited by M. Billerbeck and A. Neumann-Hartmann. [Corpus fontium historiae Byzantinae. Series Berolinensis; Volume 43.4] Boston, MA: De Gruyter, 2016.

Şükrullah. *Behcetü't Tevârîh*. Edited and translated by H. Almaz. Istanbul: Mostar Yayınevi, 2010.

Tafur, P. *Pero Tafur Travels and Adventures, 1435–1439*. Translated by M. Letts. Piscataway, NJ: Gorgias Press, 2007.

Theophanes. *Theophanes Continuatus, Ioannes Cameniata, Symeon Magister, Georgius Monachus*. Edited by I. Bekker. Bonn: E. Weber, 1838.

Theophanes. *Theophanis Chronographia*. Edited by C. de Boor. Leipzig: B.G. Teubner, 1883 and 1885.

Secondary Sources

Abu-Lughod, J. L. "The Islamic City – Historic Myth, Islamic Essence, and Contemporary Relevance." *International Journal of Middle Eastern Studies* 19 (1989): 155–76.

Acun, F. "A Portrait of the Ottoman Cities." *The Muslim World* 92, no. 3-4 (2002): 255-85.

Ådahl, K., ed. *C. G. Löwenhielm: Artist and Diplomat in Istanbul, 1824-1827*. Uppsala: Uppsala University Press, 1993.

Aflaki. *Manaqib al-'Arifin: Les saints des derviches tourneurs*. Edited and translated by C. Huart. 2 Vols. Paris: E. Leroux, 1918-1920.

Afroditi, K. "Prusa (Antiquity)." In *The Encyclopaedia of the Hellenic World, Asia Minor* (published online, August 29, 2008) and accessed online October 15, 2018.

Agnew, J. "Representing Space: Space, Scale and Culture in Social Science." In *Place/ Culture/ and Representation*, edited by J. Duncan and D. Ley, 251-71. London: Routledge, 1993.

Ahunbay, Z. "Decorative Coatings on Some Eighteenth-Century Buildings in Istanbul." In *Afife Batur'a Armağan Mimarlık ve Sanat Tarihi Yazıları*. (Essays on Architectural and Art History in Honor of Afife Batur), edited by A. Ağır, D. Mazlum and G. Cephanecigil, 205-14. Istanbul: Literatür Yayınları, 2005.

Akdağ, M. "Osmanlı İmparatorluğunun Kuruluş ve İnkişafı Devrinde Türkiye'nin İktisadi Vaziyeti." (Turkey's Economic Condition During the Establishment and Growth Eras of the Ottoman Empire). *Belleten* 13 (1949): 497-571.

Akdağ, M. *Türkiye'nin İktisadi ve İçtimaî Tarihi*, Second edition. 2 Vols. *(The Economic and Social History of Turkey)*. Istanbul: Cem Yayınları, 1959.

Akışık, A. "A Complicating Narrative: Laonikos Chalkokondyles on Ottoman Fratricide." Forthcoming.

Aktuğ-Kolay, İ. "The Influence of Byzantine and Local Western Anatolian Architecture on the 14th Century Architecture of the Turkish Principalities." *Sanat Tarihi Defterleri/ Özel Sayı - Okzident und Orient* 6 (2002): 199-213.

Ali Bahgat Bey and A. Gabriel. *Les fouilles d'al-Foustat et les origines de la maison arabe en Égypte*. Paris: E. de Boccard, 1921.

Allsen, T. *Culture and Conquest in Mongol Eurasia*. Cambridge, New York: Cambridge University Press, 2001.

Allsen, T. *Commodity and Exchange in the Mongol Empire: A Cultural History of Islamic Textiles*. New York: Cambridge University Press, 1997.

Altınsapan, E., Z. Demirel Gökalp, H. Yılmazyaşar, and A. Gerengi, "2010-2014 Kazıları Işığında Eskişehir Karacahisar Kalesi." (The Karacahisar Castle in the Light of 2010-2014 Excavations). *ASOS* 10, no. 3 (2015): 621-33.

Ambraseys, N. and C. Finkel. *The Seismicity of Turkey and Adjacent Areas: A Historical Review, 1500-1800*. Istanbul: Eren Yayınları, 1985.

Anderson, B. *Imagined Communities: Reflections on the Origins and Spread of Nationalism*. London and New York: Verso, 1983.

Anderson, B. "The Complex of Elvan Çelebi: Problems in Fourteenth-Century Architecture." *Muqarnas* 31 (2014): 73-97.

Anhegger, R. "Beiträge zur Frühosmanischen Baugeschichte." In *Zeki Velidi Togan Armağanı/Symbolae in honorem Zeki Velidi Togan*, 301–30. Istanbul: Maarif Basımevi, 1950.

Arnakis, G. G. "Gregory Palamas Among the Turks and Documents of His Captivity as Historical Sources." *Speculum* 26 (1951): 104–18.

Arnakis, G. G. "The Futuwwa Traditions in the Ottoman Empire Akhis, Dervishes and Craftsmen." *The Journal of Near Eastern Studies* 12, no. 4 (1953): 232–47.

Artuk, İ. "Early Ottoman Coins of Orhan Gāzī as Confirmation of His Sovereignty." In *Near Eastern Numismatics Iconography, Epigraphy and History: Studies in Honor of George C. Miles*, edited by D. K. Kouymjian, 457–63. Beirut: American University of Beirut, 1974.

Aslanapa, O. *Turkish Art and Architecture*. New York: Praeger, 1971.

Aslanapa, O. *Yüzyıllar Boyunca Türk Sanatı. (14. Yüzyıl)* (Turkish Art Through the Ages, 14th Century). Ankara: Milli Eğitim Bakanlığı, 1977.

Aslanapa, O. *Osmanlı Devri Mimarisi*. (The Architecture of the Ottoman Period). Istanbul: İnkilap Kitabevi, 2005.

Ataş, M. *Bursa Klavuzu*. (Bursa Guide). Istanbul: Baha Matbaası, 1944.

Avcıoğlu, N. "Istanbul: The Palimpsest City in Search of Its Architext." *RES: Anthropology and Aesthetics* 53–54 (2008): 190–210.

Avramea, A. "Land and Sea Communications, Fourth–Fifteenth Centuries." In *The Economic History of Byzantium: From the Seventh through the Fifteenth Century*, edited by A. E. Laiou, Vol. 1, 57–90. Washington, D.C.: Dumbarton Oaks Research Library and Collection, 2002.

Ayverdi, E. H. "Dimetoka'da Sultan Çelebi Mehmet Câmii." *Vakıflar Dergisi* 3 (1957): 13–16.

Ayverdi, E. H. " Bursa'da Orhan Gazi Camii ve Osmanlı Mimarisinin Menşei Meselesi." (The Origins of Ottoman Architecture and the Case of the Mosque of Orhan) *Vakıflar Dergisi* 6 (1965): 69–83.

Ayverdi, E. H. *Istanbul Mi'marî Çağının Menşe'i Osmanlı Mi'mârîsinin İlk Devri (1230-1402)*. (The Origins of the Istanbul Architecture and the First Period of the Ottoman Architecture), Vol. 1. Istanbul: Istanbul Fetih Cemiyeti, 1966.

Ayverdi, E. H. "Yıldırım Bayezid'in Bursa Vakfiyesi ve Bir İstibdalnamesi." (Bursa Waqf Charter and a Document on Exchange of Properties). *Vakıflar Dergisi* 8 (1969): 37–46.

Ayverdi, E. H. *Osmanlı Mimarisinde Çelebi ve Sultan Murad Devri*. (Ottoman Architecture during the reigns of Çelebi and Sultan Murad), Vol. 2. Istanbul: Istanbul Fetih Cemiyeti, 1972.

Ayverdi, E. H. *Osmanlı Mimarisinde Fatih Devri 855-886 (1451-1481)*. (Ottoman Architecture During the Reign of Mehmed II 855–886 (1451–1481)), Vol. 3. Istanbul: Istanbul Fetih Cemiyeti, 1973.

Balard, M. *La Romanie génoise (XIIe -début du XVe siécle)*. Rome: École française de Rome, 1978.

Balivet, M. "Byzantins Judaisants et juifs islamises des *Kuhhan* (Kahin) aux *Xionai* (Χιόνιος)." *Byzantion* 52 (1982): 24–59.

Bakirtzis, C. "The Urban Continuity and Size of Late Byzantine Thessaloniki." *DOP* 57, no. 45 (2003): 35–64.

Barkan, Ö. L. "İstila Devirlerinin Kolonizatör Türk Dervişleri ve Zaviyeler." (Turkish Dervishes and Lodges in the Age of Raids). *Vakıflar Dergisi* 2 (1942): 279–304.

Barkan, Ö. L. and E. Meriçli. *Hüdavendigar Livası Tahrir Defterleri*. (Tax Registers of the Hüdavendigar Province). Ankara: Türk Tarih Kurumu Basımevi, 1988.

Barkan, Ö. L. and E. H. Ayverdi. *Istanbul Vakıfları Tahrir Defteri: 1546 Tarihli*. (1546 Cadastral Register from Istanbul). Istanbul: Baha Matbaası, 1970.

Barmore, F. E. "Turkish Mosque Orientation and the Secular Variation of the Magnetic Declination." *Journal of Near Eastern Studies* 44, no. 2 (1985): 81–98.

Baykal, K. *Tarihte Bursa Yaygınları*. (Fires in the History of Bursa). Bursa: Bursa Eski Eserleri Sevenler Kurumu Yayınları, 1948.

Baykal, K. *Bursa ve Anıtları*. (Bursa and Its Monuments). Bursa: Hakimiyet Yayınları, 1950.

Baykal, K. "Bursa'da Saray ve Köşk." (Palace and Kiosk in Bursa). In *Milli Saraylar Sempozyumu: Bildiriler*, 31–4. Ankara: Kültür ve Turizm Bakanlığı Yayınları, 1984.

Baxandall, M. *Painting and Experience in Fifteenth-Century Italy*. Oxford: Oxford University Press, 1986.

Bekker-Nielsen, T. *Urban Life and Local Politics in Roman Bithynia: The Small World of Dion Chrysostomos*. Aarhus: Aarhus University Press, 2008.

Beldiceanu-Steinherr, I. "*La conquête d'Andrinople par les Turcs: la pénétration turque en Thrace et la valeur des chroniques ottomans*." *Travaux et Mémoires* 1 (1965): 439–61.

Beldiceanu-Steinherr, I. *Recherches sur les actes des règnes des sultans Osman, Orkhan et Murad I*. Monaco: Societas academică română, 1967.

Belke, K. ed. *Tabula Imperii Byzantini 13: Bithynien und Hellespontos*. Vienna: Austrian Academy of Sciences, 2020.

Bernard, C. A. *Les bains de Brousse en Bithynie*. Constantinople: Mille frères, 1842.

Blessing, P. *Rebuilding Anatolia after the Mongol Conquest: Islamic Architecture in the Lands of Rum 1240-1330*. Farnham, Surrey, UK and Burlington, VT: Ashgate, 2014.

Blessing, P. "Seljuk Past and Timurid Present." *Gesta* 56, no. 2 (2017): 225–50.

Blessing, P. "Urban Space Beyond Walls: Siting Islamic Funerary Complexes in Konya." In *Tomb-Memory-Space, Concepts of Representation in Pre-Modern Christian and Islamic Art*, edited by F. Giese, A. Pawlak and M. Thome, 25–43. Berlin, Boston: De Gruyter, 2018.

Blessing, P. and R. Goshgarian. *Architecture and Landscape in Medieval Anatolia, 1100-1500*. Edinburgh: Edinburgh University Press, 2017.

Bloom, J. "On the Transmission of Designs in Islamic Architecture." *Muqarnas* 10 (1993): 21-8.

Bhabha, H. *The Location of Culture*. London and New York: Routledge, 1994.

Bornstein-Makovetsky, L. "Bursa (Prousa)." *The Encyclopedia of Jews in the Islamic World*. (Consulted Online October 1, 2018).

Bouras, C. "The Impact of Frankish Architecture on Thirteenth-Century Byzantine Architecture." In *The Crusades from the Perspective of Byzantium and the Muslim World*, edited by A. E. Laiou and R. P. Mottahedeh, 247-62. Washington, D.C.: Dumbarton Oaks Research Library and Collection, 2001.

Bouras, L. "Templon." *Oxford Dictionary of Byzantium*, 3, 2023-24. New York: Oxford University Press, 1991.

Boykov, G. "The T-Shaped Zaviye/İmarets of Edirne: A Key Mechanism for Ottoman Urban Morphological Transformation." *Journal of the Ottoman and Turkish Studies Association* 3, no. 1 (2016): 29-48.

Broquière, Bertrandon de la. *The Voyage d'outremer*. Translated and edited by G. R. Kline. New York: Peter Lang, 1988.

Bryson, N. "The Gaze in the Expanded Field." In *Vision and Visuality*, edited by H. Foster, 87-108. Seattle: Bay Press, 1988.

Buchwald, H. "Lascarid Architecture." *Jahrbuch Österreichischen Byzantinistik* 28 (1979): 261-96.

Bulliett, R. *The Patricians of Nishapur: A Study of Medieval Islamic Social History*. Cambridge, MA: Harvard University Press, 1972.

Burns, R. *Origins of the Colonnaded Streets in the Cities of the Roman East*. Oxford: Oxford University Press, 2017.

Büyükkolancı, M. "Ayasuluk'ta Yeni Bulunan Kale Köşkü ve Hamamı." (The Recently Discovered Citadel Palace and the Bathhouse in Ayasoluk). In *XIII. Ortaçağ ve Türk Dönemi Kazıları ve Sanat Tarihi Araştırmaları Sempoyzumu Bildirileri*, 143-54. Denizli: Pamukkale Üniversitesi Fen- Edebiyat Fakültesi Yayınları, 2009.

Cahen, C. "Mouvements populaires et autonomisme urbain dans l'Asie musulmane du moyen âge, I." *Arabica* 5, no. 3 (1958): 225-50.

Cahen, C. "Mouvements populaires et autonomisme urbain dans l'Asie musulmane du moyen âge, II." *Arabica* 6, no. 1 (1959): 25-56.

Cahen, C. *Pre-Ottoman Turkey: A General Survey of the Material and Spiritual Culture and History c. 1071-1330*. Translated by J. Jones-Williams. London and Dublin: Sidgwick & Jackson, 1968.

Cahen, C. *The Formation of Turkey. The Seljuk Sultanate of Rum: Eleventh to Fourteenth Centuries*. Translated by P. M. Holt. Harlow: Longman, 2001.

Calvino, I. *Invisible Cities*. Translated by W. Weaver. San Diego: Harcourt, 1974.

Camille, M. *The Gothic Idol: Ideology and Image-Making in Medieval Art*. Cambridge and New York: Cambridge University Press, 1989.

Casey, E. *Getting Back into Place: Toward a Renewed Understanding of the Place World*. Bloomington: Indiana University Press, 1993.

Cerasi, M. "The Perception of Divan Yolu Through History." In *Afife Batur'a Armağan Mimarlık ve Sanat Tarihi Yazıları*. (Essays on Architectural and Art History in Honor of Afife Batur), edited by A. Ağır, D. Mazlum and G. Cephanecigil, 111–24. Istanbul: Literatür Yayınları, 2005.

Charanis, P. "Monk as an Element of Byzantine Society." *Dumbarton Oaks Papers* 25 (1971): 61–84.

Christie, R., R. McKane, and T. S. Halman, *Beyond the Walls: Selected Poems by Nazım Hikmet*. London: Anvil Press Poetry, 2002.

Constable, O. R. *Housing the Stranger in the Mediterranean World: Lodging, Trade, and Travel in Late Antiquity and the Middle Ages*. Cambridge and New York: Cambridge University Press, 2003.

Cosgrove, D. "Landscape and Landschaft." *German Historical Institution*, no. 35 (2004): 57–71.

Covel, J. *Dr. John Covel: Voyages en Turquie 1675–1677*. Edited by J.-P. Grélois, Réalités Byzantinés Éditions 6. Paris: P. Lethielleux, 1998.

Crane, H. "The Ottoman Sultan's Mosques." In the *Ottoman City and Its Parts*, edited by I. A. Bierman, R. A. Abou-El-Haj and D. Preziosi, 173–243. New Rochelle, NY: A. D. Caratzas, 1991.

Creswell, K. A. C. *A Short Account of Early Muslim Architecture*. Revised edition by J. W. Allen. Aldershot: Scolar Press, 1989.

Crinson, M. *Empire Building Orientalism and Victorian Architecture*. New York and London and New York: Routledge, 1996.

Cutler, A. "Reuse or Use? Theoretical and Practical Attitudes Toward Objects in the Early Middle Ages." *Settimane di Studio del Centro Italiano di Studi sull'Alto Medioevo* 46 (1999): 1055–83.

Cutler, A. and M. Johnson. "Synthronon." *Oxford Dictionary of Byzantium*. New York: Oxford University Press, 3, 1991: 1996.

Çağaptay, S. "The Church at Choma (Elmalı, Antalya) and Its Materials." Unpublished MA Thesis, Bilkent University, 2001.

Çağaptay, S. "The Church at Choma: A Revisiting of the Development of a Regional Style." *Byzantine Studies Conference Abstracts* 28 (2002): 62–3.

Çağaptay, S. "Visualizing the Cultural Transition in Bithynia (ca. 1300–1402): Architecture, Landscape, and Urbanism." University of Illinois at Urbana-Champaign (2007).

Çağaptay, S. "How Western Is It? The Palace at Nymphaion and Its Architectural Setting." *First International Sevgi Gönül Memorial Symposium on Byzantine Studies*, 357–63, Istanbul: Koç Üniversitesi Yayınları, 2010.

Çağaptay, S. "Frontierscape: Reconsidering Bithynian Structures and Their Builders on the Byzantine–Ottoman Cusp." *Muqarnas* 28 (2011): 155–91.

Çağaptay, S. "Prousa/Bursa, a City within the City: Chorography, Conversion, and Choreography." *Byzantine and Modern Greek Studies* 35, no. 1 (2011): 45–69.

Çağaptay, S. "The Road from Bithynia to Thrace: Gazi Evrenos' Imaret in Komotini and Its Architectural Framework." *Byzantinische Forschungen* 30 (2011): 429–42.

Çağaptay, S. "The Church of the Panagia Pantobasilissa in Trigleia (ca. 1336) Revisited: Content, Context, and Community." *Annual Bulletin of the Istanbul Research Institute* 1 (2012): 45–59.

Çağaptay, S. "Archaeology Report: Results of the Tophane Area GPR Surveys, Bursa, Turkey." *Dumbarton Oaks Papers* 68 (2014): 387–404.

Çağaptay, S. "Bilecik." In *The Encyclopaedia of Islam*, THREE, edited by Kate Fleet, Gudrun Krämer, Denis Matringe, John Nawas, and Everett Rowson. Consulted online on February 6, 2019, http://dx.doi.org/10.1163/1573-3912_ei3_COM_2 5314.

Çağaptay, S. "Prousa to Bursa: The Reinvention of an Ottoman Capital." In *Remembering and Forgetting the Ancient City*, edited by S. Ottewill-Soulsby and J. Martínez Jiménez. Cambridge: Cambridge University Press, 2021, forthcoming.

Çelik, Z. *The Remaking of Istanbul: Portrait of an Ottoman City in the Nineteenth Century*. Seattle: University of Washington Press, 1986.

Çelik, Z. *Displaying the Orient: Architecture of Islam at Nineteenth-Century World's Fairs*. Berkeley: University of California Press, 1992.

Çelik, Z., D. Favro and R. Ingersoll, ed. "Introduction." In *Streets: Critical Perspectives on Public Space*. 1–9. Berkeley: University of California Press, 1994.

Çetin, O. *Sicillere Göre Bursa'da İhtida Hareketleri ve Sosyal Sonuçları*. (Religious Conversions According to the Ottoman Registries and Its Social Impacts), 2nd ed. Ankara: Türk Tarih Kurumu Basımevi, 1999.

Çetintaş, S. *Türk Mimari Anıtları: Osmanlı Devri, Bursa'da Murad I ve Bayezid I Binaları*. (Turkish Works of Architecture: The Ottoman Period, The Buildings of Murad I and Bayezid I). Istanbul: Milli Eğitim Basımevi, 1952.

Çetintaş, S. *Yeşil Cami ve Benzerleri Cami Değildir*. (The Green Mosque and the Like Are Not Mosques). Istanbul: Maarif Basımevi, 1958.

Çıtakoğlu, H. "Bursa/Hisar Bölgesi Mozaikleri ve Geometrik Desen Repertuarı." (Bursa/Hisar Region Mosaics and Geometric Pattern Repertoire). *International Journal of Social Inquiry* 9 (2016): 1–32.

Ćurčić, S. "Architecture in the Age of Insecurity: An Introduction to Secular Architecture in the Balkans, 1300–1500." In *Secular Medieval Architecture in the Balkans 1300-1500 and Its Preservation*, edited by S. Ćurčić and E. Hadjitryphonos, 19–51. Thessaloniki: Aimos, 1997.

Ćurčić, S. "Architecture in the Byzantine Sphere of Influence around the Middle of the Fourteenth Century." In *Dečani i Vizantijska umetmost sredinom XIV veka*, edited by V. Djurić, 55–69. Belgrade: Serbian Academy of Sciences and Arts, 1989.

Ćurčić, S. and E. Hadjitryphonos. *Secular Medieval Architecture in the Balkans 1300-1500 and Its Preservation*. Thessaloniki: Aimos, 1997.

DaCosta Kaufmann, T. *Towards a Geography of Art*. Chicago and London: The University of Chicago Press, 2004.

Dagron, G. "The Urban Economy, Seventh–Twelfth Centuries." In *Economic History of Byzantium*, edited by A. E. Laiou, 393–461. Washington, D.C.: Dumbarton Oaks Research Library and Collection, 2002.

Dallaway, J. *Constantinople Ancient and Modern: With Excursions to the Shores and Islands of the Archipelago and to the Troad*. London: Cadell, 1797.

Darrouzès, J. *Epistoliers byzantins du Xe siècle*. Paris: Institut français d'études byzantines, 1960.

Dei, B. *La cronica dall'anno 1400 all'anno 1500*. Edited by R. Barducci. Florence: F. Papafava, 1985.

Demiriz, Y. *Örgülü Bizans Döşeme Mozaikleri*. (Interlaced Byzantine Mosaic Pavements). Istanbul: Yorum, 2002.

Denny, W. B. "Quotations In and Out of Context: Ottoman Turkish Art and European Orientalist Painting." *Muqarnas* 10 (1993): 219–30.

Diez, E. *Die Kunst der islamischen Völker*. Berlin: Neubabelsberg, 1915.

Doğan, A. I. *Osmanlı Mimarisinde Tarikat Yapıları, Tekkeler, Zaviyeler ve Benzer Nitelikteki Fütuvvet Yapıları*. (Tarikat Structures, Dervish Lodges, Zaviyes and Similar Futuwwa Buildings in Ottoman Architecture). Istanbul: Istanbul Teknik Üniversitesi Yayınevi, 1977.

Dörner, F. K. "Prusa ad-Olympium." *Pauly Wissowa* 1957/ 23: 1071–86.

Dunn, R. E. *The Adventures of Ibn Battuta: A Muslim Traveler of the 14th Century*, 145–6. Berkeley: University of California Press, 1986.

Efendi, İ. "Türk Hakimiyetinde Museviler." *Dergâh Mecmuası* 1338, no. 2 (1919): 19–23.

Eldem, E., D. Goffmann, and B. Masters. "Introduction." In *The Ottoman City Between East and West–Aleppo, Izmir, and Istanbul*, 1–18. Cambridge and New York: Cambridge University Press, 1999.

Eldem, S. H. "Bursa'da Şehadet Camii Konusunda bir Araştırma." (A Research on Şehadet Camii). *Türk Sanatı Tarihi Araştırma ve İncelemeleri* 1 (1963): 313–26.

Elisséeff, N. "Khan." *The Encyclopaedia of Islam*, 2, 4 (1990): 1010–11.

Elsner, J. "Significant Details: Systems, Certainties and the Art Historian as Detective." *Antiquity* 64 (1990): 950–2.

Emir, S. *Erken Osmanlı Mimarlığında Çok-İşlevli Yapılar: Kentsel Kolonizasyon Yapıları Olarak Zaviyeler*. (Multifunctional Buildings in Early Ottoman Architecture: Zaviyes as Urban Colonizing Edifices), 2 Vols. İzmir: Akademi Kitabevi, 1994.

Erbahar, A. "Etz Ahayim Synagogue, Bursa." *The Encyclopedia of Jews in the Islamic World*. (Consulted Online October 1, 2018).

Ergenç, Ö. *XVI. Yüzyılın Sonlarında Bursa. Yerleşimi, Yönetimi, Ekonomik ve Sosyal Durumu Üzerine bir Araştırma*. (Bursa at the End of the Sixteenth Century. A Research on Its Settlement, Administration, Economic and Social Aspects). Ankara: Türk Tarih Kurumu Yayınları, 2006.

Ersoy, A. "Architecture and the Search for Ottoman origins in the Tanzimat Period." *Muqarnas* 24 (2007): 79–102.

Ersoy, A. *Architecture and the Late Ottoman Historical Imaginary*. New York: Routledge, 2015.

Eyice, S. "Osmanlı Türk Mimarisinin İlk Devrinin Bir Cami Tipi Hakkında." (On an Early Ottoman-Turkish Mosque Type). Paper Presented at *Milletlerarası I. Türk Sanatları Kongresi Tebliğleri*, 19-24 Ekim 1959, 187–8. Ankara: Kültür Bakanlığı Yayınevi, 1962.

Eyice, S. "Bursa'da Osman ve Orhan Gazi Türbeleri." (The Mausolea of Osman and Orhan in Bursa). *Vakıflar Dergisi* 5 (1963): 131–47.

Eyice, S. "Two Mosaic Pavements from Bithynia." *Dumbarton Oaks Papers* 17 (1963): 373–83.

Eyice, S. "İlk Osmanlı Devrinin Dini – İçtimai Bir Müessesesi: Zaviyeler ve Zaviyeli Camiler." (A Social and Religious Organization of the Early Ottoman Era: Zaviyes and Zaviye Mosques). *Istanbul Üniversitesi İktisat Fakültesi Mecmuası* 23, no. 1–2 (1963): 1–80.

Eyice, S. "Çorum Mecitözü'nde Aşık Paşa-Oğlu Elvan Çelebi Zaviyesi." (Aşık Paşa-Oğlu Elvan Çelebi Zaviyesi at Mecitözü in Çorum). *Türkiyat Mecmuası* 15 (1969): 211–46.

Eyice, S. "Monuments byzantins anatoliens inédits ou peu-connus." *Corsi di Cultura sull'arte Ravennate e Bizantina* 18 (1971): 309–32.

Eyice, S. *Son Devir Bizans Mimarisi*. (Late Byzantine Era Architecture), Revised edition. Istanbul: Türkiye Turing ve Otomobil Kurumu, 1980.

Faroqhi, S. "In Search of Ottoman History." In *New Approaches to State and Peasant in Ottoman History*, edited by H. Berktay and S. Faroqhi, 211–41. London: Frank Cass, 1992.

Favro, D. "Meaning and Experience: Urban History from Antiquity to the Early Modern Period." *Journal of the Society of Architectural Historians* 58, no. 3 (1999): 364–73.

Favro, D. "Ancient Rome through the Veil of Sight." In *Sites Unseen: Landscape and Vision*, edited by D. Harris and D. F. Ruggles, 111–30. Pittsburgh, PA: University of Pittsburgh Press, 2007.

Fleet, K."The Treaty of 1387 between Murad I and the Genoese." *Bulletin of the School of Oriental and African Studies* 56, no. 1 (1993): 13–33.

Fleet, K. *European and Islamic Trade in the Early Ottoman State.* Cambridge, New York: University of Cambridge Press, 1999.

Flood, B. F. "The Medieval Trophy as an Art Historical Trope: Coptic and Byzantine 'Altars' in Islamic Contexts." *Muqarnas* 18 (2001): 41–72.

Flood, B. F. "Umayyad Survivals and Mamluk Revivals: Qalawunid Architecture and the Great Mosque of Damascus." *Muqarnas* 14 (1997): 57–79.

Flood, B. F. "Pillars, Palimpsests, and Princely Practices: Translating the Past in Sultanate Delhi." *RES: Anthropology and Aesthethics* 43 (2003): 95–116.

Finkel, C. *Osman's Dream: The Story of the Ottoman Empire, 1300-1923.* New York: Basic Books, 2005.

Foss, C. "The Defenses of Asia Minor against the Turks." *The Greek Orthodox Theological Review* 27, no. 2 (1982): 145–205.

Foss, C. "Prusa." *The Oxford Dictionary of Byzantium.* New York and Oxford, 1991, no. 3: 1750.

Foss, C. and D. Winfield. *Byzantine Fortifications: An Introduction.* Pretoria: University of South Africa, 1986.

Franco, M. *Essai sur l'histoire des Israélites de l'Empire Ottoman depuis les origines jusqu'à nos jours.* Paris: A. Durlacher, 1897.

Gabriel, A. "Bursa'da Murad I Camii and Osmanlı Mimarisinin Menşei Meselesi." (The Mosque of Murad I in Bursa and the Question of the Origins of Ottoman Architecture). *Vakıflar Dergisi* 2 (1942): 36–45.

Gabriel, A. *Une capitale turque, Brousse-Bursa*, 2 Vols. Paris: E. de Boccard, 1958.

Galanté, A. *Histoire des Juifs d'Anatolie*, 2 Vols. Istanbul: Imp. M. Babok, 1937–39.

Galavaris, G. *An Eleventh Century Hexaptych of the Saint Catherine's Monastery at Mount Sinai.* Athens: Mount Sinai Foundation, 2009.

Geertz, C. *Local Knowledge.* New York: Basic Books, 1983.

Gerber, H. *Economy and Society in an Ottoman City: Bursa, 1600-1700.* Jerusalem: The Hebrew University of Jerusalem, 1988.

Gerlach, S. *Tage-Buch der von zween glorwürdigsten Römischen Käysern.* Frankfurt: J.D. Zunners, 1674.

Geyer, B. "Physical Factors in the Evolution of the Landscape and Land Use." In *The Economic History of Byzantium*, edited by A. E. Laiou, Vol. 1, 32–45. Washington, D.C.: Dumbarton Oaks Research Library and Collection, 2002.

Geyer, B. "Donnés Géographiques." In *La Bithynie au Moyen Âge* , edited by B. Geyer and J. Lefort, 23–40. Paris: P. Lethielleux, 2003.

Gibb, H. A. R. ed., *The Travels of Ibn Battuta, A.D. 1325-1354.* 2 Vols. Cambridge: Hakluyt Society, 1958 –1962.

Gibbons, H. A. *The Foundations of the Ottoman Empire.* New York: Century Co., 1916.

Giorgiali, Ch. and S. Loumakis, "Prousa (Byzantium)." In *The Encyclopaedia of the Hellenic World, Asia Minor* (published online September 1, 2018 and accessed online October 15, 2018).

Gökbilgin, T. *Osmanlı Müesseseleri Teşkilatı ve Medeniyeti Tarihine Genel Bakış.* (A General View into the History of the Organization of the Ottoman Institutions and Civilization). Istanbul: Edebiyat Fakültesi Yayınları, 1977.

Goodwin, G. *A History of Ottoman Architecture.* London: Thames and Hudson, 1971.

Goodwin, G. "The Reuse of Marble in the Eastern Mediterranean in Medieval Times." *Journal of the Royal Asiatic Society* (1977): 17–30.

Goshgarian, R. "Beyond the Social and the Spiritual: Redefining the Urban Confraternities of Late Medieval Anatolia." Unpublished PhD dissertation, Harvard University, 2008.

Goshgarian, R. "Opening and Closing: Coexistence and Competition in Associations Based on Futuwwa in Late Medieval Anatolian Cities." *British Journal of Middle Eastern Studies* 40, no. 1 (2013): 36–52.

Goshgarian, R. "Social Graces and Urban Spaces: Brotherhood and the Ambiguities of Masculinity and Religious Practice in Late Medieval Anatolia." In *Architecture and Landscape in Medieval Anatolia, 1100–1500*, edited by P. Blessing and R. Goshgarian, 114–31. Edinburgh: Edinburgh University Press, 2017.

Grabar, O. *The Formation of Islamic Art.* New Haven: Yale University Press, 1987.

Graves, M. S. "The Lamp of Paradox." *Word & Image* 34, no. 3 (2018): 237–50.

Gross, E. *Das Vilâjet-nâme des Haǧǧi Bektasch: Ein türkisches Derwischevangelium.* Leipzig: Türkische Bibliotek, 1927.

Grossman, H. "Syncretism Made Concrete: The Case for a Hybrid Moreote Architecture in Post-Fourth Crusade Greece." In *Archaeology in Architecture: Papers in Honor of Cecil L.Striker*, edited by D. Deliyannis and J. Emerick, 65–73. Mainz: Von Zabern, 2005.

Güleryüz, N. *The Synagogues in Turkey.* Istanbul: Gözlem Yayınları, 2008.

Gurlitt, C. "Die Bauten Adrianopels." *Orientalisches Archiv* 1 (1909–1910): 51–2.

Hamlin, C. *Among the Turks.* London: Robert Carter & Brothers, 1878.

Hammer-Purgstall, J. *Umblick auf einer Reise von Constantinopel nach Brussa und von da zurück über Nicäa und Nicomedien.* Pesth: A. Hartleben, 1818.

Harris, D. "Postmodernization of Landscape." *Journal of Society of Architectural Historians* 58, no. 3 (1999–2000): 434–43.

Harris, D. and D. F. Ruggles, ed. "Introduction." *Sites Unseen: Landscape and Vision*, 5–29. Pittsburgh, PA: University of Pittsburgh Press, 2007.

Hartmann, R. *Im neuen Anatolien: Reiseeindrücke.* Leipzig: Hinrichs, 1928.

Hasluck, F. W. "Bithynica." *The Annual of the British School at Athens* 13 (1906-1907): 287-308.

Hasluck, F. W. *Cyzicus*. Cambridge: The University Press, 1910.

Hasluck, F. W. "Ambiguous Sanctuaries and Bektashi Propaganda." *Annual of the British School of Athens* 20 (1913-14): 94-119.

Hasluck, F. W. *Christianity and Islam under the Sultans*. 2 Vols. Oxford: The Clarendon Press, 1929.

Hazeem, S. "The Development of the Cairene *qā'a*: Some Considerations." *Annales Islamologiques* 23 (1987): 31-53.

Heisenberg, A. "Kaiser Johannes Batatzes der Barmherzige." *Byzantinische Zeitschrift*, 14 (1905): 160-233.

Hendy, M. F. *Studies in Byzantine Monetary Economy 300-1450*. Cambridge and New York: Cambridge University Press, 1985.

Heywood, C. "Boundless Dreams of the Levant: Paul Wittek, the George Kreis, and the Writing of Ottoman History." *Journal of the Royal Asiatic Society* 1 (1988): 7-25.

Heywood, C. "The 1337 Bursa Inscription and Its Interpreters." *Turcica* 36 (2004): 215-30.

Hillenbrand, R. "Madrasa, III. Architecture." *The Encyclopaedia of Islam*, TWO, 5 (1990): 1136-8.

Hızlı, M. "Bursa'da Selâtîn İmaretleri." (Bursa's Sultanic Imarets). *Uludağ Üniversitesi İlahiyat Dergisi* 10, no. 1 (2001): 33-62.

Hoffman, E. "Pathways of Portability: Islamic and Christian Interchange from the Tenth to the Twelfth Century." *Art History* 24 (2001): 17-50.

Holub, R. C. *Crossing Borders: Reception Theory, Poststructuralism, Deconstruction*. Madison, WI: University of Wisconsin Press, 1992.

Horden, P. and N. Purcell. *The Corrupting Sea: A Study of Mediterranean History*. Oxford and Malden, MA: Blackwell Publishers, 2000.

Humphreys, S. *Islamic History: A Framework for Inquiry*. Princeton, NJ: Princeton University Press, 1991.

Hüsameddin, Hüseyin. " Orhan Bey'in Vakfiyesi." (Orhan's Endowment Deed). *Türk Tarih Encümeni Mecmuası* 17, no. 7 (1926-1927): 284-301.

Imber, C. "The Ottoman Dynastic Myth." *Turcica* 19 (1987): 7-27.

Imber, C. *The Ottoman Empire 1300-1481*. Istanbul: Isis Press, 1990.

Imber, C. "The Legend of Osman Gazi." In *The Ottoman Emirate, 1300-1389*, edited by E. Zacharidou, 66-76. Rethymnon: Crete University Press, 1993.

Imber, C. "Canon and Apocrypha in Early Ottoman History." In *Studies in Ottoman History in Honour of Professor V. L. Ménage*, edited by C. Heywood and C. Imber, 117-37. Istanbul: Isis Press, 1994.

İnalcık, H. "Osmanlı İmparatorluğunun Kuruluş ve İnkişafı Devrinde Türkiye'nin İktisadi Vaziyeti Uzerine bir Tetkik Münasebetiyle." (An Assessment on the Economy in the Formative Period of the Ottomans). *Belleten* 15 (1951): 629–84.

İnalcık, H. "Bursa XV. Asır Sanayi ve Ticaret Tarihine Dair Vesikalar." *Belleten* 24 (1960): 45–102.

İnalcık, H. "The Conquest of Edirne (1361)." *Archivum Ottomanicum* 3 (1971): 185–210.

İnalcık, H. *The Ottoman Empire: The Classical Age 1300-1600*. New York: Prager, 1973.

İnalcık, H. "Osmanlı İdare, Sosyal ve Ekonomik Tarihiyle İlgili Belgeler: Bursa Kadı Sicillerinden Seçmeler." (Documents on Ottoman Administrative, Social and Economic History: Selections from Court Records in Bursa). *Belgeler* 10 (1980–1981): 1–91.

İnalcık, H. "The Question of the Emergence of the Ottoman State." *International Journal of Turkish Studies* 2/2 (1981–82): 71–80.

İnalcık, H. "Osmanlı İdare, Sosyal ve Ekonomik Tarihiyle İlgili Belgeler: Bursa Kadı Sicillerinden Seçmeler." (Ottoman Records on Administrative, Social and Economic History: A Group of Court Records from Bursa). *Belgeler* 1988 (13): 1–41.

İnalcık, H. "Bursa." *The Encyclopedia of Islam* TWO, 1 (1990): 1333–86.

İnalcık, H. "Istanbul: An Islamic City." *Journal of Islamic Studies* 1 (1990): 1–23.

İnalcık, H. "Murad I." *Türkiye Diyanet Vakfı İslam Ansiklopedisi* 31 (1991): 159–62.

İnalcık, H. "The Status of the Greek Patriarchate under the Ottomans." *Turcica* 21–3 (1991): 407–36.

İnalcık, H. "Edirne'nin Fethi (1361)." (The Conquest of Edirne, 1361) In *Edirne: Edirne'nin 600. Fetih Yıldönümü Armağan Kitabı*, edited by O. N. Peremeci, 137–59. Ankara: Türk Tarih Kurumu Yayınları, 1993.

İnalcık, H. "Kanunname." *Türkiye Diyanet Vakfı İslam Ansiklopedisi* 24 (2001): 333–7.

İnalcık, H. "The Struggle Between Osman Gazi and the Byzantines of Nicaea." In *İznik Throughout History*, edited by I. Akbaygil, 59–85. Istanbul: Türkiye İş Bankası Kültür Yayınları, 2003.

İntepe, N. *Dibâce*. Istanbul: Kaynak Yayınları, 2009.

Ivancević, R. "Two Thirteenth-Century Portals in Istria: Models of Traditional and Innovative Uses of Classical Art." *Hortus Artium Medievalium* 1996 (2): 57–64.

Jacoby, D. "Silk in Western Byzantium Before the Fourth Crusade." *Byzantinische Zeitschrift* 84–85 (1991–1992): 452–500.

Jacoby, D. "Silk Economics and Cross-Cultural Artistic Interaction: Byzantium, the Muslim World, and the Christian West." *Dumbarton Oaks Papers* 58 (2004): 197–240.

Janin, R. *Les églises et les monastéres des grands centres byzantins*. Paris: Institut Français d'études byzantines, 1975.

Jones, M. W. "Principles of Design in Roman Architecture. The Setting Out of Centralized Buildings." *Papers of the British School at Rome* 57 (1989): 106–51.

Kafadar, C. *Between Two Worlds: The Construction of the Ottoman State*. Berkeley: University of California Press, 1995.

Kafescioğlu, Ç. "Constantinopolis / Istanbul: Cultural Encounter, Imperial Vision, and the Construction of the Ottoman Capital." University Park: Pennsylvania State University Press, 2009.

Kalas, V. "Cappadocia's Rock-Cut Courtyard Complexes: A Case Study for Domestic Architecture in Byzantium." In *Housing in Late Antiquity: From Palaces to Shops*, edited by L. Lavan, L. Özgenel, and A. C. Sarantis, 393–414. Leiden and Boston: Brill, 2007.

Kaplanoğlu, R. "Bursa Kiliseleri." (Churches of Bursa). *Bursa Araştırmaları Dergisi* 30, no. 8 (2010): 10–25.

Kaplanoğlu, R., et al., *1455 Tarihli Kirmasti Defterine Göre Osmanlı Kuruluş Devri Vakıfları*. (Early Ottoman Period According to the 1455 Kirmasti Defter). Bursa: Avrasya Etnografya Vakfı Yayınları, 2014.

Kandes, V. Προύσα ετη αρχαιολογικα ιστορικη γεωγραφικη και εκκλησιαστικα περιγραφη αυτες. Athens: Asmodaios, 1883.

Kastritsis, D. *The Sons of Bayezid: Empire Building and Representation in the Ottoman Civil War 1402-1413*. Leiden: Brill, 2007.

Kastritsis, D. "Ottoman Urbanism before 1453 and the Question of Early Ottoman Capital Cities." In *Traces of the Ancient City in the Eastern Mediterranean: Erasure, Exposure and Other Urban Responses*, edited by L. Blanke, S. Çağaptay, E. Key Fowden, E. Zychowicz-Coghill. Cambridge University Press, Forthcoming.

Katz, D. "A Changing Mosaic: Multicultural Exchanges in the Norman Palaces of Twelfth-Century Sicily." Unpublished PhD dissertation, University of Toronto, 2016.

Kepecioğlu, K. *Bursa Hamamları*. Bursa: Halkevi Yayınları, 1935.

Kermeli, E. "Osman I." In *Encyclopedia of the Ottoman Empire*, edited by G. Ágoston and B. Masters, 444–5. New York: Facts on File, 2009.

Kiel, M. "The Oldest Monuments of Ottoman-Turkish Architecture in the Balkans." *Sanat Tarihi Yıllığı* 12 (1982): 117–44.

Kiourtzian, G. "L'Époque Protobyzantine À Travers les Monuments Épigraphiques." In *La Bithynie au moyen âge*, edited by B. Geyer and J. Lefort, 43–64. Paris: E. Lethielleux, 2003.

Kiprovska, M. "Plunder and Appropriation at the Borderland: Representation, Legitimacy and Ideological Use of Spolia by Members of the Ottoman Frontier Nobility." In *Spolia Reincarnated: Second Life of Spaces, Materials, Objects in Anatolia from Antiquity to the Ottoman Period*, edited by Jevtić and S. Yalman, 51–69. Istanbul: Koç University Publications, 2018.

Kitapçı Bayrı, B. *Warriors, Martyrs, and Dervishes: Moving Frontiers, Shifting Identities in the Land of Rome (13th–15th Centuries)*. Leiden: Brill, 2020.

Kleonymos, M. and Chr. Papadopoulos. Βιθυνίκα, Επίτομος Μονογραφία της Βιθυνίας και των πόλεων αυτής. Constantinople: Typois I. A. Vretou, 1867.

Koder, J. *Gemüse in Byzanz: Die Frischgemüseversorgung Konstantinopels im Licht der Geoponika*. Vienna: Fassbaender, 1993.

Koder, J. "Fresh Vegetables for the Capital." In *Constantinople and Its Hinterland*, edited by C. Mango, G. Dagron and G. Greatrex, 49–56. Aldershot: Ashgate, 1995.

Komaroff, L. "The Transmission and Dissemination of a New Visual Language." In *The Legacy of Genghis Khan: Courtly Art and Culture in Western Asia 1256-1353*, edited by L. Komaroff and S. Carboni, 168–95. New York and New Haven: MET and Yale University Press, 2002.

Kontolaimos, P. "A Landscape for the Sultan, an Architecture for the Eye: Edirne and Its Fifteenth-Century Royal Tower." *Landscape History* 37, no. 2 (2016): 19–33.

Kopytoff, I. "The Cultural Biography of Things: Commoditization as Process." In *The Social Life of Things: Commodities in Cultural Perspective*, edited by A. Appadurai, 64–94. Cambridge: Cambridge University Press, 1986.

Kostof, S. "Architectural History and the Student Architect: A Symposium." *Journal of the Society of Architectural Historians* 26, no. 3 (1967): 189–91.

Kostof, S. *The City Shaped: Urban Patterns and Meanings Through History*. London: Thames and Hudson, 1999.

Kotoula, D. "Maniera Cypria and Thirteenth Century Icon Production on the Island of Cyprus: A Critical Approach." *Byzantine and Modern Greek Studies* 28 (2004): 89–100.

Koukoules, P. I. *Βυζαντινών βίος και πολιτισμός*, 5 Vols. Athens: Institut français d'Athène, 1948–1957.

Koyunluoğlu, M. T. *İznik ve Bursa Tarihi*. (The History of İznik and Bursa). Bursa: Vilayet Matbaası, 1935.

Köseoğlu, N. *Tarihte Bursa Mahalleleri, 15. ve 16. Yüzyıllarda*. (Bursa's Neigborhoods through the Ages, 15th and 16th Centuries). Bursa: Ant Basımevi, 1946.

Kramer, J. "Kämpferkapitelle mit den Monogrammen Kaiser Justinus II. und seiner Gemahlin, der Kaiserin Sophia in Yalova Kaplıcaları (Termal)." In *Festschrift für Klaus Wessel zum 70. Geburtstag*, edited by M. Restle, 173–90, Münich: Editio Maris, 1988.

Krautheimer, R. "Introduction to an Iconography of Medieval Architecture." *Journal of the Warburg and Courtauld Institutes* 5 (1942): 1–33.

Krautheimer, R. *Early Christian and Byzantine Architecture*. Fourth edition with S. Ćurčić. New Haven: Yale University Press, 1984.

Krautheimer, R. *Rome: Profile of a City, 312-1308*. Princeton: Princeton University Press, 2000.

Kreiser, K. "Zur Kulturgeschichte der Osmanischen Moschee." In *Türkische Kunst und Kultur aus osmanischer Zeit*, edited by H.-C. von Bothmer, B. Kellner-Heinkele and D. Rohwedder, 2 Vols. 75–86. Recklinghausen: Aurel Bongers, 1985.

Kuban, D. *Istanbul, an Urban History: Byzantion, Constantinopolis, Istanbul*. Istanbul: Türkiye İş Bankası Kültür Yayınları, 1996.

Kubler, G. *The Shape of Time: Remarks on the History of Things*. New Haven: Yale University Press, 1962.

Kuran, A. *The Mosque in Early Ottoman Architecture*. Chicago: University of Chicago Press, 1968.

Kuran, A. "A Spatial Study of Three Ottoman Capitals: Bursa, Edirne and Istanbul." *Muqarnas* 13 (1996): 114–31.

Kut, G. and A. Y. Ocak. "Aşık Paşa." *Türkiye Diyanet Vakfı İslam Ansiklopedisi* 4 (1991): 1–3.

Laborde, L. de. *Voyage de l'Asie Mineure*. Paris: Firmin Didot, 1838.

Laila, A. I. "Residential Architecture in Mamluk Cairo." *Muqarnas* 2 (1984): 47–59.

Laiou, A. E. *Constantinople and the Latins: The Foreign Policy of Andronicus II, 1282–1328*. Cambridge, MA: Harvard University Press, 1972.

Laiou, A. E. "The Agrarian Economy, Thirteenth–Fifteenth Centuries." In *The Economic History of Byzantium*, edited by A. E. Laiou, 311–75. Washington D.C.: Dumbarton Oaks Research Library and Collection, 2002.

Lapidus, I. "The Evolution of Muslim Urban Society." *Comparative Studies in Society and History* 15 (1978): 21–50.

Launay, M. de. *Usul-i Mi'mari-i 'Osmani/ L'architecture ottomane/ Die ottomanische Baukunst*. Istanbul, 1873.

Lee, P. M. "'Ultramoderne': Or, How George Kubler Stole the Time in Sixties Art." *Grey Room* 2 (2001): 46–77.

Lee, P. M. *Chronophobia: On Time in the Arts of the 1960s*. Cambridge: MIT 2004.

Lefebvre, H. *The Production of Space*. Translated by D. Nicholson-Smith. Oxford, UK, Cambridge, MA: Blackwell, 1991.

Lefort, J. "Tableau de la Bithynie au XIIIe siècle." In *The Ottoman Empire (1300-1389)*, by E. Zachariadou, 101–17. Rethymnon: Crete University Press, 1993.

Lefort, J. "Les communications entre Constantinople et a Bithynie." In *Constantinople and Its Hinterland*, edited by C. Mango and G. Dagron, 207–18. Aldershot: Ashgate, 1995.

Lermer, A. and A. Shalem. *After One Hundred Years: The 1910 Exhibition "Meisterwerke Muhammedanischer Kunst" Reconsidered*. Leiden and Boston: Brill, 2010.

Lézine, A. "Les salles nobles des palais mamelouks." *Annales islamologiques* 10 (1972): 63–148.

Lindner, R. P. *Nomads and Ottomans in Medieval Anatolia*. Bloomington: University of Indiana Press, 1983.

Lindner, R. P. "How Mongol Were the Early Ottomans?" In *The Mongol Empire and Its Legacy*, edited by R. Amitai-Preiss and D. O. Morgan, 282-90. Leiden, Boston: Brill, 1999.

Lindner, R. P. *Explorations in Ottoman Prehistory*. Ann Arbor: University of Michigan Press, 2007.

Lowry, H. *Ottoman Bursa in Travel Accounts*. Bloomington: Indiana University Press, 2003.

Lowry, H. *The Nature of the Early Ottoman State*. Albany: State University of New York Press, 2003.

Lowry, H. "Random Musings on the Origins of Ottoman Charity: From Mekece to Bursa, Iznik and Beyond." In *Feeding People, Feeding Power: Imarets in the Ottoman Empire*, edited by N. Ergin, C. K. Neumann, and A. Singer, 69-79. Istanbul: Eren, 2007.

Lowry, H. *The Shaping of the Ottoman Balkans, 1350 -1550: The Conquest, Settlement and Infrastructural Development of Northern Greece*. Istanbul: Bahçeşehir University Publications, 2007.

Lowry, H. and A. Bryer, "Introduction." In *Continuity and Change in Late Byzantine and Early Ottoman Society*, edited by H. W. Lowry and Anthony Bryer, 1-8. Birmingham, UK, Washington, D.C.: Birmingham Centre for Byzantine Studies and Dumbarton Oaks Research Library and Collection, 1986.

Lubenau, R. *Beschreibung der Reisen des Reinhold Lubenau herasgegeben*. 3 Vols. Königsberg: Pr. Beyer, 1914-1915.

MacDonald, W. *The Architecture of the Roman Empire. An Introductory Study*. 2 Vols. New Haven and London: Yale University Press, 1986.

Magdalino, P. "The Byzantine Aristocratic Oikos." In *The Byzantine Aristocracy: IX to XIII Centuries*, edited by M. Angold, 92-111. BAR International Series 221. Oxford: British Archaeological Reports, 1984.

Maguire, H, "The Medieval Floors of the Great Palace." In *Byzantine Constantinople: Monuments, Topography and Everyday Life*, edited by N. Necipoğlu, 153-74. Leiden: Brill, 2001.

Malusardi, F. *Luigi Piccinato e l'urbanistica moderna*. Rome: Officina, 1993.

Mamboury, E. *Istanbul touristique*. Istanbul: Çituri Biraderler Matbaası, 1951.

Mandel, G. *I caravanserragli Turchi*. Bergamo: Lucchetti, 1988.

Mango, C. and I. Ševčenko. "Some Churches on the South Shore of the Sea of Marmara." *Dumbarton Oaks Papers* 18 (1973): 235-77.

Mansel, A. M. *Yalova ve Civarı. Yalova und Umgebung*. Istanbul: Istanbul Müzeleri Neşriyatı, 1936.

Mantran, R. "Les inscriptions arabes de Brousse." *Bulletin d'Ètudes Orientales de L'Institut Français de Damas* 14 (1952-1954): 88-114.

Marçais, G. "L'Islamisme et le vie urbaine." *Comptes rendus des séances de l'Académie des Inscriptions & Belles-Lettres* 72, no.1 (1928): 86–100.

Martiny, G. "Zur Entwicklungsgeschichte der Osmanischen Moschee." *Ars Orientalis* 4 (1961): 107–12.

Mathews, T. and A.-C. Daskalakis Mathews. "Islamic Style Mansions in Byzantine Cappadocia and the Development of the Inverted-T-Plan." *Journal of the Society of Architectural Historians* 56.3 (1997): 294–315.

Matschke, K.-P. "The Late Byzantine Urban Economy, Thirteenth–Fifteenth Centuries." In *The Economic History of Byzantium: From the Seventh through the Fifteenth Century*, edited by A. E. Laiou, Vol. 2, 435–95. Washington D.C.: Dumbarton Oaks Research Library and Collection, 2002.

Meinecke, M. *Patterns of Stylistic Changes in Islamic Architecture: Local Traditions versus Migrating Artists*. New York: New York University Press, 1996.

Melikoff-Sayar, I. *La Destan d'Umur Pasha (Düstürname-i Enveri)*. Paris: Bibliothèque byzantine, 1954.

Melikoff, I. *La Geste de Melik Danishmend 1: Etude critique du Danishmendname*. Paris: Maisonneuve, 1960.

Melville, C. "The Itineraries of Shāhrukh b. Timur (1405–47)." In *Turko-Mongol Rulers, Cities and City Life*, edited by D. Durand-Guédy, 285–315. Leiden and Boston: Brill, 2013.

Menthon, B. *Une terre de légendes: l'Olympe de Bithynie: ses saints, ses couvents, ses sites*. Paris: Bonne Presse, 1935.

Meyer, E. "Turquerie and Eighteenth-Century Music." *Eighteenth-Century Studies* 7, no. 4 (1974): 474–88.

Meyendorff, J. "Grecs, Turcs, et Juifs en Asie Mineure au XIVe Siècle." *Byzantinische Forschungen* 1 (1966): 211–16.

Miklosich, F. and J. Müller, *Acta et Diplomata Graeca Medii Aevi Sacra et Profana* Volume I. Athens: Ch. I. Spanos, 1862.

Miller, R. A. "Religious v. Ethnic Identity in Fourteenth-Century Bithynia: Gregory Palamas and the Case of the Chionai." *International Journal of Turkish Studies* 13, no. 1–2 (2007): 27–42.

Millet, G. *Monuments byzantins de Mistra: matériaux pour l'étude de l'architecture et de la peinture en Grèce aux XIVe et XVe siècles*. Paris: E. Leroux, 1910.

Morris, R. *Monks and Laymen in Byzantium (843–1118)*. Cambridge: Cambridge University Press, 1995.

Morrisson, C. and J. C. Cheynet. "Prices and Wages in the Byzantine World." In *The Economic History of Byzantium*, edited by A. E. Laiou, 2: 815–78. Washington D.C. Dumbarton Oaks Research Library and Collection, 2002.

Mordtmann, A. D. *Anatolien, Skizzen und Reisebriefe aus Kleinasien 1850–1859*. Hannover: Orientbuchhandlung H. Lafaire, 1925.

Mundell–Mango, Marlia. "Thermae, Balnea/ Loutra, Hamams: The Baths of Constantinople." In *Istanbul and Water*, edited by P. Magdalino and N. Ergin, 129–60. Ancient Near Eastern Studies Supplement 47. Leuven: Peeters, 2015.

Murphey, R. *Exploring Ottoman Sovereignty: Tradition, Image and Practice in the Ottoman Imperial Household, 1400–1800*. London: Bloomsbury, 2008.

Muthesius, A. "Constantinople and Its Hinterland: Raw Silk Supply." In *Studies in Byzantine and Islamic Silk Weaving*, edited by A. Muthesius, 315–35. London: The Pindar Press, 1995.

Necipoğlu, G. "From International Timurid to Ottoman: A Change of Taste in Sixteenth-Century Ceramic Tiles." *Muqarnas* 7 (1990): 136–70.

Necipoğlu, G. *Architecture, Ceremonial and Power: The Topkapı Palace in the Fifteenth and Sixteenth Centuries*. New York: Architectural History Foundation, 1991.

Necipoğlu, G. "The Life of an Imperial Monument: Hagia Sophia after Byzantium." In *Hagia Sophia from the Age of Justinian to the Present*, edited by R. Mark and A. Çakmak, 195–225. Cambridge and New York: Cambridge University Press, 1992.

Necipoğlu, G. "An Outline of Shifting Paradigms in the Palatial Architecture of the Pre-Modern Islamic World." *Ars Orientalis* 23 (1993): 3–24.

Necipoğlu, G. "Anatolia and the Ottoman Legacy." In *The Mosque: History, Architectural Development and Regional Diversity*, edited by M. Frischman and H. Uddin-Khan, 141–53. London: Thames & Hudson, 1994.

Necipoğlu, G. "Dynastic Imprint on the Cityscape: The Collective Message of Imperial Funerary Mosque Complexes in Istanbul." In *Cimètiers et traditions funéraires dans le monde islamique (Acte du colloque international, Istanbul 28-30 September 1991)*, edited by J.-L. Bacqué-Grammont and A. Tibet, 23–36. 2 Vols. Ankara: Türk Tarih Kurumu Yayınları, 1996.

Necipoğlu, G. *The Age of Sinan: Architectural Culture in the Ottoman Empire*. London: Reaktion, 2005.

Necipoğlu, G. "Creation of a National Genius: Sinan and the Historiography of Classical Ottoman Architecture." *Muqarnas* 14 (2007): 141–83.

Necipoğlu, G. "Visual Cosmopolitanism and Creative Translation: Artistic Conversations with Renaissance Italy in Mehmed II's Constantinople." *Muqarnas* 29 (2012): 1–81.

Necipoğlu, N. "State and Future of Byzantine Studies in Turkey." In *Aptullah Kuran için Yazılar-Essays in Honor of Aptullah Kuran*, edited by Ç. Kafescioğlu and L. Thys-Şenocak, 23–6. Istanbul: Yapı Kredi Yayınları, 1999.

Nelson, R. and S. R. Shiff. *Critical Terms for Art History*. Chicago: University of Chicago Press, 1996.

Nora, P., ed. *Realms of Memory: Rethinking the French Past*. Vol. 3: Symbols. (with L. Kritzmann). New York: Columbia University Press, 1999.

Ocak, "Ahi (akhī)." In *The Encyclopaedia of Islam*, THREE, edited by Kate Fleet, Gudrun Krämer, Denis Matringe, John Nawas, and Everett Rowson. Consulted online October 12, 2018, http://dx.doi.org.ezp.lib.cam.ac.uk/10.1163/1573-3912_e i3_COM_23942.

Ocak, A. Y. "Zaviyeler, Dini, Sosyal ve Kültürel Tarih Açısından Bir Deneme (Zaviyes: Religious, Social, Cultural and Historical Review)." *Vakıflar Dergisi* 12 (1978): 247–69.

Ocak, A. Y. "Elvan Çelebi." *Türk Diyanet Vakfı İslam Ansiklopedisi* 11 (1995): 63–4.

Öcalan H. B., S. Sevim and D. Yavaş, ed. *Bursa Vakfiyeleri*. (Bursa Waqfs). Bursa: Bursa Kültür Sanat ve Turizm Vakfı Yayınları, 2013.

Oğuz, Z. "Multifunctional Buildings of the T-Type in the Ottoman Context: A Network of Identity and Territorialization." Unpublished MA thesis, METU, 2006.

Oğuz Kursar, Z. "Sultans as Saintly Figures in Early Ottoman Mausolea." In *Sacred Spaces and Urban Networks*, edited by S. Yalman and H. A. Uğurlu, 67–88. Istanbul: Koç Üniversitesi Yayınları, 2019.

Okçu, R. "Prusia ad Olympum Mozaikleri." (Mosaics from Prusia ad Olympum). *Journal of Mosaic Research* 3 (2009): 31–51.

Olwig, K. *Landscape, Nature and the Body Politic: From Britain's Renaissance to America's New World*. Madison: University of Wisconsin Press, 2002.

Öney, G. "Anadolu Selçuklu Mimarisinde Antik Devir Malzemesi." (Ancient Period Spolia in Anatolian Seljuk Architecture). *Anadolu* 12 (1968): 17–38.

Orbay, İ. *Bursa*. MIT: Aga Khan Awards Ceremony Local Office, 1983.

Ötüken, S. Y. *Forschungen im nordwestlichen Kleinasien, Antike und byzantinische Denkmäler in der Provinz Bursa*. Tübingen: Ernst Wasmuth Verlag, 1996.

Ousterhout, R. G. "The Byzantine Heart." *Zograf* 17 (1986): 36–44.

Ousterhout, R. "Review of the Byzantine Fortifications: An Introduction." *Journal of the Society of Architectural Historians* 48, no. 2 (1989): 182–3.

Ousterhout, R. "Constantinople, Bithynia and Regional Developments in Later Byzantine Architecture." In *The Twilight of Byzantium*, edited by D. Mouriki and S. Ćurčić, 75–110. Princeton: Princeton University Press, 1991.

Ousterhout, R. "Ethnic Identity and Cultural Appropriation in Early Ottoman Architecture." *Muqarnas* 12 (1995): 48–62.

Ousterhout, R. *Master Builders of Byzantium*. Princeton: Princeton University Press, 1999.

Ousterhout, R. "In Pursuit of the Exotic Orient." *Journal of Aesthetic Education* 35, no. 4 (2001): 113–18, Book Review of *Venice and the East: The Impact of the Islamic World on Venetian Architecture 1100–1500*, by Deborah Howard. New Haven: Yale University Press, 2000.

Ousterhout, R. "Architecture as Relic and the Construction of Sanctity: The Stones of the Holy Sepulchre." *Journal of the Society of Architectural Historians* 62, no. 1, (2003): 4–23.

Ousterhout, R. "Secular Architecture." In *The Glory of Byzantium: Art and Culture of the Middle Byzantine Era A.D. 843–1261*, edited by H. C. Evans and W. D. Wixom, 193–200. New York: MET, 2004.

Ousterhout, R. "The East, the West, and the Appropriation of the Past in Early Ottoman Architecture." *Gesta* 43, no. 2 (2004): 165–81.

Ousterhout, R. *A Byzantine Settlement at Çanlı Kilise*. Washington D.C.: Dumbarton Oaks Research Library and Collection, 2006.

Ousterhout R. and C. Bakirtzis. *The Byzantine Monuments of Evros/Meriç River Valley*. Thessaloniki: European Center for Byzantine and Post-Byzantine Monuments, 2007.

Özendes, E. *The First Capital Bursa*. Istanbul: YEM Yayınları, 1999.

Özer, M. *Edirne Sarayı (Saray-ı Cedid-i Amire) Kısa Bir Değerlendirme*. (The Palace at Edirne: A Short Analysis). Istanbul: Bahçeşehir Üniversitesi Yayınları, 2014.

Özkan, E. and F. Ünal. *Hisarkeoloji*. (The Archaeology of the Castle). Bursa: Osmangazi Belediyesi Yayınları, 2009.

Özkılınç, A. ed. *166 Numaralı Muhasebe-i Vilayet-i Anadolu Defteri (937/1530): Hüdavendigâr, Biga, Karesi, Saruhan, Aydın, Menteşe, Teke ve Alâiye Livâları*. (Number 166 Registry of the Anatolian Province Accounts). Ankara: Başbakanlık Devlet Arşivleri Genel Müdürlüğü, 1995.

Pancaroğlu, O. "Architecture, Landscape, and the Patronage in Bursa: The Making of an Ottoman Capital City." *Turkish Studies Association Bulletin* 20, no. 1 (1995): 40–55.

Pancaroğlu, O. "Caves, Borderlands and Configurations of Sacred Topography in Medieval Anatolia." *Mésogeios* 25–26 (2005): 249–82.

Pancaroğlu, O. "Visible/Invisible: Sanctity." In *Eastern Mediterranean Port Cities: A Study of Mersin, Turkey– From Antiquity to Modernity*, edited by F. Yenişehirlioğlu, E. Özveren and T. Selvi Ünlü, 79–91. Cham: Springer, 2019.

Pancaroğlu, P. "Devotion, Hospitality and Architecture in Medieval Anatolia." *Studia Islamica* 108, no. 1 (2013): 48–81.

Pantelić, B. *The Architecture of Decani and the Role of Archbishop Danilo II*. Wiesbaden: Reichert, 2002.

Papademetriou, T. *Render unto the Sultan: Power, Authority, and the Greek Orthodox Church in the Early Ottoman Centuries*. Oxford: Oxford University Press, 2015.

Papaioannou, S. *Michael Psellos: Rhetoric and Authorship in Byzantium*. Cambridge: Cambridge University Press, 2013.

Papazotos, Th. "The Identification of the Church of 'Profitis Elias' in Thessaloniki." *Dumbarton Oaks Papers* 45 (1991): 121–7.

Pardoe, Julia. *The City of the Sultan and Domestic Manners of the Turks in 1836.* 2 Vols. London: Henry Colburn, 1838.
Parvillée, L. *Architecture et décoration turques au XVe siècle.* Paris: Ve A. Morel, 1874.
Patrinelis, G. F. "Ειδήσεις για την Ελληνική κοινότητα της Προύσας (15ος-17ος αι.)." (News for the Greek Community in Bursa). Δελτίο Κέντρου Μικρασιατικών Σπουδών. (Bulletin of the Center for Asia Minor Studies) 7 (1988): 9–50.
Peacock, A. C. S. "Court and Nomadic Life in Saljuq Anatolia." In *Turko-Mongol Rulers, Cities and City Life*, edited by D. Durand-Guédy, 191–221. Leiden and Boston: Brill, 2013.
Pekak, M. S. *Zeytinbağı (Trigleia) Bizans Dönemi Kiliseleri.* (Byzantine Churches of Trigleia). Unpublished PhD dissertation, Hacettepe University, Ankara, 1991.
Pekak, M. S. "Zeytinbağı/Trilye Bizans Dönemi Kiliseleri." In (The Byzantine Churches of Trigleia) *XIII. Kazı ve Araştırma Sonuçları Toplantısı*, 48–53. Ankara: Kültür ve Turizm Bakanlığı Yayınları, 1995.
Piccinato, L. "L'esperienza del piano di Bursa." *Urbanistica* 36–7 (1962): 110–36 with an English summary, 30–1.
Pickett, J. "Water and Empire in the *De aedificiis* of Procopius." *Dumbarton Oaks Papers* 71 (2018): 95–125.
Pinatsi, C. "New Observations on the Pavement of the Church of Haghia Sophia in Nicaea." *Byzantinische Zeitschrift* 99, no. 1 (2006): 119–26.
Pinon, P. "The Ottoman Cities of the Balkans." In *The City in the Islamic World*, edited by R. Holod, S. Jayussi, A. Petruccioli and A. Raymond, 143–58. Leiden and Boston: Brill, 2008.
Pococke, R. *A Description of the East and Some Other Countries.* 2 Vols. London: W. Bowyer, 1743–1745.
Pollock, G. "Beholding Art History: Vision, Place, and Power." In *Vision and Textuality*, edited by S. Melville and B. Readings, 38–66. Macmillan: Imprint Palgrave, 1995.
Pralong, A. "Matériel Archéologique Errant." In *La Bithynie au moyen âge*, edited by B. Geyer and J. Lefort, 225–86. Paris: P. Lethielleux, 2003.
Pralong, A. and J. P. Grélois, "Tombeau d'Orcan à Brousse." In *Byzance Retrouvée érudites et voyageurs français (XVIe–XVIIIe siècles)*, edited by M.-F. Auzépy, 138–9. Paris: Publications de la Sorbonne, 2001.
Pralong, A. and J. P. Grélois, "Les monuments byzantins de la ville haute de Brousse." In *La Bithynie au Moyen Âge*, edited by B. Geyer and J. Lefort, 134–49. Paris: P. Lethielleux, 2003.
Prohorov, G. M. "Prenie Grigorija Palamys Chiony: Turki'i Problema Zidovskaja Mudrostvujuscih." *Trudy Otdela Drevnerusskoj Literatury* 27 (1972): 329–69.
Rabbat, N. "Mamluk Throne Halls: *Qubba* or *Iwān*?" *Ars Orientalis* 23 (1993): 201–18.

Rabbat, N. *Mamluk History Through Architecture: Monuments, Culture and Politics in Medieval Egypt and Syria*. London: I. B. Tauris, 2010.

Rabinow, P. ed. *The Foucault Reader*. New York: Pantheon, 2010.

Raymond, A. "Islamic City, Arab City: Orientalist Myths and Recent Views." *British Journal of Middle Eastern Studies* 21, no. 1 (1994): 3–18.

Redford, S. "The Alaeddin Mosque in Konya Reconsidered." *Artibus Asiae* 51, no. 1–2 (1991): 57–74.

Redford, S. "The Seljuks of Rum and the Antique." *Muqarnas* 10 (1993): 148–56.

Redford, S. "Thirteenth-Century Rum Seljuk Palaces and Palace Imagery." *Ars Orientalis* 23 (1993): 215–32.

Redford, S. "Byzantium and the Islamic World, 1261–1557." *Byzantium: Faith and Power 1261–1557*, edited by H. Evans, 389–415. New York: MET, 2004.

Redford, S. "City Building in Seljuq Rum." In *Seljuqs: Politics, Society and Culture*, edited by C. Lange and S. Mecit, 256–76. Edinburgh: Edinburgh University Press, 2011.

Renouard de Bussierre, M. T. *Lettres sur l'Orient: écrites pendant les années 1827 et 1828*. Paris: Levrault, 1829.

Robert, L. *Études anatoliennes: recherches sur les inscriptions grecques de l'Asie Mineure*. Paris: E. de Boccard, 1937.

Robert, L. "Sur un type monétaire de Prousa de l'Olympe et sur des épigrammes." *Hellenica* 2 (1946): 94–102.

Robert, L. *A travers l'Asie Mineure: poètes et prosateurs, monnaies grecques, voyageurs et géographie*. Athens and Paris: Diffusion de Boccard, 1980.

Rose, G. *Feminism and Geography*. Minneapolis: University of Minnesota Press, 1993.

Ruggles, D. F. *Gardens, Landscape, and Vision in the Palaces of Islamic Spain*. Pennsylvania: Pennsylvania State University Press, 2000.

Ruggles, D. F. "The Dual Heritage of Sicilian Monuments." *The Cambridge History of Arabic Literature: The Literature of Al-Andalus*, edited by R. Menocal, R. Scheindlin and M. Sells, 25–9. Cambridge: Cambridge University Press, 2000.

Ruggles, D. F. *Islamic Gardens and Landscapes*. Philadelphia: University of Pennsylvania Press, 2008.

Sackett, J. R. "Style and Ethnicity in Archaeology: The Case of Isochretism." In *The Uses of Style in Archaeology*, edited by M. Wright Conkey and C. A Hastorf, 32–43. Cambridge: Cambridge University Press, 1989.

Sahas, D. "Gregory of Palamas on Islam." *The Muslim World* 73, no. 1 (1983): 1–21.

Saladin, H. *Manuel d'art musulman, l'architecture I*. Paris: Librairie Alphonse Picard, 1907.

Salgırlı, S. "Architectural Anatomy of an Ottoman Execution." *Journal of the Society of Architectural Historians* 72, no. 3 (2013): 301–21.

Salgırlı, S. "Soap Bars and Silk Cocoons: Microecologies of Connectivity in Late Medieval Mediterranean Architecture." *Journal of Early Modern History* 23 (2019): 121–51.

Salmeri, G. "Dio, Rome, and the Civic Life in Asia Minor." In *Dio Chrysostom Politics, Letters, and Philosophy*, edited by S. Swain, 53–92. Oxford: Oxford University Press, 2000.

Şaman Doğan, N. "Bursa Murad Hüdavendigar Camii ve Niğde Ak Medrese'nin Düşündürdükleri." (Some Thoughts on the Mosque of Murad Hüdavendigar and Niğde Ak Medrese). In *Prof. Dr. Zafer Bayburtluoglu Armağanı–Sanat Yazıları*, edited by M. Denktaş and Y. Özbek, 211–20. Kayseri: Kayseri Büyükşehir Belediyesi, 2001.

Sauer, C. "The Morphology of Landscape." *University of California Publications in Geography* 2, no. 2 (1925): 19–54.

Sauvaget, J. "L'enceinte primitive de la ville d'Alep." *Mélanges de l'Institut Français de Damas. Section Des Arabisants* 1 (1929): 131–59.

Sauvaget, J. "Le plan antique de Damas." *Syria* 26, no. 3–4 (1949): 314–58.

Scanlon, G. T. "Preliminary Report: Excavations at Fustat." *Journal of the American Research Center in Egypt* 4 (1965): 7–30.

Scanlon G. T. and W. B. Kubiak. "Fusṭāṭ Expedition Preliminary Report 1971, Part I." *Journal of the American Research Center in Egypt* 16 (1979): 103–24.

Schneider, A. M. *Die römischen und byzantinischen Denkmäler von Iznik-Nicaea*. Berlin: Archäologisches Institut des Deutschen Reiches, 1943.

Schiltberger, J. *The bondage and travels of Johann Schiltberger : a native of Bavaria, in Europe, Asia, and Africa, 1396-1427*. Edited by J. Buchan Telfer. New York: B. Franklin, 1970.

Schlemmer, U. *Johannes Schiltberger: Als Sklave im Osmanischen Reich und bei den Tataren: 1394–1427*. Stuttgart: Thienemann, 1983.

Schultze, V. *Altchristliche Städte und Landschaften*. 2 Vols. Gütersloh: C. Bertelsmann, 1922.

Selçuk, İ. "State Meets Society: A Study of *Bozakhāne* Affairs in Bursa." In *Feeding People, Feeding Power: Imarets in the Ottoman Empire*, edited by N. Ergin, C. K. Neumann, and A. Singer, 23–48. Istanbul: Eren, 2007.

Selçuk, İ. "State and Society in the Marketplace: A Study of Late Fifteenth-Century Bursa." Unpublished PhD dissertation, Harvard University, 2009.

Selçuk, İ. "Suggestions on the Social Meaning and Functions of the *Akhi* Communities and Their Hospices in Medieval Anatolia." In *Architecture and Landscape in Medieval Anatolia, 1100–1500*, edited by P. Blessing and R. Goshgarian, 95–113. Edinburgh: Edinburgh University Press, 2017.

Sestini, D. *Voyage dans La Grèce asiatique, à la péninsule de Cyzique à Brusse et à Nicée*. London and Paris: Chez Leroy, 1789.

Sevim, S. "1. Murad'ın Vakıfları ve Temlikleri." In *Sultan 1. Murad Hüdavendigar ve Dönemi*. (Murad I Hüdavendigar and His Period), edited by İ. Selimoğlu, 371–94. Bursa: Osmangazi Belediyesi Yayınları, 2012.

Shahid, I. "Lakhmids." *The Encyclopaedia of Islam*, TWO, 5 (1984): 632–4.

Sims, E. "Markets and Caravanserais." In *Architecture of the Islamic World; Its History and Social Meaning*, edited by G. Michell, 97–111. London: Thames and Hudson, 1984.

Singer, A. "Enter, Riding on an Elephant: How to Approach Early Ottoman Edirne." *Journal of the Ottoman and Turkish Studies Association* 3, no. 1 (2016): 89–109.

Smith, Th. "An Account of the City of Prousa in Bithynia." *Philosophical Transactions* 14 (1684): 431–3.

Sölch, J. "Historisch-geographische Studien über bithynische Siedlunge." *Byzantinische-Neugriechische Jahrbücher* 1 (1920): 263–83.

Spon, J. and G. Wheler. *Voyage d'Italie, de Dalmatie, de Grece et du Levant: fait aux années 1675 et 1676*. La Haye: Alberts, 1724.

St. Laurent, B. "Léon Parvillée: His Role as Restorer of Bursa's Monuments after the 1855 Earthquake and His Contribution to the Exposition Universelle of 1867." In *L'Empire Ottoman; la République de Turquie et del la France*, edited by J.-L. Bacqué Grammont and H. Batu, 247–82. Paris: Isis, 1986.

St. Laurent, B. "Ottomanization and Modernization: The Architectural and Urban Development of Bursa and Genesis of Tradition." PhD dissertation, Harvard University, 1989.

Stotz, C. L. "The Bursa Region of Turkey." *The Geographical Review* 29 (1939): 81–100.

Swain, S. *Dio Chrysostom Politics, Letters, and Philosophy*. Oxford: Oxford University Press, 2000.

Swift, E. H. *Roman Sources of Christian Art*. New York: Columbia University Press, 1951.

Tabbaa, Y. *Constructions of Power and Piety in Medieval Aleppo*. University Park, PA: Pennsylvania State University Press, 1997.

Tabbaa, Y. "Defending Ayyubid Aleppo: The Fortifications of al-Ẓāhir Ghāzī (1186–1216): Muslim Military Architecture in Greater Syria." In *Muslim Military Architecture in Greater Syria: From the Coming of Islam to the Ottoman Period*, edited by H. Kennedy, 176–82. Leiden, Boston: Brill, 2005.

Taeschner, F. "Beiträge zur frühosmanischen Epigraphik und Archäologie." *Der Islam* 20 (1932): 109–86.

Taeschner, F. "Beiträge zur frühosmanischen Epigraphik und Archäologie." *Der Islam* 22 (1935): 69–73.

Tagg, J. "Introduction/Opening." In *Grounds of Dispute: Art History, Cultural Politics and the Discursive Field*, edited by J. Tagg, 1–39. Minneapolis: University of Minnesota Press, 1992.

Tak, E. "Diplomatik Bilimi Bakımından XVI–XVII. Yüzyıl Kadı Sicilleri ve Bu Sicillerin İhtiva Ettiği Belge Türlerinin Form Özellikleri Ve Tanımlanması." (16th and 17th Century Court Registers and Their Examinations and Contents in Accordance with Diplomacy). Unpublished PhD dissertation, Marmara University, 2009.

Tanman, M. B. "Erken Dönem Osmanlı Mimarisinde Memlük Etkileri." (The Mamluk Impact on Early Ottoman Architecture). In *Osmanlı Mimarisinin 7 Yüzyılı: Uluslararası Bir Miras*. N. Akın, A. Batur, S. Batur, 82–90. Istanbul: YEM Yayınları, 2001.

Tanman, M. B. "Mamluk Influences in the Architecture of the Anatolian Emirates." In *The Arts of the Mamluks in Egypt and Syria: Evolution and Impact*, edited by D. Behrens Abouseif, 283–300. Goettingen: Bonn University Press, 2012.

Tanman, M. B. "Ekrem Hakkı Ayverdi'nin Erken Devir Osmanlı Mimarisine Dair Tespitleri." In *Osmanlı Mimarlık Kültürü: Ekrem Hakkı Ayverdi'nin Hâtırasına*, H. Aynur and A. H. Uğurlu, 231–53. Istanbul: Kubbealtı Neşriyatı, 2016.

Tanpınar, A. H. *Beş Şehir*. Ankara: Ülkü Matbaası, 1946.

Tanpınar, A. H. "Bursa'nın Daveti." In *Yaşadığım Gibi*, edited by B. Emil, 215–16. Istanbul: Dergâh Yayınları, 1996.

Tekinalp, V. M. "Remodelling the Monastery of Hagios Ioannes Prodromos in Prusa ad Olympum (Modern Bursa, Turkey)." In *The Architecture of Byzantium and Kievan Rus from the 9th to the 12th Centuries*, 164–79. St. Petersburg: Transactions of the State Hermitage Museum, 2010.

Terezakis, G. "The Diocese of Prousa." *The Encyclopaedia of the Hellenic World, Asia Minor* (published online September 20, 2018 and accessed online October 1, 2018).

Texier, C. F. *Description de l'Asie Mineure*. Paris: Firmin Didot, 1839.

Texier, C. F. and R. P. Pullan. *Byzantine Architecture: Illustrated by Examples of Edifices Erected in the East During the Earliest Age of Christianity*. London: Day & Son, 1864.

Thevénot, J. *The Travels of Monsieur de Thevénot into the Levant*. Edited by A. Lowell. London: H. Clark, 1687.

Thys-Şenocak, L. "The Yeni Valide Mosque Complex in Eminönü, Istanbul (1597–1665)." In *Women, Patronage, and Self-Representation in Islamic Societies*, edited by D. F. Ruggles, 69–89. Albany: State University of New York Press, 2000.

Tournefort, J. P. de. *Voyage d'un botaniste*. Edited by S. Yerasimos. Paris: F. Maspero, 1982.

Trachtenberg, M. "Gothic and Italian Gothic: Toward a Redefinition." *Journal of the Society of Architectural Historians* 50 (1991): 22–37.

Trachtenberg, M. *Dominion of the Eye: Urbanism, Art and Power in Early Modern Florence*. Cambridge and New York: Cambridge University Press, 1997.

Trepanier, N. "Harvesting Garden Semantics in late Medieval Anatolia." In *Architecture and Landscape in Medieval Anatolia, 1100–1500*, edited by P. Blessing and R. Goshgarian, 187–99. Edinburgh: Edinburgh University Press, 2017.

Tunay, M. I. "Masonry of Late Byzantine and Early Ottoman Periods." *Zograf* 12 (1981): 76–9.

Turğut, Vedat. "Orhan Gazi Dönemi Ve Vakıfları." *Orhan Gazi ve Kocaeli Tarihi Araştırmaları* 10 (2019): 1–84.

Ubicini, A. *La Turquie actuelle*. Paris: Hachette, 1855.

(Usman) Anabolu, M. "Olympos Dağı Eteklerindeki Prusa (Bursa) Sikkesindeki Therme ile İlişkili Olarak." *Belleten* 59, no. 226 (1995): 583–4.

Uysal, A. O. "Zaviyeli Camilerde Minare Problemi." (The Problem of a Minaret in Zawiya Mosques). *Türk Etnografya Dergisi* 20 (1997): 47–63.

Uzunçarşılı, İ. H. "Gazi Orhan Bey Vakfiyesi." (The Endowment Deed of Orhan) *Belleten* 19, no. 5 (1941): 277–88.

Van Berchem, M. "Origine de la madrasah." *Matériaux pour un Corpus Inscriptionum Arabicarum* 1, no. 1–2 (1894–1896): 254–69.

Veinstein, G. "The Ottoman Town (Fifteenth–Eighteenth Centuries)." In *The City in the Islamic World*, edited by R. Holod, S. Jayussi, A. Petruccioli and A. Raymond, 205–17. Leiden and Boston: Brill, 2008.

Von Erlach, J. B. *Entwurff Einer Historischen Architektur*. Leipzig: Selbstverl, 1725.

Von Thünen, J. H. *Der isolierte Staat in Beziehung auf Landwirthschaft und Nationalökonomie*. Hamburg: F. Perthes, 1826.

Vryonis, S. *The Decline of Medieval Hellenism in Asia Minor and the Process of Islamization from the Eleventh through the Fifteenth Century*. Berkeley and London: University of California Press, 1971.

Walsh, P. G. *Pliny the Younger, Complete Letters*. Oxford: Oxford University Press, 2006.

Ward-Perkins, B. *Roman Imperial Architecture*. Third edition. New Haven: Yale University Press, 1994.

Watt, J. C. Y. "A Note on Artistic Exchanges in the Mongol Empire." In *The Legacy of Genghis Khan: Courtly Art and Culture in Western Asia 1256–1353*, edited by L. Komaroff and S. Carboni, 62–73. New York: MET, 2002.

Weiker, W. *Ottomans, Turks and the Jewish Polity: The History of the Jews of Turkey*. Lanham: University Press of America, 1992.

Weyl Carr, A. "Correlative Spaces: Art, Identity and Appropriation in Lusignan Cyprus." *Modern Greek Studies Yearbook* 14–15 (1998–1999): 59–80.

Wheler, G. *A Journey into Greece*. London: William Cademan, 1682.

Wilde, H. *Brussa: eine entwickelungsstäte türkischer architektur in Kleinasien unter den ersten Osmanen*. Berlin: E. Wasmuth, 1909.

Wittek, P. "Le Sultan de Rûm." *Annuaire de l'Institute Philologie et d'Histoire Orientales et Slaves* 6 (1938): 361–90.
Wittek, P. *The Rise of the Ottoman Empire.* London: Royal Asiatic Society, 1938.
Wittek, P. "Chiones." *Byzantion* 21 (1951): 421–3.
Wolper, S. E. "Khidr, Elwan Çelebi and the Conversion of Sacred Sanctuaries in Anatolia." *The Muslim World* 90 (2000): 309–22.
Wolper, S. E. *Cities and Saints: Sufism and the Transformation of Urban Space in Medieval Anatolia.* University Park, PA: Pennsylvania State University Press, 2003.
Yalman, S. "Building the Sultanate of Rum: Memory, Urbanism and Mysticism in the Architectural Patronage of 'Ala al-Din Kayqubad (r. 1220–1237)." Unpublished doctoral dissertation, Harvard University, 2011.
Yavuz, A. T. "Anadolu Selçuklu Dönemi Kervansarayları Tipolojisi." (Typology of the Anatolian Seljuk Caravanserais) *IV. Milli Selçuklu Kültür ve Medeniyeti Semineri Bildirileri, Konya,* 183–98. Konya: Selçuklu Araştırma MeYayınları, 1995.
Yavuz, A. T. "Kervansaraylar." *Anadolu Selçlukluları ve Beylikler Dönemi Uygarlığı Kitabı,* edited by A. Y. Ocak, 435–45. Ankara: Kültür ve Turizm Bakanlığı Yayınları, 2006.
Yenal, E. *Bir Zamanlar Türkiye – Turkey As It Was. Carl Gustaf Löwenhielm Bir İsveç Elçisinin 1820'lerdeki Türkiye Albümü – A Swedish Diplomat's Turkish Portfolio in the 1820s.* İstanbul: Yapı Kredi Yayınları, 2003.
Yerasimos, S. *La fondation de Constantinople et de Sainte-Sophie dans le traditions turques.* Paris: IFEA and Jean Maisonneuve, 1990.
Yıldız, S. N. "From Cairo to Ayasoluk: Hacı Paşa and the Transmission of Islamic Learning to Western Anatolia in the Late Fourteenth Century." *Journal of Islamic Studies* 25 (2014): 263–97.
Yılmaz, H. *Caliphate Redefined. The Mystical Turn in Ottoman Political Thought.* Princeton: Princeton University Press, 2018.
Yılmaz, İ. "Bursa Sur Kapıları ve Taht-ı Kale Kapısı Rekonstrüksiyonu." (City Gates of Bursa and the Restoration Project at the Tahta Kale Gate) *Uludağ Üniversitesi Fen-Edebiyat Fakültesi Sosyal Bilimler Dergisi* 26, no. 1 (2014): 87–105.
Yılmazyaşar, H. "İznik Ayasofya Kilisesi'nde Osmanlı Dönemi Yapısal Düzenlemeleri." (The Ottoman Interventions at the Nicaean Saint Sophia) *Ebru Parman'a Armağan: Sanat Tarihi ve Arkeoloji Yazıları,* edited by A. O. Alp, 361–84. Ankara: Alter Yayınları, 2009.
Yüksel Muslu, C. *The Ottomans and the Mamluks: Imperial Diplomacy and Warfare in the Islamic World.* London: I.B. Tauris, 2014.
Yürekli, Z. *Architecture and Hagiography in the Ottoman Empire: The Politics of Bektashi Shrines in the Classical Age.* Farnham: Ashgate, 2012.

Yürekli, Z. "Architectural Patronage and the Rise of the Ottomans." In *A Companion to Islamic Art and Architecture*, edited by F. Barry Flood and Gülru Necipoğlu, 734–54. Hoboken, NJ: Wiley Blackwell, 2017.

Yürekli-Görkay, Z. "Osmanlı Mimarisinde Aleni Devşirme Malzeme: Gazilerin Alamet-i Farikasi." In *Gelenek, Kimlik, Bireşim: Kültürel Kesişmeler ve Sanat; Günsel Renda'ya Armağan = Tradition, Identity, Synthesis: Cultural Crossings and Art; Essays in Honor of Günsel Renda*, edited by Z. Yasa Yaman and S. Bağcı, 273–82. Ankara: Hacettepe Üniversitesi Yayınları, 2011.

Zachariadou, E. "The Conquest of Adrianople by the Turks." *Studii Veneziani* 12 (1970): 211–17.

Zachariadou, E. *Trade and Crusade: Venetian Crete and the Emirates of Menteshe and Aydın (1300–1415)*. Venice: Istituto ellenico di studi bizantini e postbizantini di Venezia per tutti i paesi del mondo, 1983.

Zachariadou, E. "Notes sur la population de l'Asie Mineure turque au XIVe siècle." *Byzantinische Forschungen* 12 (1987): 223–34.

Zachariadou, E. "Religious Dialogue between Byzantines and Turks during the Ottoman Expansion." In *Religionsgespräche im Mittelalter*, edited by B. Lewis and F. Niewöhner, 289–304. Wiesbaden: Harassowitz, 1992.

Index

Abdal Murad viii, *16*, 161 n.19
  (dervish convent) shrine of 81–2
Abdülaziz 66, 152 n.105, 165 n.67
Abdülhamid II 125 n.18
Abdülmecid I 18
Abu-Lughod, J. L. 119 n.33
accommodation 8, 17, 19, 35, 46,
  132 n.81, 156 n.34
  külliye and 87, 88, 89, 96, 98
  nonconfessional 30
acropolis. *See* old city
Aflaki 85, 161 n.29
ahis 4, 70–1, 143 n.23, 153–4
  n.6, 154 n.14
  külliye and 85, 87, 89, 90, 98
Ahmedi 5, 168 n.87
Ahmed Vefik Paşa 20, 104, 170 n.15
Ahunbay, Z. 157 n.37
Akdağ, M. 95, 166–7 n.81
Akışık, A. 93, 134 n.101, 165 n.71,
  166 n.72
Ak *Madrasa* (Niğde) 57
Aktuğ-Kolay, İ. 124 n.9
al-'Umari 168 n.87
Alaeddin Keykubat I 99
Alaeddin Mosque (Bursa) 36–7, 44, 64
Alaeddin Mosque (Konya) 64,
  147 n.50, 151 n.97
al-Dimishqi, Ali ibn Musheimesh 64
Alexander the Great 150–1 n.90
al-Hiri (central large room flanked by
  side rooms) 75
al-majlis (sitting/meeting places) 76
al-Masudi 75
al-Mutawakkil 75
Alp Arslan 72
alternating brick-and-stone
  construction 74, 87, 91–3,
  99, 107, 108
  convent-*masjids* and Friday mosques
  and 51, 55, 58, 64, 66, 67
  transition and 27, 33, 37, 38
Altınsapan, E. 112 n.4
Ambraseys, N. 121 n.50

Anatolia 4–5, 7–9, 11–13, 18, 21,
  146 n.41, 152 n.103, 169 n.99
  hybridity and 56–8, 61–5, 67
  inverted-T plan and 69–73
  külliye and 85, 92, 94, 95, 96
  map in mid-fourteenth century *3*
  medieval 113 n.14, 124 n.9
  pseudo-spolia in 147 n.50
  transition and 24, 27, 29, 43
  Turkish-occupied 95, 167 n.82
  urban landscape of 15
Anatolian principalities (Beyliks) 24,
  29, 65, 96
ancestral capital 92–5
Anderson, B. 43, 124 n.9, 137 n.133
Angelokoma/İnegöl 23
Anhegger, R. 62
Antioch 13
Apamea Myrlea 116 n.2
appropriation 7, 8, 10, 23–5, 67, 70, 106,
  107, 124 n.11, 152 n.104
Apulia 9, 55
arches 20, 27, 33, 107, 145 nn.35,
  37–8, 148 n.62
  hybridity and 51–3, 57, 58, 62–4, 66
  külliye and 87, 98, 99
architectural transference 23
Armenian Catholic church 142 n.17
Armenian Gregorian church 142 n.17
Arnakis, G. G. 127 n.37, 143 n.23, 153 n.6
Arrian of Nicomedia 117 n.5
Artuk, İ. 149 n.76
aşağı hisar. *See* lower city
ashlar masonry 9, 27, 58–9, 63, 64,
  67, 90, 92–3
Aşık Paşa 43
Aşıkpaşazade 29, 95, 111 n.1, 123 n.5,
  125 n.16, 128 n.43, 133 n.98,
  134 n.103, 153 n.2, 168 n.87
Aslanapa, O. 147 n.44, 151 n.96
Ataş, M. 127 n.35
Athenaios of Naukratios 32
atrophied Greek cross 66
Avcıoğlu, N. 128 n.41

Avramea, A. 167 n.84
Ayasofya Mosque. *See* Church of Saint Sophia, Nicaea
Ayasoluk 15, 64
Aydinid İsa Bey Mosque (Ayasoluk) 64, 151 n.96, 153 n.107
Aydinids 8, 15, 64, 96, 127 n.38, 133 n.97
Ayverdi, E. H. 6, 38, 43, 61, 71, 88, 124 n.7, 126 nn.26, 29, 127 n.35, 128 n.42, 129 n.53, 130 n.67, 131 n.77, 132 n.81, 133 nn.92, 94, 96, 144 nn.28–9, 146 nn.41–2, 149 n.70, 150 nn.80, 84, 154 n.19, 155 n.21, 161 n.17, 162 nn.38, 42, 163 nn.43, 48, 53–4, 165 nn.66–7, 69
Ayyubids 9, 57, 64, 76, 158 n.54

Balard, M. 117 n.7
Balıkpazarı neighborhood 49, 50
Balivet, M. 143 n.23
Balkans 15, 18–19, 21, 56–7, 62, 89, 94, 120 nn.38, 43, 146 n.38
Barkan, Ö. L. 85, 118 n.15, 141 n.6, 160 n.6
Barmore, F. E. 155 n.21
basilical type structure 20, 44, 45, 46, 61–2, 103, 139 n.146
basilika therma, significance of 32–3
bathhouses 13, 14, 23, 30, 34, 38, 84, 88
 evolution of 30–3, 38
 imarets and 88–9
Battle of Ankara (1402) 26
Battle of Köse Dağ (1243) 12
Battle of Manzikert (1071) 12
Battle of Nikopolis (1396) 62, 102
Baxandall, M. 108
Bayezid I 15, 25, 29, 33, 53, 80, *84*, 146 n.41, 150 n.90, 151 n.100.
 See also convent-*masjids*; Friday mosques
 as Alexander the Great 150–1 n.90
 captivity of 101, *102*
 defeating Crusade armies 102
 külliye sponsored by 16, 83, *84*, 90–1
 Noble Lodge and Pleasant İmaret (endowment deed) 90
 as *Sultan-ı Rum* 62
Baykal, K. 62, 121 n.49, 125 n.18, 127 n.34, 129 nn.48, 53, 131 n.77, 142 n.11

Bayri, Kitapçı 154 n.6
 Warriors, Martyrs, and Dervishes 4
Bekker, I. 129 n.51
Bekker-Nielsen, T. 32, 117 n.5, 118 nn.18, 23, 119 n.26, 126 nn.21, 32
Beldiceanu-Steinherr, I. 112 n.5, 162 n.35, 163 nn.44, 46
Belke, K. 152 n.102
Benedetto Dei 97, 168 n.87
Bernard, C. A. 36, 137 n.126
Bey Saray (palace of rulers/Bursa Palace) 26, 28–30, 101, *109*
Bezasistan (Bedesten) 51, 87, 90
Bilecik 52, 66
Bithynia 3, 5, 7, 13, 15, 23, 29, 52, 63, 72, 73, 80, 95, 117 nn.5–6, 118 n.15, 138 n.143, 160 n.6, 167 n.82
Blessing, P. 4, 113 n.14, 140 n.3, 152 n.107, 155 n.27, 156 n.34
 Rebuilding Anatolia after the Mongol Conquest 4
Bloom, J. 151 n.96
Bornstein-Makovetsky, L. 141 n.10
Boykov, G. 83 nn.23–4, 120 n.36
bozahane 49–50
Broquière, Bertrandon de la 2, 125 n.18, 127 n.37, 143 n.21, 160 n.9, 168 n.87
Bryer, A. 140 n.4, 141 n.5, 152 n.103
Bryson, N. 108
Burns, R. 118 n.23, 127 n.32
Bursa 1. *See also individual entries*
 as ancestral capital 92–5
 Archaeological Museum 27, 28, 46, 103, 122 n.56, 127 n.36
 salvage excavations 28, 103 n.10, 127 n.36
 architectural recycling in 24
 Byzantine, Roman roots of 13–15
 as commercial center 2
 conquest of 125 n.16
 Court Registers 30
 as *dar al-mulk* (abode of sovereignty) 94
 as emerging Ottoman identity 11–13
 as emporium of silk 81, 98, 100, 105, 108, 169 n.105, 172 n.31
 1827 view *2*
 geographical location of 11
 hans in 98–9

Index

inverted-T in 77 (*see also* inverted-T structures)
invisibility of 10, 101–10
modern day 79–80
modern urban fabric of 109–10
until 1950s 79–81
non-Muslim communities in 97–8, 141 n.6
Ottomanization of 7, 12, 18–19, 25, 38–9, 47, 67, 80, 96
past, reconstruction of 19–21
transitional architectural culture in 67
transition from Prousa to 15
walls and gates of 25–8
Bursa-style arch 58, 148 n.62
Büyükkolancı, M. 127 n.38
Byzantine viii–ix, 65, 140 n.4. *See also* individual entries
   Roman roots and 13–15
   domes 39–42

cadastral registers 48, 49, 50, 71, 118 n.15, 141 n.6
Cahen, C. 117 n.7, 119 n.33, 141 n.9
Calvino, I. 101
Camille, M. 124 n.11
Canon's House (Poreč, Dalmatia) 55
capital city, notion of 28–30, 94–5
caravanserais 85, 98, 167 n.83
Cassas 40, 41, 43, 108
Catenacci 40, 41, 43, 44, 108
Cave of Seven Sleepers 123 n.3
Çekirge *31*, 88, 89
Çelik, Z. 121 n.51, 122 n.52, 160 n.4, 171 n.15
Cerasi, M. 122 n.52
Çetintaş, S. 43, 71, 88, 129 n.53, 144 n.29, 155 n.21
Chalkokondyles, Laonikos 93, 134 n.101, 166 n.72, 168 n.87
Chelebowski, S. 101
Cheynet, J. C. 160 n.7
Chionai (Islamized Jews) 50, 143 n.23
chorography 106
Christianity and Islam under the Sultans (Hasluck) 23
churches, transformation of 138–9 n.146
Church of Panagia Paregoritissa 55
Church of Pantobasilissa (Trigleia) 47, 65

Church of Saint John Prodromos 15, 34, 39, 45, 103
Church of Saint Sophia. *See also* Saint Sophia
   Adrianople/Edirne 19
   Istanbul 61
   Mistra 42
   Nicaea 18–19, 24, 42, 147 n.44
   Ohrid 55, 123 n.5, 133–4 n.99
   Trebizond 42
Church of Saint Stephanos (Fatih Cami) (Trigleia). *See* Fatih Cami
Church of Saint Theodore (Mistra) 41
Church of Saint Irene 139 n.147
Church of Santo Stefano 53
Church of Taxiarches 49, 142 n.13
Church of the Holy Apostles 40, 41, 49, 142 n.13
Çifte Minareli *Madrasa* (Erzurum) 72
citadel 7–9, 19, 48–9, 82, 125 n.18, 163 n.43
   inner 28, 46, 127 n.36
   mosques in 34–8
   Ottoman urban enterprise and 82–6
   transition and 23, 25, 28–30
   upper 36, 131 n.77
colonnaded street/road system viii, 13, 14, 83, 118 n.23, 127 n.32
Constable, O. R. 169 nn.102, 104
Constantine IV 27
Constantine V Kopronymos (Iconomachos) 139 n.147
Constantine VI 31
Constantine VII Porphyrogennetos 31, 168 n.90
Constantinople viii, 11, 14, 15, 18, 19, 32, 41, 48–50, 52, 53, 62, 94, 112 n.5, 125 n.16, 139 n.147, 172 n.29. *See also* Istanbul
   Theodosian Walls of 27
convent-*masjids* 47, 69, 77
   of Bayezid I 58–9, *84*
      ashlar masonry 58–9
      façade *59*
   of Murad I *31*, 54–8
      Byzantine practice in 56
      façade *55*, *56*, *57*
      isometric view of *54*

scholars' knowledge on 57
of Orhan 8, 50–4, *51*
façade 51–2, *52*
inverted-T structure 51
conversion 7–8, 18–19, 84, 100,
123 nn.4–6, 127 n.37,
132 n.79, 133 n.99, 134 n.105,
152 nn.101, 103
Friday mosques and convent-*masjids*
and 47, 59–61, 66
transition and 23–4, 30, 34–5,
38, 43, 45–6
Cosgrove, D. 106, 171 n.26
Covel, J. 27, 28, 30, 35, 36, 41, 43,
44, 81, 86, 108, 125 n.18,
132 n.83, 136 n.119
Crane, H. 101
Creswell, K. A. C. 146 n.38
Crusaders, ix, 9, 12, 14–5, 18, 57, 102
Ćurčić, S. 5, 52, 120 n.43, 145 nn.35, 38,
146 n.43, 169 n.102
Cutler, A. 125 n.14

Dagron, G. 117 n.6, 160 n.8
Dallaway, J. 137 n.126
Dalmatian architecture 55
Danişmendname (epic) 8
Daskalakis-Mathews, A.-C. 76, 158 n.47,
159 nn.58–9
Davud-i Kayseri 38
decumanus maximus 27, 127 n.32
defters 140 n.4
Demiriz, Y. 42, 136 nn.119,
123, 137 n.127
Demirkapı neighborhood 49, 88
dervishes 70, 71, 81, 82, 85,
89, 156 n.34
de Tournefort, J. 1
Didymoteichon/Dimetoka 15, 19, 53,
94, 120 n.43
Diez, E. 155 n.26
Dio of Prousa (Dio Cocceianus
Chrysostom) 13, 14,
31, 89, 103
Discourses (*Orations*) (Dio of Prousa) 13
distanciated gaze 106, 171 n.26
Doğan, A. 70, 71, 153 n.2
Doğan, Şaman, N. 147 n.52
Doukas, John 168 n.87
dual heritage 74

durqa'a (central square in hall)
76
durqa'a-iwan 76
Düsturname (Enveri) 8, 116 n.39

Edirne/Adrianople 15, 18, 19, 29,
62, 92, 94, 149 n.66,
151 n.91, 165 n.67
conquest of 112 n.5
as *dar al-ghuzat* (abode of
gazis) 166 n.76
as frontier capital 94
Edirne Palace 29, 128 n.45
1855 earthquake 8, 18, 20, 34, 37, 38,
44, 61, 62, 66, 82, 89, 90, 104,
116 n.41, 127 n.32, 133 nn.92,
98, 144 n.29
1862 Cadastral Map 9, 25, *26*, 86, 106
Eldem, S. H. 62 n.84
Emir, S. 72, 144 n.29, 155 n.21, 156 n.31
Emir Sultan 49
endowment deed 85–90, 94,
146 n.42, 150 n.80, 162 n.35,
163 n.44, 166 n.74
Ephesos 9, 13, 15
Ephraim of Ainos 45,
137 n.126, 139 n.148
Erbahar, A. 142 n.12
Ergenç, Ö. 141 n.7, 142 n.18
Ersoy, A. 121 n.51, 152 n.105, 157 n.43,
165 n.67, 171 n.15
Ertuğrul 95, 124 n.7
Ethnika (Stephen of Byzantium) 32
Etz Ahayim synagogue 49, 142 n.12
Evliya Çelebi 2, 35, 36, 43, 61, 81, 82,
97–8, 109, 132 n.82, 136 nn.119,
123, 144 n.25, 161 nn.11, 17
Eyice, S. 34, 39, 42, 43, 46, 70–2,
132 n.79, 136 nn.119, 123,
138 n.138, 154 n.16, 155 n.26

façade 9, 20, 76, 93, 98
hybridity and 51–3, *52*, 55,
55–7, *59*, 62–4
transition and 32, *35*, 39, 40, 44
fakihs 71
Faroqhi, S. 168 n.87
Fatih Cami (Church of Saint
Stephanos) 24, 44, 123–4
n.6, 152 n.101

Index

Favro, D.   91, 122 n.59, 160 n.4
Finkel, C.   121 n.50
Fleet, K.   96, 168 n.87
Flood, F. B.   125 n.14, 152 n.104
Florentines   97, 168 n.91
fortifications   7, 14, 20, 26, 58, 126 n.28
Foss, C.   111 n.3, 126 n.28
Franco, M.   141 n.10
fratricide, practice of   93–4
Friday mosques. *See also Şehadet*
   (Martyrdom) Mosque; *Ulu*
   Cami (Holy/ Grand Mosque)
   of Bayezid   9, *51*, 62–5
      as *Makam-ı Hamis* (fifth
         sanctuary)   63
      as *Ulu Cami*   63–4
   of Murad I   61–2, *109*
   of Murad II   149 n.66
   of Orhan   26, 34, *35*, 36, *37*, 38,
      60–1, 132 n.81
      1337 inscription   60–1
   significance of   47–8, 59–60
frontier   4, 5, 15, 58, 66, 74, 81, 82, 89,
   94, 100, 154 n.6, 166 n.71
funduqs   99
Fustat (Egypt)   75, 76
futuwwa groups   48, 70. *See also*
   convent-*masjids*

Gabriel, A.   6, 43, 61, 101,
   126 nn.26, 29, 127 n.32,
   129 n.53, 131 n.77, 132 n.79,
   144 n.29, 146 n.42, 150 n.80,
   155 n.21, 165 n.69, 170 n.1
Galanté, A.   141 n.10
Galavaris, G.   130 n.70
gardens, significance of   1, 30, 51, 80–1,
   91, 95, 105, 160 n.7, 161 n.12,
   164 n.58, 166 n.79
gaza (holy war)   5, 60, 149 n.71
gaze, significance of   10, 106, 171–2 n.26
Gazi thesis   5, 8, 89, 94, 166 n.76
   significance of   60, 149 n.71
Genghis Khan   73
Genoese   ix, 12, 58, 96, 97, 98, 103,
   108, 148 n.58, 168 nn.87,
   91, 169 n.94
Gerber, H.   167 n.83, 169 n.105
Germiyan, Germiyanid
   principality   29, 94

Gerush synagogue   142 n.12
Geyikli Baba   70
Gibb, H. A. R.   127 nn.37, 39, 132 n.79
Gibbons, H.   4
   History of the Ottoman Empire, The   4
Gökbilgin, T.   146 n.42, 150 n.80,
   162 n.35, 163 nn.44, 46
Gökdere River   98
Gök *Madrasa* (Sivas)   72
Goodwin, G.   144 n.28, 149 n.66,
   152 nn.104–5
Goshgarian, R.   4, 113 n.14,
   153 n.6, 154 n.14
   "Beyond the Social and the
      Spiritual"   4
Graves, M. S.   63
Great Seljuks   12, 70
Gregoras, Nikephoros   15, 45, 168 n.87
Grélois, J. P.   43, 134 n.105, 136 n.122
ground-penetrating radar (GPR)
   survey   20–1, 28, 122 n.57,
      127 n.35, 133 n.96
   results of   45–6
Güleryüz, N.   142 n.12
Gurlitt, C.   159 n.59

Hacı İlbeyi   112 n.5
Hacı Paşa   133 n.97
Hadjitryphonos, E.   120 n.43, 169 n.102
Hadrian   14
Hamlin, C.   116 n.41
Hammer-Purgstall, J.   28, 39,
   125 n.18, 127 n.34, 134 nn.100,
   105, 137 n.126
Hannibal   117 n.5
hans (inns)   51, 87, 167 n.83
   Cocoon Han   *99*, 98–100 n.105
   as commercial institutions   96
   Emir Han   82, 87
   Kapan Han   96, 99, 169 n.105
   Ottoman period   98
   separating travelers from city
      inhabitants   96–7
   types of   99–100
   urban   98–9
Harris, D.   171 n.26
Hartmann, R.   131 n.77
Hasluck, F. W.   5, 23, 136 n.119
Heisenberg, A.   112 n.5, 121 n.44
Hexapytergos   34

Heywood, C. 5
Hilfat Gazi 8
Hisar kapı (fort gate) 27
Hızlı, M. 162 n.35, 163 n.54
Hoca Sadeddin Efendi 62, 133 n.98
Horaia Pege viii, 14
Horden, P. 147 n.51
hot springs 30–2
Hüdavendigar (master teacher/devotee of God) 89
Humphreys, S. 123 n.4
hybridity 3, 9, 47, 58, 65, 66, 69, 73–5, 93, 107–9, 172 n.28.
See also convent-masjids; Friday mosques

Ibn Battuta 1, 28, 32, 35, 70–1, 108, 127 nn.37, 39, 132 n.80, 168 n.87
Ibn Tulun 75
İbrahim I 61
Iconoclastic period (726–87, 814–42) 44
imarets (hospices) 19, 47, 50, 70, 72, 82, 86–92, 93, 143 n.21, 145 n.34, 162 n.38
    bathroom 88–9
Imber, C. 4, 5, 111 n.1, 113 n.13, 117 n.7
İnalcık, H. 112 n.5, 117 n.7, 118 nn.15–16, 141 n.6, 148 n.58, 166 nn.72, 81, 167 n.83, 168 n.93
İntepe, N. 120 n.39
interregnum period 54, 93, 102
inverted-T structures 9, 69, 148 n.61, 156 n.31, 159 n.59
    abrupt change and 77
    continuity in 75–7
    hybrid architecture and 48, 51, 61, 62, 73–5
    identity, origin, and function of 70–3
    külliye and 83, 90, 93
    in Mediterranean region 76–7
Irene (wife of John III Vatatzes) 15, 31, 45
Irgandı Bridge 16, 97–8, 97, 103
İsa Bey Mosque Ayasoluk, Aydinid 64
Islamic city, notion of 17, 119 n.33
Istanbul 2, 4, 11, 60, 61, 95, 103, 105, 109, 116 n.3, 141 n.7, 162 n.34.
    See also Constantinople

İvaz Paşa 165 n.66
iwan 72. See also convent-masjids

Jacoby, D. 113 n.9
Janin, R. 39, 119 n.27, 134 n.105
Joaillier, P. and Sebah, J. P. 109
John III Vatatzes 121 n.44
    Irene, wife of 15, 31, 45
John VIII Xiphilinos viii
Justinian 32, 46
    Theodora, wife of 32
Justin II 32

Kabalos 34
Kafadar, C. 5, 114 n.20, 118 n.16, 149 n.73, 152 nn.103–4, 162 n.33, 165 nn.67, 71, 166 n.76
Kafescioğlu, Ç. 4, 120 n.36, 131 n.72, 141 n.7, 161 n.13, 171 n.25
    Constantinopolis/Istanbul 4
Kallistos, Anastasios 49
Kandes, V. 116 n.41, 141 n.6, 142 n.13
Kantakouzenos, John 168 n.87
Kaplanoğlu, R. 142 n.17, 169 n.103
Kaplıca kapı (the hot springs gate) 27
Karacahisar 112 n.4
Karamanids 26, 27, 62, 87, 127 n.32, 144 n.28
    Ali Bey 57
Kara Mustafa Baths. See Kükürtlü Hamam (sulfur baths)
Karınca River 49
Kastritsis, D. 93, 143–4 n.23, 149 n.66, 150 n.90, 152 n.106, 165 nn.67, 70, 166 n.74
Katib Celebi 29, 128 n.42
Katz, D. 77
Kayabaşı neighborhood 49
Kazeruni, Ebu Ishak 70
Keçecizade Fuad Paşa 18, 120 n.39
Kermeli, E. 111 n.1
khutbas 60, 71, 84
Kiourtzian, G. 126 n.31
Kiprovska, M. 115 n.38, 123 n.3, 124 n.9
Kirmasti/Mustafakemalpaşa 23, 98, 106
Kitapçı Bayrı, B. 4, 154 n.6
Kline, G. R. 168 n.91
Komotini/Gümülcine 15, 19
Kontolaimos, P. 128 n.45
Konya 15, 126 n.25, 140 n.3

Köprülü, M. Fuat   156 n.31
  Anadolu'da İslamiyet (Köprülü)   4–5
  Les origines de l'empire ottoman   5
Kostof, S.   19, 91, 121 n.48,
    122 n.59, 160 n.4
Krautheimer, R.   136 n.122,
    147 n.44, 157 n.45
Kreiser, K.   151 n.91
Kubler, G. A.   77, 159 n.63
Kükürtlü bath   89, 130 n.66
  Hamam (sulfur baths)   32, 33
külliye (socioreligious complexes)   9, *16*,
    19, *31*, 38, 59, 62, 71, 80, 106,
    109, 161 n.27
  Bayezid's complex and   90–1
  commercial networks and *hans*
    and   95–100
  gardens in   95
  of Mehmed I and Murad II   92–5
  Murad I's complex and   88–9
  neighborhoods and   *16*, 49
  Orhan's complex and   86–8
  Ottoman urban enterprise and   82–6
  significance of   47–8
  as urban choreography   9–10, 91
  waqf system and   164 n.58
Kuran, A.   72, 116 n.3, 131 n.77,
    144 n.28, 154 n.16, 155 nn.26–
    7, 169 n.102

Laborde, L. de   136 n.119, 137 n.126
La Chanson de Roland   82
Laiou, A. E.   95, 160 n.7, 167 n.82
Lala Şahin *Madrasa* (Bursa)   38
Lala Şahin Mausoleum
    (Mustafakemalpaşa)   98,
    133 n.98, 147 n.47
landscape   viii, 1, 6, 7, 11, 15, 18, 23, 48,
    161 n.12, 165 n.65
  cultural   105, 109, 116 n.1, 172 n.35
  invisible Prousa and   104–6, 110
  külliye and   79, 80, 83, 86, 91–2, 95
  significance of   106
  viewing of   171 n.26
Lapidus, I.   119 n.33, 120 n.37
Lefebvre, H.   164 n.64
Leo VI   31
Lindner, R. P.   5, 13, 73, 111 n.1, 156 n.31
local knowledge   74. *See also* convent-
    masjids; Friday mosques
Lombard frieze   56

Löwenhielm, C. G.   1, 40, 43, 44, 62, 109
lower city   9, *51*, 62, 132 n.81,
    161 n.27, 163 n.43
  monuments and memory and   79,
    83, 85, 86, 88, 90, 96
  transition and   25, 35, 38
Lowry, H.   5, 12, 50, 82,
    113 n.9, 116 n.41, 118 nn.14–15,
    120 n.43, 129 n.53, 138 nn.140–
    1, 140 n.4, 141 nn.5–6, 10,
    143 n.21, 144 n.25, 149 nn.70–1,
    160 n.9, 161 nn.9, 11, 19, 162
    n.30, 167 n.83, 168 n.93
Lubenau, R.   30, 80, 81, 125 n.18

MacDonald, W.   104
madrasa   26, 38, 46, 72,
    115 n.37, 123 n.5, 133 nn.96, 98,
    139 n.152, 151 n.96
  convent-*masjids* and Friday mosques
    and   47, 54, 57
  külliye and   84, 86, 88–90, 92, 93,
    100
Magdalino, P.   91
Maguire, H.   41
mahalles (boroughs/neighborhoods)   15,
    16, 32, 48–50, 103, 108,
    126 n.25, 141 nn.6–7, 142 n.12
  külliye and   79, 80, 83, 85,
    88, 91–2, 100
  Lowry on   50
  non-Muslim   49
  Schiltberger on   50
mahfils (meeting rooms)   76
Mahmud II   49
Malik Shah   72
Malusardi, F.   171 nn.16, 19
Mamboury, E.   159 n.59
Mamluk workmanship   4, 9, 29, 76, 89,
    92, 151 n.97, 155 n.26, 158 n.55
  hybridity and   47, 53, 57–9, 63–5, 67
Manastır (Monastery)   39, 134 n.103
Mango, C.   5, 124 n.6, 138 n.143
Manisa, *Ulu Cami*, Saruhanid, 63–5
Mansel, A. M.   138 n.142
marble revetments, significance
    of   137 n.126
Maringhi, Giovanni di
    Francesco   168 n.93
Maritza river   29
Marmara-basin economy   95

Mathews, T.   76, 158 nn.47, 58, 159 nn.58–9
mausolea   7, 15, 23, 94. *See also*
    Orhan; Osman
Mayor synagogue   142 n.12
Medikion   14
Mehmed I (*Yeşil*)   16, 26, 27, 29, 49, 102
  külliye of (*Yeşil* Complex)   92–3
    Green Mausoleum   104
  marriage to Sitt Hatun   29
  mosque of, Dimetoka   53
  mosque of, Söğüt   66, 165 n.67
  Old Mosque (Edirne) of   92,
    149 n.66
Mehmed II   19
Mehmed IV   30
Mehmed Bey of Birgi, Aydinid
    principality   8, 127 n.39
Meinecke, M.   64
Melikoff, I.   133 n.98
Menteshe, Menteshid
    principality   96, 149 n.76
Menthon, B.   14, 119 n.27, 132 n.79
Meriçli, E.   118 n.15, 141 n.6, 160 n.6
Metropolitan Church of Saint John the
    Theologian   49
Michael VIII Palaiologos   12
mihrab   54, 61, 63, 71, 154 n.16, 155 n.21
Miletopolis/Karacabey   23
minaret   36, 62, 63, 71, 116 n.41,
    155 nn.21–2, 163 n.46
minbar   63, 64, 71
monasteries on holy mountains,
    significance of   152 n.102
Monastery of Docheiariou
    (Mount Athos)   55
Mongol–Ilkhanids   ix, 7, 15, 18, 58, 72,
    73, 126 n.25, 149 n.76, 156 n.31
Mongol influence   73, 156 nn.31, 34
monumentality   20, 63, 90–2, 106,
    131 n.72. *See also külliye*
Mordtmann, A.   61
mosaics   20, 44, 110, 122 n.56,
    129 n.53, 139 n.147
movable dwelling, notion of   127–8 n.39
Mount Olympus   9, 11, 14, 31, 32, 79, 81,
    82, 116 n.41
  monasteries on   119 n.27
multi-functionality, of buildings   9,
    18, 48, 71–3, 140 n.1. *See also*
    convent-*masjids*

Murad I   8, 10, 15, 20, 25, 29, *31*, 33,
    34, 37, 48, 60, 80, 130 n.66,
    148 n.58. *See also* convent-
    masjids; Friday mosque
  İmaret-i Kapluca (endowment
    deed) and   88–9
  külliye sponsored by   16, *31*, 83–5, 91
    bathhouse imaret   88–9
  as martyr, *ahi* and holy
    figure   88–9, 163 nn.45, 51
Murad II (*Muradiye*)   86, 106,
    112 n.5, 149 n.66
  külliye of   16, 92, 93–5
  marriage to Mara Branković
    29
  marriage to Sultan Hatun   29
  mausoleum of   166 n.73
Murphey, R.   112 n.5
Mustafa I   61
Muthesius, A.   113 n.9

Namazgah   49
Namazgah River   49
Necipoğlu, G.   48, 59, 72, 85, 134 n.99,
    148 n.58, 150 n.90, 151 n.97,
    152 n.107, 157 n.44, 161 n.27,
    162 n.34, 171 n.25
Neşri   38, 50, 87, 134 n.100, 144 n.26
Nicaea/İznik   15, 18, 23, 28, 50, 52,
    74, 106, 107
Nicomedia/İzmit   15, 23
Nilüfer (Odrysses) River   11
Nizam-al Mulk   72
nonconfessional
  accommodations   30
  continuity   33
  loci   89
Nora, P.   106
Norman Sicily   76, 77

Ocak, A. Y.   70
Öcalan, H. B.   162 n.35
Oğuz, Z.   140 n.1, 154 nn.16, 20
Oğuz Kursar, Z.   88, 163 n.45
Old Bath (*Eski Kaplıca*)   31–3, *31*, 89,
    129 nn.50, 53
old city   8, 9, 12, 15, *16*, 19, *26*,
    48–9, 60–1, 132 n.81,
    139 n.152, 144 n.25
  framing of   25–8

invisible Prousa and 103, 104, *109*, 110
külliye and 79–80, 83–6, 90, 92, 94
transition and 25, *26*, 30, 32, 34–8, *35*, *37*
Öney, G. 124 n.9
Orhan 15, 20, 25, 80, 96, 127 n.37. *See also* convent-*masjids;* Friday mosques; *madrasa;* old city
   building conversions in the old city 26, 34–43, *35–7, 40*
   Davud-i Kayseri on 38
   fratricide, practice of 93
   külliye sponsored by *16*, 83, 86–8
   Mausolea (tomb) of 2, 21, 24, 25, *26*, 34, 35, *36*, 38–42, *40, 42, 109*
     GPR results 45–6
     new evidence on 43–5
     opus sectile panel 41–2, *42*, 44
   Palamas and 50
   as Sultan of Bursa 28
Orhan Mosque (Biga) 123 n.5
Orhan Mosque (Bilecik) 52, 66
orthogonal city planning 17
Oruç 168 n.87
Osman 1, 95, 124 n.7
   Mausolea (tomb) of 2, 21, 24, 25, *26*, 34, *36*, 39, *40, 109*
     GPR results 45–6
     new evidence on 43–5
Ottoman. *See individual entries*
Ötüken, S. Y. 138 n.142
Ousterhout, R. 5–6, 66, 73, 76, 124 n.6, 133 n.99, 136 n.122, 138 n.146, 144 n.28, 145 n.33, 147 nn.47, 50, 152 n.105, 159 nn.58–9
Özendes, E. 98, 169 n.99
Özer, M. 128 n.45
Özkan, E. 122 n.56, 127 n.36

Pachymeres, George 29, 45, 139 n.148, 160 n.7, 168 n.87
Palaiologan Constantinople 53
Palamas, Gregory 50, 127 n.37, 143 n.23
Palatine Anthology 32, 130 n.59
Pancaroğlu, O. 11, 73, 87, 116 n.3, 123 n.3, 132 n.80, 154 n.14, 156 n.34, 162 n.38, 163 n.46, 164 n.58, 167 n.83

Pantobasilissa 52, 65–6
Papadopoulos, Chr. 123
Papazotos, T. 134 n.104
Pardoe, Julia 136 n.119
Parvillée, L. 20, 170 n.15
Peacock, A. C. S. 128 n.39
Pekak, M. S. 124 n.6
Peremeci, O. N. 112 n.5
Philadar neighborhood. *See* Kayabaşı neighborhood
Piccinato, L. 25, 104–5, 171 nn.16, 17
Pınarbaşı 150 n.88
Pinatsi, C. 42
Pinon, P. 120 n.38
Pir Emir 49
Pliny the Elder 117 n.5
Pliny the Younger 13, 89
   correspondence with Trajan 14, 31
Polykarpos 112 n.5
Pralong, A. 43, 134 n.105, 136 n.122, 138 n.142
pre-interregnum period 92
pre-Ottoman neighborhoods 141 n.6
prime object/prime building 77
Procopius 32, 130 n.60, 139 n.157
Prost, H. 104
Prousa. *See* Bursa
Prousias I viii, 11, 117 n.5
Psellos, Michael viii
pseudo-spolia 57, 147 n.50
Pullan, R. 31, 129 n.51, 136 n.119
Purcell, N. 147 n.51
Pythia (Yalova) 32, 44, 46, 134 n.105, 138 n.142, 167 n.84

qa'a 76, 158 n.55

rab' (collective housing area) 76
Rabbat, N. 158 n.55
Ran, N. H. viii
Redford, S. 124 n.9, 128 nn.39, 46, 134 n.100, 151 n.97, 152 nn.103–4
remodeling 14, 20, 90, 125 n.18, 126 n.26, 127 n.32, 128 n.42, 133 n.92, 163 n.48

hybridity and 49, 53
  transition and 26, 27, 35
Renouard de Bussierre, T. 137 n.126
restoration 7, 20, 103, 122 n.54,
    127 n.32, 130 n.67, 137 n.127,
    165 n.67, 170 n.15
  hybridity and 51, 61, 63
  külliye and 80, 87–90, 97, 98
  transition and 26–8, 33, 34,
    36, 37, 46
reuse, architectural 47, 67,
    115 n.38, 124 n.9, 125 n.14,
    134 n.105, 152 n.104
  transition and 24–5, 30, 34, 37,
    38, 44, 46
ritual/resort, theme of 31
riwaq (frontal gallery) 76
Robert, L. 117 n.5, 129 n.51, 130 n.56
Roman *fora* 83, 91
Rose, G. 171–2 n.26
Ruggles, D. F. 6, 157 n.39, 161 n.12,
    166 n.79, 169 n.105, 171 n.26
Rum Seljuks ix, 7, 12, 18, 58, 70, 83,
    92, 96, 126 n.25; 140 n.3,
    151 n.97, 156 n.34
  Abbasid rulership and 60
  hans of 98
  urbanism of 26
Ruy González de
    Clavijo 126 n.23, 168 n.87

Sackett, J. R. 148 n.60, 172 n.28
St. Laurent, B. 121 nn.51–2, 138 n.140
Saint Zoni (Samos) monastery
    169 n.102
Sakkoudion 14
Salgırlı, S. 101, 140 n.1, 169 n.105
Salmeri, G. 118 n.23
Saltanat kapı (gate of sovereignty) 20,
    27, 28, 126 n.28
Saltukname 166 n.76
Saroz 7, 18, 125 n.16
Saruhanid 64, 65
Schiltberger, J. 2, 50, 86
Schlemmer, U. 113 n.10,
    142 n.21, 161 n.9
Schultze, V. 134 n.105
Şehadet (Martyrdom) Mosque 34,
    35, 37, 60, 84, 109. See also
    Friday mosques

Selçuk, I. 4, 50, 71, 153 n.6, 154 n.14
  State and Society in the
    Marketplace 4
sericulture 2, 113 n.9
Sestini, D. 134 n.100,
    137 n.126, 161 n.11
Setbaşı bridge 103–4
Setbaşı neighborhood 49, 50
Ševčenko, I. 5, 124 n.6, 138 n.143
Severan dynasty 32
Şeyh Bedreddin viii
Sheikh 1, 70, 71, 85, 87, 88
silver-domed tomb (Gümüşlü
    Kümbet) 25, 39,
    125 n.14, 134 n.102
Singer, A. 29, 94, 112 n.5, 129 n.46
Smith, T. 36, 45, 109, 125 n.18, 127 n.34,
    129 n.48, 132 n.83, 139 n.147
Söğüt 66, 92, 112 n.4, 156 n.31
Sölch, J. 116 n.1
spolia/spoliation 7, 20, 27, 67, 75
  in Anatolian context 124 n.9
  Byzantine 24, 43, 57
  in Islamic context 152 n.104
  significance of 115 n.37
Spon, J. 30, 81, 108, 125 n.18,
    129 n.48, 136 n.119
spontaneous/irregular city planning 17
Stephen of Byzantium 32, 117 n.5
Stotz, C. L. 116 n.41
Strabon 117 n.5
Su kapı (the water gate) 27
Şükrullah 168 n.87
sulfurous hot spring 32
Sultaniya 85
Sultan Mahmud of Gazna 72
synthronon 44

Tabriz 85
Taeschner, F. 131 n.77
Tafur, P. 80, 161 n.9, 168 n.91
tahrir defters. See cadastral registers
Tak, E. 146 n.42, 162 nn.30, 35,
    163 nn.44, 54
Tanman, B. 53, 64, 151 nn.96–7
Tanpınar, A. H. *Beş Şehir* (Five Cities) 6,
    103, 170 n.7
Tekinalp, V. M. 43, 132 n.83, 134 n.105,
    135 n.112, 136 n.122
tekke (as dervish convent) 166 n.79

tekke (as hospice)   85
Texier, C.   31, 39, 98, 109, 129 nn.51, 53, 134 n.105, 136 n.119, 169 n.99
Theodore I Laskaris   27
Thessaloniki/Selanik   15, 19, 39, 40
Thevénot, J.   2
1326 period   1, 12, 19, 23, 26, 50, 66, 107, 125 n.16, 152 n.101
1337 inscription   5, 34, *35*, 37, 46, 60–1
Timur   viii, 67, 101, *102*,102
Timurids   18, 26, 27, 53, 59, 67, 101, 102
Timurid sack   viii, 12, 18, 26, 27, 29, 54, 67, 92, 102
Tokat buildings   72
Tophane (Park)   45, 122 n.55, 127 n.35
Trachtenberg, M.   91, 145 n.37, 164 n.59
Trajan   13, 14
   correspondence with Pliny the Younger   14, 31
transitional architectural culture   67
translation   67, 74
Trebizond   15, 42, 101
Trigleia   24, 44, 65, 123 n.6, 152 n.101
triumphalist appropriation   7, 8, 107, 115 n.37
triumphalist impulse   66
Tunay, M. I.   145 n.33
Turcoman   12, 28, 98

Ubicini, A.   33, 82, 130 n.70
Ukhaidir (Iraq)   75
Ukhaidir *majlis*   77
Ulu Cami (Holy/ Grand Mosque)   24, *51*, 58, 62, 63, 84, 87, 90, 132 n.81.
   See also Friday mosques
umma (community of believers)   17
Umur Bey, Aydinid principality   8, 116 n.39, 133 n.98
Ünal, F.   122 n.56, 127 n.36
urbanism   ix, 1, 4, 6–11, 13–19, 21, 47, 50, 61, 71, 121 n.52, 160–1 n.8, 165 n.65, 171 n.16
   colonnaded streets and   118 n.23
   continuity, conversion, and reuse and   23–6, 31, 34, 38, 45
   Cordoba and   161 n.12
   cultural landscape and   172 n.35
   and enterprise   82–6
   hans and   98–9
   invisible Prousa and   101, 103–10

külliye and   79–81, 89, 91–2, 96, 98
   Laskarid interventions of   112 n.5, 121 n.44
   Ottoman interventions in Balkans of   120 n.43
   urban armature and   104
   urban choreography and   9–10, 91
   urban memory and   105, 107
   and urban process, notion of   80, 160 n.4
   waqf system and   164 n.58
utilitarian opportunism   7, 8, 66, 72, 100
Uysal, A. O.   155 n.21
Uzunçarşılı, I. H.   162 n.35

Venetians   ix, 96, 97, 168 nn.87, 91
Vilayetname of Hacı Bektaş   157 n.43, 166 n.79
visibility   20, 23, 41, 44, 51, 56, 91, 92, 101–10, 131 n.77
visuality, concept of   108
von Erlach, J. B. F.   36, 61, 109, 132 n.84
von Thünen, J. H.   159 n.1
Vryonis, S.   5, 123 n.5, 168 n.90

wakalas   99
walls and gates   2, 25–8, *26*, *109*
waqf system   33, 88, 99, 130 n.66, 150 n.80, 164 n.58
Wheler, G.   30, 81, 108, 125 n.18, 129 n.48, 136 n.119, 143 n.21, 161 n.11
Wilde, H.   144 n.29, 159 n.59
Winfield, D.   126 n.28
Wittek, P.   5, 60, 143 n.23, 149 n.70, 150 n.90
   Rise of the Ottoman Empire, The   5
Wolper, E. S.   43, 73, 124 n.9, 147 n.51, 154 n.14, 156 n.34
   Cities and Saints   73

Yalman, S.   4
   "Building the Sultanate of Rum"   4
Yenişehir   29, 52, 66, 74, 128 n.39
Yerasimos, S.   166 n.76
Yer kapı (the ground gate)   20, 27, 88
Yeşilova (Great Plain)   11
Yıldırım   49
Yıldız, S. N.   133 n.97

Yılmaz, H. 60–1, 89, 122 n.54, 133 n.97, 149 nn.70, 76
Yılmazyaşar, H. 112 n.4, 123 n.5
Yüksel Muslu, C. 128 n.40
Yürekli, Z. 115 nn.37, 38, 123 n.3, 124 n.9, 146 n.41, 151 n.100, 153 n.107, 163 n.45
Yürekli–Görkay, Z. 115 n.37, 124 n.9
Zachariadou, E. 112 n.5, 117 n.7, 143 n.23, 167 n.82
zaviyes (convent/lodges) 70–2, 86, 87, 88, 90, 162 n.38
Zindan kapı (dungeon gate) 27

www.ingramcontent.com/pod-product-compliance
Lightning Source LLC
Chambersburg PA
CBHW072232290426
44111CB00012B/2057